BPM Excellence in Practice 2009

Innovation, Implementation and Impact

BPM Excellence in Practice 2009

Innovation, Implementation and Impact

Award-winning Case Studies in Workflow and Business Process Management

Edited by

LAYNA FISCHER

Future Strategies Inc.
Lighthouse Point, Florida, USA

BPM Excellence in Practice 2009: Innovation, Implementation and Impact
Copyright © 2009 by Future Strategies Inc.
ISBN13: 978-0-9819870-2-6

Published by Future Strategies Inc., Book Division

2436 North Federal Highway, #374, Lighthouse Point FL 33064 USA
954.782.3376 / 954.719.3746 fax
www.FutStrat.com
books@FutStrat.com

Cover: Hara Allison www.smallagencybigideas.com

Publisher's Cataloging-in-Publication Data

ISBN: 978-0-9819870-2-6
Library of Congress Control Number: 2009936835

BPM Excellence in Practice 2009: Innovation, Implementation and Impact /Layna Fischer

p. cm.

Includes bibliographical references and appendices.

1. Technological Innovation. 2. Organizational Change. 3. Business Process Management. 4. Information Technology. 5. Total Quality Management. 6. Management Information systems. 7. Office Practice-Automation. 8. Knowledge Management. 9.
Workflow. 10. Process Analysis

Fischer, Layna.

Table of Contents

Section 5: South and Central America

Section 6 Appendix

Introduction
BPM Excellence in Practice:
Innovation, Implementation and Impact

Layna Fischer, Editor and
Awards Executive Director

The prestigious annual **Global Excellence Awards for BPM and Workflow** are highly coveted by organizations that seek recognition for their achievements. Now evolved into their 18th year, originally starting with, and moving through, imaging, documentation, knowledge management and more, as our industry moved forward, these awards not only provide a spotlight for companies that truly deserve recognition, but also provide tremendous insights for organizations wishing to emulate the winners' successes.

These winners are companies that successfully used BPM in gaining competitive advantage within their industries.

CRITERIA

The criteria for submitting an entry are fairly simple: the project should have been operational for six months prior to nomination, and have been installed within the past two years. The submission guidelines, however, are more detailed. To be recognized as winners, companies must address three critical areas: excellence in *innovation*, excellence in *implementation* and excellence in strategic *impact* to the organization. Details at www.bpmf.org.

Innovation

Innovation encompasses the innovative use of technology for strategic business objectives; the complexity of the underlying business process and IT architecture; the creative and successful deployment of advanced workflow and imaging concepts; and process innovations through business process reengineering and/or continuous improvements.

- Innovative use of BPM technology to solve unique problems
- Creative and successful implementation of advanced BPM concepts
- Level of integration with other technologies and legacy systems
- Degree of complexity in the business process and underlying IT architecture

Implementation

Hallmarks of a successful *implementation* include extensive user and line management involvement in the project while successfully managing change during the implementation process. Factors impacting the level of difficulty in achieving a successful implementation include the system complexity; integration with other advanced technologies; and the scope and scale of the implementation (e.g. size, geography, inter-company processes).

- Successful BPM and/or workflow implementation methodology
- Size, scope and quality of change management process
- Scope and scale of the implementation (e.g. size, geography, inter-and intra-company processes)

Impact

Impact is the bottom line, answering the question, "What benefit does BPM deliver to my business? Why should I care?"

- Extent and quantifiable impact of productivity improvements
- Significance of cost savings
- Level of increased revenues, product enhancements, customer service or quality improvements
- Impact of the system on competitive positioning in the marketplace
- Proven strategic importance to the organization's mission

- Degree to which the system enabled a culture change within the organization and methodology for achieving that change

Using BPM for Competitive Advantage

Examples of potential benefits include: productivity improvements; cost savings; increased revenues; product enhancements; improved customer service; improved quality; strategic impact to the organization's mission; enabling culture change; and—most importantly—changing the company's competitive position in the market. The visionary focus is now toward strategic benefits, in contrast to marginal cost savings and productivity enhancements.

While successes in these categories are prerequisites for winning a Global Excellence Award, it would reward all companies to focus on excelling in *innovation, implementation* and *impact* when installing BPM and workflow technologies. Companies must recognize that implementing innovative technology is useless unless the organization has a successful approach that delivers—and even surpasses—the anticipated benefits.

SUBMIT AN ENTRY

Submissions for the annual **Global Excellence Awards for BPM and Workflow** open in the September timeframe. The Awards program is managed by Future Strategies Inc., the Awards Director is Layna Fischer in collaboration with Derek Miers of BPM Focus.org, with sponsorship from WfMC, OMG and BPM.com.

General information and guidelines may be found at www.bpmf.org or contact:

Layna Fischer, Layna@FutStrat.com

Future Strategies Inc., www.FutStrat.com Phone +1 954 782 3376, Fax +1 954 719 3746

TABLE OF CONTENTS AND CHAPTER ABSTRACTS

Guest Chapters:

SOCIAL TECHNOLOGIES WILL DRIVE THE NEXT WAVE OF BPM SUITES

Clay Richardson, Forrester Research, USA

When you spend time taking a sober look at a market's maturity—like we did with our recently published BPM Tech Radar report—some technologies make you yawn, but then other technologies give you goose bumps. The primary purpose of the BPM Tech Radar was to map the maturity of the 15 most critical technologies that make up the BPM landscape. This included tried and true technologies such as workflow, process modeling, document imaging, and business rules; in addition to bleeding and leading edge technologies such as process data management and process mashups.

THINKING GLOBAL, ACTING LOCAL: HOW BI AND BPM SUPPORTS SMART CITIES IN A GLOBALIZED ECONOMY

Lewis Carr, Oracle Corp., USA

Even cities with multi-billion dollar budgets and over 10,000 employees are still using combinations of Excel, Project, siloed databases, homegrown dashboards and other poorly suited tools. This paper looks at the challenges local governments face and how BI and BPM will make cities smarter about how they plan and implement budgets and sourcing, programs, and infrastructure. The paper discusses the local government business model and levers of growth and how this model may have inherent structural barriers that prevent insight and change. Finally, we provide successful cases of BI and BPM being applied from different parts of local government organizations towards the same goals of improved performance, streamlined management and transparency and accountability of government to its constituents.

Section 1: Europe

KPN, NETHERLANDS

Finalist, Europe. Nominated by Cordys, UK

KPN is the leading telecommunications and ICT service provider in The Netherlands, offering wireline and wireless telephony, Internet and TV to customers and end-to-end telecom and ICT services to business customers. KPN provides wholesale network services to third parties and operates an efficient IP-based infrastructure with global scale. In order to attract new customers, retain its more than 35 million existing customers and remain competitive as a multi-play provider amidst the forces of deregulation, KPN must focus on creating a more customer-centric business - and aligning its IT systems to meet this objective.

MIGROS BANK, SWITZERLAND

Gold Award, Europe. Nominated by Action Technologies Inc., USA

Migros Bank is one of the 10 leading financial institutes in Switzerland and one of the biggest Retail-Banks. Our focus is to be very close to the clients and therefore we have around 50 branches all over Switzerland and many more small contact-points that offer basic services for new clients. All in all about 1,400 employees work for Migros Bank. When we outsourced almost all of our IT to an external provider, little or no electronic workflows were in use. In addition, we were confronted with increasing regulatory and risk issues concerning the internal order processing from the regions to the centralized back-offices that were done by placing orders by paper forms and by fax. To improve these situations we initiated a project to implement electronic people-to-people workflows.

TECHSPACE AERO, BELGIUM

Silver Award, Europe. Nominated by W4, France

Techspace Aero designs, develops and produces modules, equipment and test cells for aircraft and space engines. The regulations in the domain require strict quality control of the products. The quality department, alongside the company's ambition to become the world leader in its areas of excellence, has decided to rationalize its applications for better department efficiency. At the same time, studies conducted by the IT department on the operation of the ERP used for quality management have demonstrated that a BPM solution could respond more effectively to the evolution requirements fixed by the company, and more specifically conform to the quality requirements within Techspace Aero.

Section 2: Middle East and Africa

PRUHEALTH, SOUTH AFRICA

Gold Award, Middle East and Africa. Nominated by TIBCO, France

PruHealth is a leading health insurance company which rewards members for adopting a healthy lifestyle. Launched in October 2004, PruHealth is a joint venture between Prudential and Discovery, the South African health insurance leader. Its model is based on a successful concept launched in South Africa. Prudential is a leading financial services company founded in 1848 with over 21 million customers and 28,000 employees worldwide.

Section 3: North America

CITY OF EDMONTON, ALBERTA, CANADA

Finalist, North America. Nominated by Computronix, Canada

We describe the basic concepts, workflow design and robust implementation of an electronic circulation system using the POSSE® Business Process Management tool suite. A key business process for the City of Edmonton is the consultation of internal and external stakeholders on applications for new licenses, permits, bylaw amendments and certain key City-wide initiatives. In the past, documents were circulated by sending paper copies to stakeholders who then returned the annotated copies. The comments from the various stakeholders were manually collated into a single document for the subsequent decision process. This paper based circulation process was slow and fairly labour intensive. In 2006, we developed and implemented a leading edge POSSE® Web-based Land Development

Application (LDA) system that allowed the applicant to submit electronic copies of application documents.

DICKINSON FINANCIAL CORP., USA

Finalist, North America. Nominated by Adobe Systems Inc., USA

Motivated by competitive pressure to improve its customer service, standardize its forms and increase potential future growth, Dickinson Financial Corporation (DFC) had the opportunity to implement new solutions that would ultimately reduce internal costs, improve scalability and customer services, generate ROI, ensure compliance with bank processes and attain better risk management. DFC chose to put into action automated document processes based on Adobe technologies in an effort to achieve its business goals of increased customer satisfaction and a "paperless bank."

OFFICE OF THE SECRETARY OF DEFENSE (OSD) FOR ACQUISITION, TECHNOLOGY & LOGISTICS (A T & L), USA

Finalist, North America. Nominated by Oracle Corp., USA

The OSD AT&L vision is to drive the capability to defeat any adversary on any battlefield. Our Enterprise Architecture must support an inspired, high-performing, boundary-less organization that delivers. We must be an agile, motivated, collaborative, and creative organization with new ideas and new ways of doing business. Based on its vision OSD AT&L chose to deploy a very agile and collaborative driven solution leveraging the latest technologies and methodologies in Business Process Management and Enterprise 2.0. With a focus on quickly delivering capabilities to the field OSD has focused on BPM and Enterprise 2.0 for secure and scalable solutions.

HIGH COURT OF JUSTICE OF THE STATE OF HIDALGO, MEXICO

Silver Award, North America. Nominated by PECTRA Technology, USA

Within the framework of e-governance developed by the Government of Mexico – with the purpose of improving the quality and transparency in management and increasing the efficiency in public services – the High Court of the State of Hidalgo implemented an Integral Program of Processes Systematization. The project included the integration of tasks of 51 first instance courts and their second instance courts, each one of them with numerous individual, complex, and manual processes. In addition, all the value chain participants – both internal and external - were integrated: Organization (Courts, Courtrooms); citizens (Lawyers, parties involved in the trial), and the Government.

U.S. XPRESS ENTERPRISES, INC., USA

Silver Award, North America. Nominated by Cordys Ltd., UK

U.S. Xpress Enterprises stands today as one of the premier transportation companies in North America. Founded in 1985, U.S. Xpress is the third-largest privately-owned truckload carrier with over 8,500 trucks and 26,000 trailers. U.S. Xpress has reshaped the landscape of transportation by developing revolutionary innovations that continually deliver unmatched levels of customer satisfaction.

US MILITARY ENTRANCE PROCESSING COMMAND, US GOVERNMENT

Gold Award, North America. Nominated by Oracle Corp., USA

The United States Military Entrance Processing Command (US MEPCOM) processes and qualifies individuals applying for military service in any one of five Armed Services (Army, Navy, Marine Corps, Air Force and Coast Guard) and their subcomponents (i.e. Reserve, National Guard). They are required to process over 1 million records a year with potentially spikes of 18,000 per day (5.6 million a year), and to maintain over 60 million current records across all the armed services. Their existing Enterprise Architecture (EA) was to antiquated and brittle to handle the growing requirements of its customer in an increasingly changing environment.

Section 4: Pacific Rim

AEGON RELIGARE LIFE INSURANCE, INDIA
Finalist, Pacific Rim. Nominated by Cordys, UK

AEGON is a leading life and pensions company with more than 40 million customers worldwide and presence in over twenty markets throughout the Americas, Europe and Asia. Religare is India's leading financial services company. AEGON Religare Life Insurance is a joint venture promoted by AEGON, Religare and Bennett, Coleman and Co. The company specializes in life insurance, pensions and investment products. The biggest challenge faced by the business was to create and implement a successful, efficient and sustainable BPM model, incorporating real-time integration of systems and data exchange across its existing IT infrastructure.

IMAN AUSTRALIAN HEALTH PLANS AUSTRALIA
Silver Award, Pacific Rim. Nominated by Polonious Pty Ltd, Australia

Australian Health Plans, a division of IMAN International Pty Ltd is a specialist provider of health plans for temporary residents working in Australia. Since 1981, the IMAN group has specialised in this niche market for health plans.

In 2004 IMAN had a problem; as their sales grew, their costs grew in proportion. Considering this, they made a strategic decision to embark on an IT improvement strategy based on implementing Open Source technology via their IT software partners Polonious Pty Ltd. Their main objective was being to control operating costs and stop costs increasing with sales as far as possible.

FULLERTON INDIA CREDIT COMPANY LIMITED, INDIA
Gold Award, Pacific Rim. Nominated by Newgen Software Technologies Ltd., India

Being a recent entrant in the retail-lending segment, Fullerton India Credit Company Limited (FICCL) plans for rapid rollout of branch network to reach a large customer base. The company's objective was to achieve lean but profit-oriented branches, reduce the turnaround-times, lower the operational costs and improve the customer experience.

Newgen offered FICCL a BPM solution based on Newgen® OmniFlowTM, which integrates with the core system, Flexcube. The solution covers the entire spectrum of loan process starting from loan initiation, de-dupe, credit verifications, deviation handling and approvals, loan booking by the back-office, and finally the loan disbursal process.

Section 5: South and Central America

NATIONAL INSTITUTE OF METROLOGY, STANDARDIZATION AND INDUSTRIAL QUALITY – INMETRO, BRAZIL
Silver Award, South America. Nominated by Cryo Technologies, Brazil

Through directives which have already been named in its strategic planning, INMETRO seeks to roll out a new process-oriented public administration model, focusing entirely on customer satisfaction and the efficiency of its processes. As an initial project, the redesign and automation of its Accreditation process, essential to guaranteeing the competitiveness of Brazilian industry, succeeded in substantially reducing the total time required to carry out this process, at the same time introducing a new paradigm for the way governmental agencies provide services in Brazil. This project's success now serves as the model for many other process automation initiatives within the organization.

ISAPRE MICROSYSTEM, CHILE
Finalist, South America. Nominated by PECTRA, USA

A process has been worked out allowing the ISAPRE - private institutions which capture workers' compulsory contribution payment and provide 18% of the Chilean population with their service – to electronically manage audit processes of health affidavits. This process is tailored according to the needs of each organization and exhibits integration on two levels: BPM solution integration with other components of documentary management and integration with each particular client's applications. The developed solution offers innovations and benefits on a business level, in processes and in marketing models: It joins users from the entire national territory together, integrates applications on a unique virtual desktop, and is brought to the market under the Software as a Service modality.

PRODUBANCO, ECUADOR

Gold Award, South America. Nominated by BizAgi Ltd., Colombia

Produbanco is one of the main financial institutions in Ecuador. In their search for a solution for the administration of credit applications they were looking for a simple system that was agile and able to integrate with their Core Banking systems as well as all areas involved throughout their organization. They decided upon BizAgi's BPM (Business Process Management) technology to automate the process of managing their consumer credit applications (personal, vehicle and credit cards) and mortgages. Today, the system manages more than 4500 cases per month, all by means of a web portal that is programmed to disburse the loans at a national level in the shortest possible time. The levels of security and control are sufficient to ensure a healthy loan portfolio in accordance with the bank's guidelines. In terms of transactions, 80% are processed automatically and 20% are processed by risk analysts and a centralized, multi-product credit factory.

TRANSFIRIENDO S.A., COLOMBIA

Finalist, South America. Nominated by TYCON S.A., Argentina

Transfiriendo S.A., a Colombian company with headquarters in Bogotá focused on providing transaction services through technological solutions related to the exchange of digital documents, has successfully implemented BIZUIT Agile Business Suite as a platform for information exchange and management of business processes that manage the issue, printing and delivery of insurance policies called SOAT (Compulsory Insurance of Motor Vehicle Accidents).BIZUIT allowed us to count - in a very short time - with a technological platform that manages approximately 70% of SOAT policies that are issued throughout Colombia, managing information from the largest and most important insurances companies in the country. The success of the business carried us to become a leader in the industry and replicate our business in Ecuador, with an overwhelming success. The BIZUIT SOA platform allowed us to reuse the majority of services and existing business processes.

Section 6 Appendix

AWARD WINNERS AND NOMINATORS CONTACT DIRECTORY

FURTHER READING, ASSOCIATIONS,

Guest
Chapters

Social Technologies Will Drive the Next Wave of BPM Suites[1]

Clay Richardson, Forrester Research, USA

When you spend time taking a sober look at a market's maturity—like we did with our recently published BPM Tech Radar report—some technologies make you yawn, but then other technologies give you goose bumps. The primary purpose of the BPM Tech Radar was to map the maturity of the 15 most critical technologies that make up the BPM landscape. This included tried and true technologies such as workflow, process modelling, document imaging, and business rules; in addition to bleeding and leading edge technologies such as process data management and process mashups.

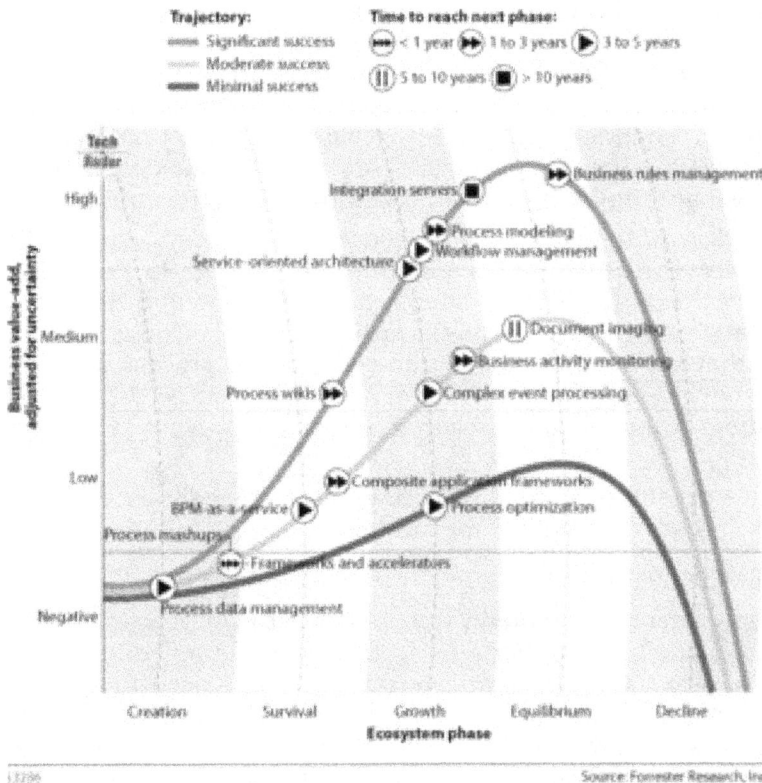

Now that I've had time to step back from the excitement of pulling the report together (that's a completely separate blog post or book unto itself), one key point has lodged itself into my subconscious—yes, I've had a few dreams about this (pretty sad, I know): Of all the technologies we evaluated, the components that generated the most buzz and excitement had some connection with social media or Web 2.0. That's not a big surprise, right? Social

---

[1] Originally posted September 2, 2009 at

http://blogs.forrester.com/business_process/2009/09/social-technologies-will-drive-the-next-wave-of-bpm-suites.html media is hot right now, it's sexy; it's the "golden child" so to speak. But BPM and social media together?

At first blush it seems an odd marriage. But take a step back. Okay, a few steps back. Let's remember what BPM is all about: Ultimately, BPM is a discipline for continually improving cross-functional, end-to-end business processes. To accomplish this, Business Process professionals spend gobs of time and money analyzing and implementing strategies to improve process collaboration, communication, interdepartmental hand-offs, and institutional process knowledge. Hmmm... collaboration, communication, updating knowledge—smells pretty social to me. In many ways, social is just the natural extension and evolution of collaboration, as Connie Moore outlined in her recent blog post "Great News For The Process World—A Sea Change Is Coming."

While the BPM suites market evolved over the past two decades to support the "known human interactions" within the enterprise, vendors continue to overlook—or can't capture—a lot of the process whitespace within organizations. Think: e-mail communication about a process, instant messaging to get a response to a process-related question, allowing business users to generate processes, allowing front-line workers to update process knowledge. Based on our BPM Tech Radar interviews—we spoke with over 65 customers, leading vendors, and BPM evangelists—it seems that social and Web 2.0 technologies are breathing new life into BPMS to tackle the remaining process whitespace that still needs to be conquered in the enterprise.

Early leaders in the "Social BPM" space include Lombardi and Software AG. Earlier this year, Software AG announced their AlignSpace offering under the banner of Social BPM. And, Lombardi is also pushing the envelope in this space with their Blueprint platform, which now offers a "friend feed" style feature that allows process users to get feeds on process model and requirements changes throughout discovery. IBM is even getting into the game by integrating some of Lotus' social components with Websphere Process Server.

So what's driving this trend of Social BPM? Three larger trends are pushing process and social media closer together:

ACCELERATED PACE OF CHANGE IN THE BUSINESS ENVIRONMENT

Business leaders who thought they had months or years to adapt their processes to changing conditions are now fossils, driven into extinction by our latest recession. Going forward, business leaders need to approach BPM using both a top-down and bottom-up approach. New technologies, such as "process wikis" allow frontline workers to update process knowledge as conditions change on the ground. This real-time feedback loop was never available before; most updates to process knowledge are only captured haphazardly or driven from the top down.

THE NEED TO PUT PROCESS COMPLETELY INTO CONTEXT

I spend a lot of time trying to read through e-mail threads to understand the complete context of a question posed to me (the snowball effect: e-mail starts off from one person, bounces around, and then ends up in my inbox). Completing a process often involves numerous conversations—via e-mail, instant messenger, voicemail, etc.—that fall outside of the BPM suite container. Imagine combining a tool like Google Wave with a BPMS: Now process-related conversations and threads can be easily traced throughout the process instance. So, instead of digging through e-mail, you can click on an activity in the process and see the entire context of conversations around the in-flight process.

DEMAND FOR USER-GENERATED CONTENT

I'm man enough to admit it: Just like you I jumped on the "get-rich building your own iPhone app" bandwagon. Why? Because I think I can code and I want the world to see my new whiz-bang idea for the iPhone. Of course none of this ever materialized (I have a full time job, remember?). But a lot of other hack and weekend developers rolled up their sleeves and contributed their own whiz-bang apps—some good, some not so good. Looks like users and department heads are also trying to get in on the act of user-generated content. Except it's not for the iPhone—it's for internal processes. "Process mashups" (such as Serena Business Mashups) and "BPM-as-a-Service" (such as Appian Anywhere) technologies are indulging the business' fantasy of automating processes without IT's help. And the verdict? Process hacks are having success generating some pretty nice processes (that run!).

Recently, I did a guest spot on CIOTalkRadio covering "human interaction management." Phil Gilbert (Lombardi Software's CEO) and Howard Smith (CTO, CSC European Group) were also guests for the segment. I kind of blew up the show by telling the host, Sanjog Aul, that I hated the term "human interaction management" since it assumes we can manage "human interactions". Really? At any rate Phil and I ended up hijacking the conversation to lay out the future of what work and processes will look like. The short of it, processes and BPM will be much more social. Phil threw out a statement that I think sums it up well: "A lot of people are looking for BPM on steroids. What we really need is BPM on Facebook."

WHY IT MATTERS

Don't discount social media's impact on business process management just because of its current level of hype and consumer focus. Over the next two to three years BPM suites will continue to incorporate social technologies and features that connect process to the real way that people work and get things done. Millennials and Gen Y employees entering the work force will likely embrace these new features and help accelerate the Social BPM trend. Business Process professionals should keep an open eye (and open mind) out for opportunities to begin leveraging Social BPM components such as process wikis, process mashups, and BPM-as-a-Service.

WHAT'S YOUR TAKE?

I want to hear from you. Let me know what you think about social media's impact on the BPM market? Do you think Social BPM represents the natural progression of BPM suites. Do you think social technologies will help BPM suites harness process-related conversations and user generated content? Or do you think this is just a mashup of two hot market segments that really don't belong together?

Thinking Global, Acting Local: How BI and BPM support Smart Cities in a Globalized Economy

Lewis Carr, Oracle Corporation, USA

ABSTRACT

Business Process Management (BPM) and Business Intelligences (BI) suites are prevalent in large and medium size private sector and central government organizations but have not fully reached down to local government. Even cities with multi-billion dollar budgets and over 10,000 employees are still using combinations of Excel, Project, siloed databases, home-grown dashboards and other poorly suited tools. This paper looks at the challenges local governments face and how BI and BPM will make cities smarter about how they plan and implement budgets and sourcing, programs, and infrastructure. The paper discusses the local government business model and levers of growth and how this model may have inherent structural barriers that prevent insight and change. Finally, we provide successful cases of BI and BPM being applied from different parts of local government organizations towards the same goals of improved performance, streamlined management and transparency and accountability of government to its constituents.

INTRODUCTION

We live in an urban world. As of last year, according to UN statistics, more than 51 percent of us now reside in urban environments. Since the turn of this century, mega-cities in the developing world have seen a full doubling of their populations and even developed-world cities and towns will see increases of over 10 percent. By 2050 over two-thirds of us will be urban dwellers—a situation that will pose several challenges and opportunities. Thomas Friedman coined the term "the world is flat" in his famous book of the same name and it was even mentioned in the Foreword with reference to the competitive pressures private sector businesses face. While I would agree with that assessment, for local government the "flat world" label applies but with a far more multi-dimensional impact than monetary profit and loss.

Cities are becoming the globalization "ground-zero" for new definitions of poverty, in fighting communicable diseases that can lead to pandemics, in combating terrorism and in dealing with international gangs and crime syndicates. But most importantly, they also act as the economic engines for new-world economies and are on the forefront of their respective national hopes and desires to compete on the international stage.

In today's economic climate, local government revenue collections, expenditures, programs, and delivered services are scrutinized more than ever before for return on investment (ROI) and outcomes. The problems arise not from the scrutiny but from the lack of understanding how and where these four areas are interconnected and how to bridge the siloed elements within them, streamline those join-up operations and produce better outcomes for a given investment. Homeowners and businesses argue for lower property taxes because they do not see direct value back to them yet in the next breath demand more infrastructure to improve quality of life and promote economic development. Of course, government understands that balancing these areas is handled by through a complex set of funding mechanisms and programs but what they do not have is the visibility into where to deliver fine-tuning or course corrections to the programs and services delivered; where they are interdependent or how to make them efficient, transparent, and ultimately transform them.

- What is the right mix of focused government programs and policies to get from where cities are today towards a vibrant and sustainable future?
- What are justifiable revenue streams from constituents and central government coffers and expenditures that can be made?
- How can cities deliver better deliver services and infrastructure to constituents without excessive demands on those very citizens and businesses being served, for further taxation and a call for wider fiscal support from central funding?

The answer to these questions is a platform with the intelligence to provide transparency and accountability and a mapping of the existing and required connection points between operational processes and programs that can, when combined, support transformation of day-to-day information and transactions into the priorities of tomorrow's focused and integrated programs. Two core components of this solution are the appropriate applications of BI and BPM.

IDENTIFY INEFFICIENCIES AND STRUCTURAL BARRIERS: THE ROADMAP TO BECOMING A SMART CITY

As described above, globalization and today's economic climate weigh heavily on the resources and citizens of most cities around the world. Many cities are faced with declining property tax bases, larger expenditures on social safety nets (unemployment insurance, job training, child welfare, etc.), and further demands to justify investment in transportation, energy distribution, education spending and other infrastructure building, while equally critical to the quality of life and economic viability of the city, these mid- to long-term investments are much harder to justify. And, even when justified, the funds must partially come through additional efficiencies gained and funds transferred from existing programs.

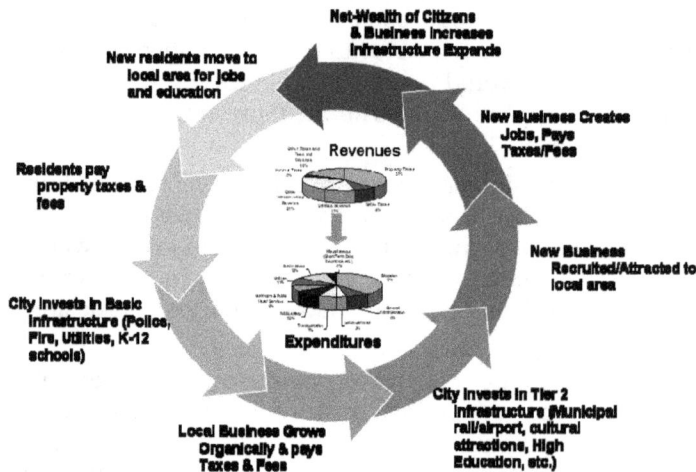

Figure 1 Conceptual Cycle of Urban Development and Municipal Growth

The goal of a BI and BPM platform is to provide the intelligence required to improve recruitment and retention of the city's economic engine which in turn fuels better quality of life for its citizens, raising their standards of living through higher paying, skilled employment which in turn raises the value of their assets—including their property and the municipal property tax base. This, in turn, with the right government policies, infrastructure investment and programs, attracts more business and the cycle repeats itself as shown in the figure above.

Through the use of BPM and BI, government executives receive unprecedented insights into emerging cyclical trends, structural characteristics of their organization and underlying operational process. By leveraging BPM and Service Oriented Architecture (SOA) governance, reusable business processes that represent best practices within government programs and their associated IT resources can be scaled up and reused across all organizations as a shared service. By leveraging BI and SOA, detailed information can be extracted from specific service delivery mechanisms and their usage such as how many permits are issued, to whom, through which channels and in which demographic segment of your constituency. The following Table provides a high-level mapping of Government Processes to typical BPM Features applied.

Characteristics of Local Government Processes	Primary BPM Feature Set Applied
Continuously Changing Policy and Downstream Changes to Procedures	Process modelling and simulation (can be combined with Enterprise Policy Automation)
Inconsistent and unwritten process from multiple departments	Process modelling and simulation
Inefficiencies in process execution	Process execution and optimization
Different employees doing different tasks at different stages of the workflow	Process execution and optimization
Required approval at different stages	Decision Services
Management reports and performance pledges	Business Activity Monitoring and Executive Dashboards
Enabling or Improving Constituent Self-Service	Process execution and optimization (can be combined with Enterprise 2.0) and Portal capabilities)
Reduction in Paper and Manual Processes (e.g. e-Records and Green Initiatives)	Process execution and optimization (can be combined with Enterprise Content Management)
Cross Government Collaboration	Service Enabled Processes (can be combined with SOA)

Table 1 Characteristics of Local Government processes mapped to primary BPM feature set applied

For example, the BI collected from SOA-enabled platforms across departments and multiple operations can be used to answer questions such as how many code violations are flagged by different departments, in turn, the results of this can be mapped to various municipal zoning areas and compared with the business process used in each of those departments. Modelling can then be done with Business Process Management to determine how to modify and apply best practices around what to flag, how to respond, how to inspect, and how to enforce infractions upon citation. Resulting changes in the process may have an impact on programs and their underlying resources, ranging from the number of inspectors, standard metrics set for evaluating their effectiveness and efficiency to consolidation of backend infrastructure or decisions to standardize on particular field hand-held devices. The process is of course cyclic, with new BI information being extracted, analyzed and placed in dashboards to determine how to further improve the programs and set annual department and program budgets.

The combination of BI and BPM are also critical to cities because core resources are changing for cities; even the definition of "employee" is evolving. Increasingly, governments are relying on part-timers and volunteers, partners, non-profits and contractors to deliver government services. Variations in employee type can lead to workflow differences particularly in expert knowledge worker roles where human to human interaction is involved. BPM can be used to identify inefficiencies across end-to-end process and, when coupled with BI, local government department and contracting managers can determine if clear and quantifiable differences in outcomes against defined metrics are being delivered. The ability to track the cost and relative effectiveness of programs and service delivery channels empowers government executives during reviews of cross-departmental operations to determine where process may need modification based on how well prior performance periods delivered against metrics, contract negotiations to negotiate the best contract with those government employees or outside contracts that are capable of meeting the needs of constituents and a host of other areas.

By using the combination of BI and BPM, governments not only monitor the relative success and efficiency of government programs, assets and channels, but relate individual and program performance measures to larger policy objectives such as reducing operational costs, decreasing crime, measuring the value of infrastructure investments in roads, sewer systems, public education, social safety nets, public healthcare and increasing economic development and developing a sustainable workforce. In other words, the combination of BI and BPM can provide transparency and proof that tax revenues were spent wisely. Through executive dashboards, mayors, city and county council members and other government executives identify the key policy objectives they need to track, and post attainment of those objectives on their website for all constituents to see; they can even build community forums to elicit discussion and feedback and embedded the dashboard results into constituent facing web sites.

SMART CITY BI AND BPM TRAILBLAZERS

It is often said that Sunshine is the best disinfectant for political systems when wielded by the appropriate controller. In some cities this has led to overlapping bureaucracies and redundant programs and resourcing. Even where it hasn't been the case, if the city is old and large, it's an unfortunate assumption city government is faced with. Many cities have embarked on programs to deliver a full account of their budgets and programs and accountability to their constituents. More often than not, these programs are being spearheaded by financial controllers at the city-wide level. A superb example of this is Boston's BAR program (Boston About Results) which provides quarterly performance and management data to its constituents directly on its public site at **www.cityofboston.gov/bar**.

The site went live in February of 2009 and provides facts and figures about the delivery, use, and cost of city services. As stated on the site, "internally, this data is used to identify trends, raise questions and devise new management strategies. To increase accountability and transparency, Mayor Menino is making consolidated performance and budget data available online for many of the City's biggest departments." Of course, a certain level of internal efficiencies and transparency must be developed by the team carrying out these reviews. It would be very difficult to do this without use of integrated Business Intelligence Suites such as Enterprise Performance Management tools back-ended by BI tools that collect the right information from the various departments built around a SOA platform spanning those silos. Dashboards have to be clear and simple but adequately and comprehensively reflect key indicators of health for critical constituent services. Cities take different approaches to setting up their points of control. In some cases, it means developing a separate department and focusing on a particular stage of government services delivery.

Hong Kong, for example, created a separate organization, Hong Kong Efficiency Unit (HKEU) in 1992 with the directive: "To pursue the Government's commitment to improve services to the community and to achieve openness and accountability by formulating, securing support for and coordinating the implementation of a programme of Public Sector Reform." The organization works as the lead oversight and project management office for cross-department, city-wide transformative including, their Single Non-Emergency Number (SNEN) service, 1823 (equivalent to US 311 systems) which launched in 2001. HKEU uses BPM with on-line city services to business, citizens and internal organizations to automate the back-end government processes to efficiently support and provision them, improve communications between staff where human to human interaction are part of the workflow and to identify bottlenecks and problem areas for overhaul and elimination.

While there may be several organizational angles from which to embark on a Smart Cities effort, they all have four things in common:

1. an executive sponsor with a constituent-centric focus as part of the mission statement at the very top level of government—in general the mayor of the city;
2. as quickly as possible, set up a shared services organization with a center-of-excellence level of resourcing in support of that organization;
3. used a combination of organizational changes and IT was simply an enabler;
4. BI and BPM as tools to support on-going continuous improvements and insight in to the process. New York City is probably the best poster-child for this set of highly effective habits by smart cities.

For the last eight years, New York has been led by Mayor Blumberg, a mayor who truly understands customer service, Information Technology, and financial management at a level unmatched by most public officials due to his Financial Services industry background. In his tenure he has established a fully integrated, on-line self service city portal, **www.nyc.gov/apps/311** and call center that consolidated over 45 call centers inclusive of over 1,000 employees. The purpose of this system was not simply to increase efficiency and transparency of city service delivery—removing the "department shuffle" that frustrates so many residents of large cities around the world - but to act as a feedback loop to determine where services should be improved and extended. Like Boston, New York City uses BI and posts reports on performance of various city services and use of public funds to its website, NYCStat **www.nyc.gov/html/ops/nycstat/html/ home/home. shtml**). New York City officials have been indoctrinated with Mayor Blumberg's business style and fully understand that technology is an enabler. New York City departments are results driven with metrics that are dashboarded with business intelligence software.

Services like NYC.gov and the 311 call center (largest in the country) have all been implemented by the Department of Information Technology & Telecommunications; a shared-services organization with more than 700 employees including software developers and systems analysts, project managers, and administrative support. As NYC's shared services organization, it operates 24x7 for several other organizations' IT infrastructure services, ERP, and front-office applications and services inclusive of a 24x7 help desk. In essence, they've built a global enterprise-class IT organization of the same quality and size of their commercial counterparts (in terms of budget and total employees).

Of course all the examples we've provided are for large cities with large budgets and employee roles but these are not pre-requisites for successful programs nor are smaller departmental organizations within large cities or mid-sized cities (down to say 50,000) without need of BI and BPM. For example, one of the fastest growing housing associations in the United Kingdom, Metropolitan Housing Partnership (MHP) in London provides quality, affordable housing solutions for tenants and leaseholders--all with a budget of roughly $400 million and 1500 employees. MHP used BPEL process orchestration, a key component of most BPM suites to re-engineer a number of their key business processes and implemented new, innovative systems to service the needs of their customers (tenants and leaseholders). With BPEL process orchestration they were able to meet changing regulatory requirements cost-effectively and at the speed of demand.

CONCLUSION

Smart Cities will be defined by tangible constituent-centric leading indicators such as single-point of contact web-based self-service for all government (the next generation of eGovernment portals), single-number non-emergency services (for example 311 in the United States), intelligent transportation systems (for example Smart parking systems), green infrastructure such as electrical grids that enable and facilitate individual business and homeowners to install solar panels that send energy back to the grid during peak hours of use and many other symbols of 21st century communities. But, behind all these successful programs, Business Intelligence and Business Process Management will be required to provide:

- Automation and orchestration of process across existing siloed multi-departmental municipal landscapes
- Extraction of key information from IT systems as it relates to workflow within the orchestrated process that can be turned into intelligence to support continuous improvement to the process
- Analysis of performance trends and operations for services delivered through dashboarding of BI and BPM results
- Operational efficiencies through streamlining workflow/process orchestration inclusive of back-end ERP systems
- Tracking and improving the effectiveness of programs, employees, peer government and service delivery partners
- Improving Government Accessibility and Transparency intra-government, between Local and Federal, and cross government and public stakeholders.
- Reducing costs of Operations in sharing and collaboration, especially in Medical and Judicial / Enforcement / Homeland Security areas

As the world's leading information-management company, Oracle understands that local government's most valuable asset is information and the efforts of its employees. The combination of BPM and Business Intelligence is designed to provide local governments with the tools necessary to empower employees in providing constituents with consistent and efficient services.

Section 1

Europe

KPN, Netherlands

Finalist, Europe

Nominated by Cordys, UK

1. EXECUTIVE SUMMARY / ABSTRACT

KPN is the leading telecommunications and ICT service provider in The Netherlands, offering wireline and wireless telephony, Internet and TV to customers and end-to-end telecom and ICT services to business customers. KPN provides wholesale network services to third parties and operates an efficient IP-based infrastructure with global scale. In order to attract new customers, retain its more than 35 million existing customers and remain competitive as a multi-play provider amidst the forces of deregulation, KPN must focus on creating a more customer-centric business—and aligning its IT systems to meet this objective. This has spurred KPN to:

1. accelerate and increase the scale of new service offerings (e.g. the 2008 mass roll-out of its All-IP network for Fiber-to-the Curb (FttC, based on VDSL) and Fiber-to-the-Home (FttH) capabilities);

2. increase customer service and satisfaction levels (e.g. improving the percentage of 'first time right' instances); and,

3. reduce overall provisioning costs (e.g. the Consumer Segment cut back a multitude of brands to three).

To help take KPN's business to a new level with these customer-centric imperatives for all its IP Consumer, Wholesale and Business Markets, KPN implemented a flexible, carrier-grade business process management platform with rapid modeling and revision of business process in real-time. The Cordys Business Operations Platform (BOP) supported KPN's multiple customer systems in CRM/Billing Support System domains to automate serviceability and provisioning operations (e.g. "zero touch activation"), and improve the percentage of "first time right" customer calls; whilst also to:

1. dramatically accelerate multiple-product market introduction cycles

2. increase the rate of rollout of its new glass network, which is estimated to enable about €900 million of cost-savings through the eventual sunset of 1400 local exchanges across the company; and,

3. support the eventual network growth from the planned 100,000 customers in the first year to 3.5 million customers in the next 2 years.

2. OVERVIEW

The KPN Glass Program Project

KPN is implementing an All-IP infrastructure by connecting 28,000 street cabinets to fiber and, from those cabinets, connecting to customers with fiber or VDSL, to set themselves apart from their competition.

The KPN Glass Program Project leverages advanced Business Process Management tools to manage commercial orchestration (provisioning, fulfillment, invoicing and servicing) of customer orders for its new product line (IP services on top of a fiber network). Through this Project, KPN now provides direct provisioning ("zero touch activation") and billing of new voice, Internet and multimedia services on new fiber network. Orders are entered from the Internet straight through to Operational Support Systems and Billing Support Systems. This requires a high level of sophistication with respect to handling complex processes with multiple situations (including management of exceptions and alerts within preset service level hierarchies), systems (legacy systems and other network technologies) and sites (national project). The platform also provides a real-time, multi-level Business Activity Monitoring dashboard for the Business Manager on the progress and performance of provisioning processes.

This has dramatically improved provisioning speed and accuracy (speed top line revenue growth), while lowering costs. The system is designed to scale from 100,000 customers in the first year to 3.5 million in the next 2 years

In terms of implementation, the KPN Glass Program has resulted in three projects to address similar - but also specific - process needs in three of its core market segments:

1. Commercial Orchestration for KPN Consumer Market (CM) Glass All-IP Program;
2. Wholesale Order Desk for All-IP Service Providers in Consumer Markets; and,
3. Commercial Orchestration for KPN's Business Market DSL and glass fiber products (ZIPB)

Project 1. Commercial Orchestration for KPN Consumer Market (CM) Glass All-IP Program

The project consists of a set of business processes for the provisioning of All-IP glass fiber products. For each All-IP product or service a unique process is available that orchestrates the creation, change, deletion, activation and deactivation of the product in the OSS-domain. Specifically, in this case, the system is a part of the process to:

1. Get available products at home address (retrieves products from product catalogue; perform customer validation, location validation, etc.)
2. Validate order and insert order in CRM-system (Siebel)
3. Execute order (retrieves order lines from CRM-system and create products in OSS-environment)
4. Accommodate customer self service (such as self-configuration, activation/deactivation of products)
5. Cancel orders
6. Upgrade / downgrade orders, including the activation / deactivation of products
7. Move a customer to another location (delete at old location, create at new location)
8. Make Administrative changes of customer data
9. Handle engineer resource allocation / planning and hardware logistics
10. Manage Process Exceptions

Project 2: Wholesale Order Desk for Service Providers;

This market for Service Providers who are resellers of KPN All-IP Products requires a robust and secure system to handle third-party orders. This process requires checking commercial product portfolios as agreed with the Services Providers. The solution focused on:

1. Orchestrating the order process (identification, authorization, validation en registration)
2. Translating incoming Service Provider-orders to an order that can be sent to the OSS-domain.
3. Managing the order database
4. Handling of Service Provider / Customer Support inquiries about Products and Installed Base
5. Managing SLA's with Service Providers
6. Analyzing Incidents

Project 3. Commercial Orchestration for KPN's Business Market DSL and glass fiber products

The Commercial Orchestration Engine for the Business Market (ZM) consists of a set of business processes for the provisioning of DSL and All-IP glass fiber products. The solution focused on:

1. Validating the order based on defined rules, and inserting order into the Order Database
2. Transforming incoming Commercial orders into outgoing Functional Orders that can be sent to the OSS-domain.
3. Orchestrating the order execution, handling dependencies between products
4. Cancelling orders
5. Upgrading / downgrading existing order
6. Moving customers to other locations (e.g. delete at old location, create at new location)
7. Handling administrative changes
8. Handling logistics for equipment delivery
9. Managing process exceptions

Benefits

- A Business Process Management platform is ideal for managing complex systems and processes in the highly dynamic and competitive Telco industries. It supports an agile development approach, which leads to quick turn-around times.
- The fully web services-based architecture enables relative ease of connective with other business applications.
- The Business Activity Monitoring module has rich value-add functionalities, giving a high level of business predictability.
- The project also benefited from the highly motivated and knowledgeable Cordys solution provider team members.

3. BUSINESS CONTEXT

KPN is the leading telecommunications and ICT service provider in The Netherlands, offering wireline and wireless telephony, Internet and TV to customers and end-to-end telecom and ICT services to business customers. KPN provides wholesale network services to third parties and operates an efficient IP-based infrastructure with global scale. The company has in the Netherlands alone:

- 4.5 million PSTN / ISDN lines
- 3.4 million broadband customers
- 0.6 million TV customers
- 7.5 million wireless customers

Telecom deregulation has placed additional pressure on KPN to compete. KPN has to provide better customer service, unified services and new services, delivered faster. KPN is also working on replacing their current copper network with an All-IP infrastructure to reduce operational and maintenance costs. These substantial cost reductions which will be partly reinvested in revenue growth and partly allocated for improving margins to 'best-in-class'.

With the All-IP network, KPN is launching a Triple Play bundle of service for their customers in Broadband, TV and VOIP. KPN requires a business process management tool to handle the complexity of orchestrating the provisioning these new service offerings to customers, while managing current legacy information and systems.

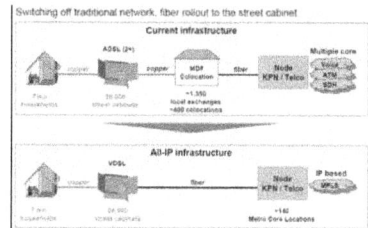

"Because of the intense time pressure we faced we were looking for a supplier who could not only provide a flexible application, but also has extensive knowledge of the subject matter so as to contribute to this strategic project." Jan Muchez, CIO of KPN.

4. THE KEY INNOVATIONS

4.1 Business

KPN is now truly becoming a customer-centric company based on a fully future-proofed next generation Business Operations Platform for Telco. They have dramatically accelerated their ability to launch new products into the market, and improve their serviceability and provisioning operations (e.g. "zero touch activation" and "first time right" customer calls).

KPN also scored in terms of improving operational efficiencies and cost-savings, by providing the technology infrastructure to eventually more quickly sunset 1400 local exchanges across the company. KPN also now has a system that customers can service themselves with, which is scalable to support a network growth from 100,000 customers in the first year to 3.5 million customers in the next 2 years.

KPN will soon demonstrate industry leadership with its successful All-IP launches, and its innovative business process management implementation will form the architectural base for all future projects. New applications and mash-applications can be added to the Cordys Business Operations Platform for additional flexibility.

4.2 Process

This was a new implementation for a new product offering to KPN. Prior to this, KPN had a mixture of legacy systems and manual processes for customer order orchestration. KPN was already using Business Process Management tools for earlier product launches, but these solutions were less robust and more labor intensive.

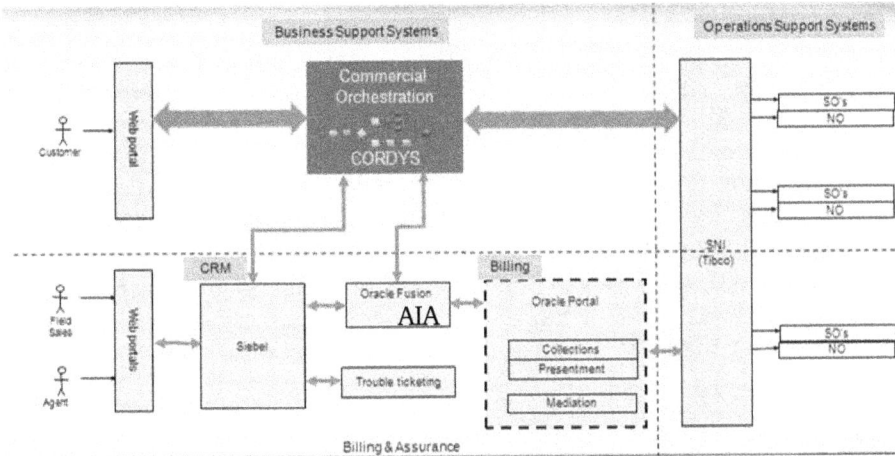

Figure 1 – KPN Commercial Orchestration for Customer Market

In terms of system's runtime adaptability, the project requirements and processes constantly evolved throughout the three implementations. In addition, the tool's can be seen in the 3 similar, but distinct requirements for the 3 projects.

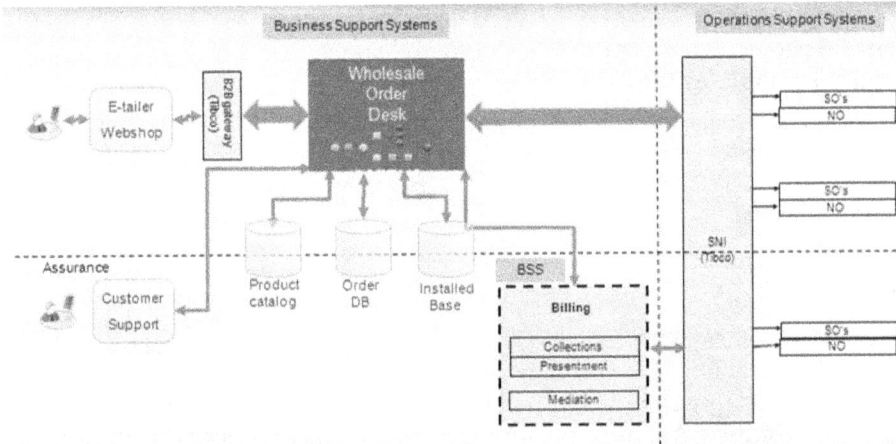

Figure 2 – KPN Commercial Orchestration for Wholesale

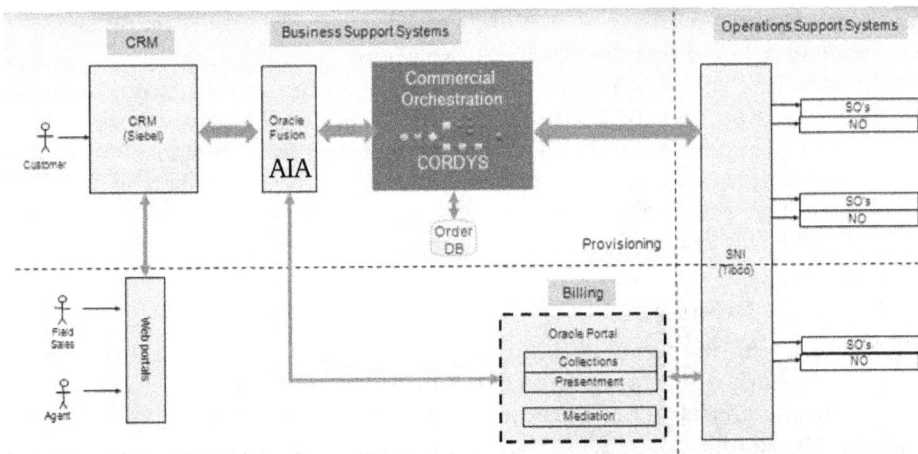

Figure 3 – KPN Commercial Orchestration for Business Customers

4.3 Organization

The whole program serves as a reference implementation of the new agile work environment within KPN, which will continue throughout the company. This was borne from management complexity of the project, which had been compounded by the multiple locations involved. The first project (Glass Program) ran at Bussum, and then moved to other locations Groningen / The Hague / Almere / India. The second project (WOD) is running in The Hague, and the third project (ZIPB) is running in Bussum again.

With this implementation, KPN is moving towards a customer self-service model – which is expected to provide a higher level of service for customers, thus freeing their employees for higher value customer service exceptions/needs.

5. HURDLES OVERCOME

The first conceptual IT architecture was implemented in this totally new business imperative introducing IP services on top of a fiber network. As a result, the project began without all of the business requirements specified. This was compounded by the scope and scale of the implementation: the first project was a national project that was part of a huge program and it included inter-company processes. The flexible implementation framework allowed KPN to make changes throughout. KPN, in partnership with its solution provider Cordys, had a team of about 25 people (partners and KPN employees included) delivered the first project within the stipulated 90 days and on budget.

This was a strategic project driven and sponsored by top management from KPN, Cordys and system implementation partners (such as Capgemini, IBM, and Accenture). Given the scale and the tight timelines involved, this was vital to the project's success.

6. BENEFITS

6.1 Cost Savings

The shift to a glass fiber network is estimated to eventually enable KPN to sunset 1400 switches across the company, saving roughly €900 million in management. In addition, this investment will help KPN be future proof: KPN intends to leverage this new BPM infrastructure to bring additional customers and services (such as Digital TV with 800000 users) in the future.

6.2 Time Reductions

Due to the competitive market, KPN has to be a very dynamic organization, making flexibility a key driver for their new solution. From a business process perspective, it is now much easier to make changes to the implementation, since almost all logic was realized by using BPMN Business Processes instead of Java programming. From a customer service perspective, instead of manually processing orders, customers can now place their orders over the web – with straight through processing from KPN backend systems. Customers now receive significantly faster (if not immediate) confirmation of orders. Less staff time is now spent servicing customers.

6.3 Increased Revenues

KPN was able to more rapidly launch, provision and invoice All-IP customers – and gain the early mover's market share of this market. However, as both product and platform were launched together, it is not possible to attribute revenues or costs directly to one cause. However, the change programme is thus far successful and the company is realizing its objectives on time.

6.4 Productivity Improvements

KPN employees can now provide a range of support levels and reports for both their direct channel to the consumer markets and their indirect sales channels (via Service Providers). They can also now focus more on handling just the exceptions and building relationships, instead of previously expending their energies on ensuring that orders were processing correctly.

7. BEST PRACTICES, LEARNING POINTS AND PITFALLS

7.1 Best Practices and Learning Points

✓ *Leverage the agile development approach for quick turnaround times. Find a technology solution that is truly flexible when working with dynamic requirements, and factor that into the professional services arrangement. Change is bound to happen during the implementation.*

✓ *Leverage a corporate-standardized platform that can be reused for other business processes (for example, projects were quickly created sprung Customer Market to Wholesale Market to Business Market, based on the base knowledge of the first project.)*

✓ *Leverage a real web service-based architecture, which can work seamlessly with your legacy systems and also work with potential future technologies*

✓ *Have the highest Executive commitment available for projects with such large strategic impact and scale*

✓ *Work with Solution Partners who have in depth knowledge of the industry*

7.2 Pitfalls

✗ *The waterfall approach does not work in such implementations, because requirements keep changing. A strong high-level decoupled architecture and a central design office is required to manage all the changes and interdependencies between the subsystems.*

✗ *Over-extending legacy systems that may not be able to serve your future needs.*

8. COMPETITIVE ADVANTAGES

Strategically, KPN has defined the following 'growth' objectives, that provides the company with competitive advantage:

Customer focus:
- Services based on customer needs
- No technology push
- Customer life-cycle management
- Multi-branding
- Segmented market approach
- Many own and third party channels
- Supported by limited number of clear and targeted brands
- Lowest cost
- Focus on operational excellence
- Competitive cost base

Proactive:
- Early exposure of All-IP to the market

KPN also has the following platforms and infrastructure directions:
- Migrate to IP (Higher quality network, with higher bandwidth and structurally lower costs)
- Simplify network processes and IT
- Switch off legacy systems

KPN has upped the ante with these new product investments, and has strengthened its position as a front runner in the market and perceived by other Telco's as such. These short and long term objectives are in alignment with the project goals to provide cost-effective ways to increase customer intimacy, improve operational efficiency and demonstrate product leadership through launching All-IP to the market.

9. Technology

By leveraging a Business Process Management layer for commercial orchestration, KPN is able to keep its current Business Applications as standard as possible. Instead of customizations made to business applications (which might be a lengthy, disruptive and costly process), configurations are made within the Cordys Business Operations Platform.

- Cordys BPM-engine is triggered by external events (customer portal, order fulfillment from Siebel, etc)
- Cordys Studio has a easily maintainable graphical design of orchestration logic, which helps in training in-house/partner resources to manage drilled-down process configurations for such large scale implementations
- Cordys orchestrates the order fulfillment at the BSS-side and calls all relevant peripheral applications, like Stream serve DMS (send letters and emails to customers), Tango engineering planning and De telefoongids Directory Services. (See Figure 5 below.)

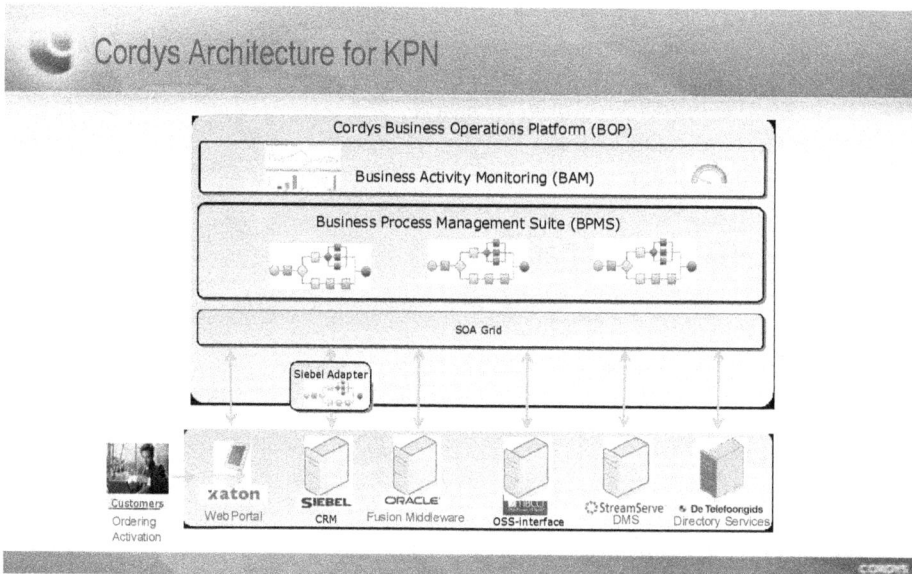

Overall process performance on the business level is monitored using Cordys Business Activity Monitoring

With this, KPN has created a very flexible infrastructure to meet its competitive needs. The project has delivered the technology boost it needs on the service and delivery front to present greater customer value, including:

- more customer self-service abilities within the solution, so that straight-through-processing (STP) capability was possible
- sophisticated, but user-friendly graphical design facilities, quick in assembly – very limited coding for short cycles, quick iterations and changes-on-the-fly

- a secure, carrier-grade and scalable architecture that allows for multiple servers to be added in case of increasing system load. (In total, the system leverages 250 different web services, where 100 web services are connecting to external systems with UDDI or HTTP connector.)

10. THE TECHNOLOGY AND SERVICE PROVIDERS

Cordys is a global provider of software for business process innovation and Enterprise Cloud Orchestration. The industry-leading Cordys Business Operations Platform (BOP) consists of a complete suite for next generation Business Process Management (BPM), Business Activity Monitoring (BAM) and innovative SaaS Deployment Frameworks (SDF), delivering a complete Platform as a Service (PaaS) solution. It includes an open, integrated set of tools & technologies including Composite Application Framework (CAF), Master Data Management (MDM) and a SOA Grid. The Cordys platform and its cutting-edge Cloud technology empowers customers to dramatically improve the speed of change, fundamentally altering the way they innovate their Business Operations to achieve a true customer-centric philosophy. Global 2000 companies worldwide have selected Cordys to achieve business performance improvements such as increased productivity, reduced time to market, higher security and faster response to ever-changing market demands. Headquartered in the Netherlands, Cordys is a global company with offices in the USA, the UK, Germany, China, India and Israel. For more information please visit www.cordys.com.

Migros Bank, Switzerland

Gold Award, Europe

Nominated by Action Technologies Inc., USA

1. EXECUTIVE SUMMARY / ABSTRACT

Migros Bank is one of the 10 leading financial institutes in Switzerland and one of the biggest Retail-Banks. Our focus is to be very close to the clients and therefore we have around 50 branches all over Switzerland and many more small contact-points that offer basic services for new clients. All in all about 1,400 employees work for Migros Bank. When we outsourced almost all of our IT to an external provider, little or no electronic workflows were in use. In addition, we were confronted with increasing regulatory and risk issues concerning the internal order processing from the regions to the centralized back-offices that were done by placing orders by paper forms and by fax. To improve these situations we initiated a project to implement electronic people-to-people workflows. Today we are capable of implementing new processes very quickly. A businessperson is able to configure structured and un-structured processes in a short time, depending on the complexity of the requested process. Migros Bank ranks in the top ten in Switzerland's Financial Services industry, but we are far smaller than our global competitors, such as Credit Suisse. An IT executive at Migros Bank, who had been a key implementer of the award-winning ServiceNet application at Credit Suisse, sought to create the same cost, speed, and quality benefits of ServiceNet within a substantially smaller organization. Any analysis of implementation costs (both fixed and variable) across industries and companies, showed that, while BPM software costs and system maintenance costs vary with scale, business process development and business process change costs do not. In fact, it is widely known that labor costs to develop a running process can often exceed software purchase costs and that process changes often cost more than annual software maintenance fees. If these fixed costs cannot be reduced, large organizations will always maintain cost advantages over their middle and smaller sized competitors.

This case study discusses new methods and inventions that eliminate cost disadvantages faced by small and mid-scale organizations, thus enabling these organizations to compete on service and specialization without incurring disadvantages of scale. Migros Bank is the first company to benefit from these methods and inventions.

2. OVERVIEW

In 1925, Gottlieb Duttweiler founded Migros in Zurich, Switzerland to sell basic foodstuffs to his customers, at convenient locations, with excellent service, at value prices. Migros has become one of Switzerland's largest enterprises. Our name comes from the French "mi" for half or mid-way and "gros", which means wholesale. Thus the word connotes prices that are halfway between retail and wholesale. Migros Bank is part of this enterprise and holds to Mr. Duttweiler's original mission - as do all Migros companies. Migros Bank is one of only five nationwide Banks in Switzerland, having a countrywide presence in Switzerland. Further, we are the fourth largest bank in the nation. We have achieved this position by relentlessly following the original mission of the firm. Maintaining a clear mission over such a long period requires effective strategies and tactics to respond to changing competition, customer preferences, and available technologies. Recently, we undertook a study of our efficiency and effectiveness in serving customers. The results of that study produced an action plan that will:

- Increase management's span of control by reducing the number of regional centers from 11 to 6
- Expand the local presence with 19 additional branches till 2010 to a total of 64 branches
- Maintain a strong sales and customer service presence in each branch while centralizing back office and IT services
- Compensate for the risks of miscommunication and poor coordination that would occur with increasing span of control and centralization moves by adding a people-to-people (P2P) Business Process Management (BPM) system

The plan, named Optima, is our single largest initiative, and is being implemented over several years. Nonetheless, a number of the plan's key steps are complete, while many more are in process. This report to the Workflow Management Coalition discusses the results of Migros Bank's people-to-people BPM system and our facilitating role in enabling Migros Bank to achieve the strategic goals through Optima.

3. BUSINESS CONTEXT

Migros Bank responded to the substantial growth of the Bank with increased centralization, specialization and division of work. Complicated processes with a lot of media breaks, the permanent growth of informal communication with order nature and the inefficient monitoring because of complexity and physical separation needed to be optimized.

We outsourced the building of business processes to a third party company, which was our core-banking supplier at that time. However, Business Process implementations were too slow and not able to fulfill our business demands for flexibility, agility, time and cost. We were obligated to radically change the way we were implementing and deploying our business processes. Separating standard retail-banking operating procedures (like payments normally provided by the core-banking platforms) from business event driven procedures (managed by people) was a key decision for successfully managing and orchestrating the new human-oriented, business-processing platform.

In-sourcing Human Driven Procedures

We intended to implement and maintain innovative, business-event and thus human driven processes like customer care processes (i.e. Complaints, Investigations, Inquiries) by our internal business people only. Most of these processes are our key differentiators from competitors in the customer service domain. We overcame the lack of a documented business case for our business event processes by empowering our business people with business configuration tools and techniques, enabling them to 'implement' the processes by themselves. Business needs will dictate how quickly we proceed with the implementation of additional people interaction processes.

Risk Mitigation

Managing human oriented processes required more than just managing the interaction between business people involved in such a process execution. It also required managing the conditions of satisfaction for fulfilling commitments between the different actors involved. Thus, these commitments needed to be defined and published as business rules in a business language and context.

Time to Market

By separating standard workflows from human-oriented processes, we were able to develop different implementation strategies. While standard workflow implementations are part of the core-banking functionality with focus on customization, the implementation of human-oriented workflows use agile software engineering methods and techniques. Using the 'agile' approach we implemented processes within days and deployed them within a week. Setting-up a new human-oriented workflow from scratch and deploying it bank-wide took less than a week.

Initial Project Scope

From the beginning, it was important to manage paper-dominated processes first. All the clients, who were not using e-banking or the predefined banker's orders placed their orders by phone or directly at the front desk, where they were sent by internal mail or fax to the back offices.

This unstructured and inefficient way of treating internal orders needed to be replaced with electronic workflows. The integration of customer's contact data and all bank business relevant data as well as the reflection of our organization including roles, competences and responsibilities were pre-requisites to succeed.

The initial project started in September 2005 and went live with the following processes in April 2006:

- ✓ Accounts balancing
- ✓ Payments CHF
- ✓ Payments foreign exchange
- ✓ Standing orders CHF
- ✓ Standing order foreign exchange
- ✓ Standing orders fees
- ✓ Securities coverage
- ✓ Checks order
- ✓ Compliance

- ✓ Complaints
- ✓ Inquiries
- ✓ New Employees management
- ✓ Employees critical change management
- ✓ New Organizational Units management
- ✓ Organizational Units critical change management
- ✓ Information synchronization management with the core-banking system
- ✓ Case delay management
- ✓ User profile management

Extended Project Scope

After setting up the people-to-people platform, our employees were trained to configure and maintain processes themselves. For this crucial purpose, a tool was developed- the Configuration Box (ConBox). With this ConBox, business people were able to configure processes and to change, test and to deploy them within a few days.

We developed and deployed another twenty-three new processes in the span of only four months (between March and June 2008). This was accomplished by just **one** of our business engineers. This was the ultimate proof statement for the successful implementation of the new people-to-people-processing system.

Expected Improvements at the Process Level

With the new people-to-people platform, business expectations for process optimization were as follows:
- Reduction of passage and process cycle time up to 30%
- Increased productivity up to 30%
- No lost information, zero lost cases

- Mitigation of operational risks
- Increased transparency
- Automated auditable documentation of formal and informal processing
- Generated process-analysis information as a baseline for further improvement

4. THE KEY INNOVATIONS

We decided to purchase Action Technologies' Metro software as a people-to-people BPM system, which uses a closed-loop human interaction model to manage the negotiations, agreements, and customer satisfaction with work performed. The system also provides real-time monitoring of every step of every process and the status of work within every commitment. To this underlying system, Action Solutions added inventions that dramatically reduced process development time and process change time. The patented interaction model is a pre-requisite for coordinated collaboration and is extremely valuable for business people.

4.1 Business

New processes, once defined by business people, are handed over to the responsible business engineers for Migros Bank Workflow. These persons, who are not software engineers, are able to configure the new processes with the ConBox. They configure defining rules and activities or create splits into other sub processes easily. This allows us to be faster and react immediately to business changes and the market without being dependent on third party companies or IT. Quality of service is faster and thru the internal development by business people, no loss of key knowledge to third parties is assured. A spreadsheet-like template enables roles and documents required for completion to be added from pick lists. At run time, the role management system allows process initiators to select individuals to perform each step. In this way, process steps, roles, people, and forms are linked together by mouse clicks to form a process that is itself just one more mouse click away from becoming a running process. After only one week of training by Action Solutions, Migros Bank personnel have developed and implemented 23 business processes in 81 person days. Currently, new processes take approximately two person-days to design and deploy. Twenty additional processes have been identified and we have every reason to believe that these additional processes will be just as cost effective to develop as our first tranche of processes. The cost with which complete, running processes can be developed shatters the barrier that has kept small and mid-sized organizations from reaping the same business process benefits as their larger brethren. The same advances by Action Solutions apply to process maintenance, and may be even more revolutionary. Once we have designed a process the Process Owner can modify it, within broad boundaries. The Process Owner is a businessperson, not an IT-person. These changes employ the same pick list/mouse-click techniques described earlier. If, for example, a new document or form has become necessary in an existing process, the process owner merely opens the process template, goes to the document list and selects the appropriate item. Behind the scenes, the rules of completeness associated with this process will change to reflect the new requirements of the process. The same method is used to add a process step, change a role, or modify conditionals. These changes take minutes, not months. Thus, like process development costs, process maintenance costs have become inconsequential in the overall cost structure of deploying a BPM system. This means that the economies of scale in BPM deployments once enjoyed by only the largest organizations have now disappeared, removing a substantial cost disadvantage formerly incurred by smaller competitors in a market.

4.2 Process

Before introducing the new solution at Migros Bank, process design and business rules definition were done in the classical . There were tools used, but their usage required skilled IT people and were often too tool specific, instead of business relevant. The following process model shows a typical process map in use at Migros Bank.

Obviously this way of publishing processes needs some further explanation, so that business people can understand. Nevertheless business people will not be able to make use of such techniques nor tools supporting it, without a deeper understanding of the underlying notations and methods. Furthermore modeling human oriented processes this way is very complex and not very useful. This is mainly because of the missing support for mapping dynamic behaviors like events, activities and policies (rules), which are not following the sequential pattern of process design. Action Technologies Inc. did modeling human-oriented workflows for more than 20 years, and pioneered its acceptance industry wide. They always used a state machine based approach with its corresponding notation.

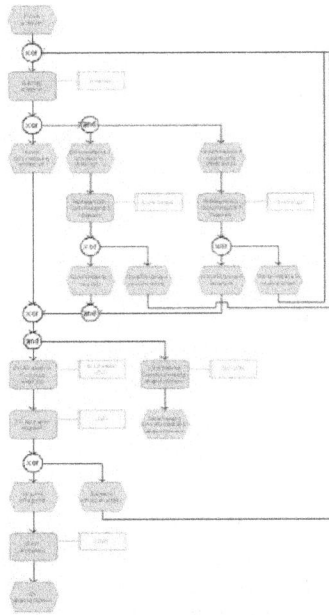

Figure 1: sequential process model

Sequential modeling is good for workflows which can execute autonomously with little outside direction, where the workflow itself primarily controls the execution and some or no user interaction is required. Whereby **state-machine oriented modeling** is good for workflows that depend heavily on outside control to guide execution, i.e. much user interaction is expected or other outside control (e.g. services) will drive the flow of execution.

For systems-oriented workflows,
Sequential workflow
modeled as flowchart

For human-oriented workflows,
State machine workflow
Modeled as state diagram

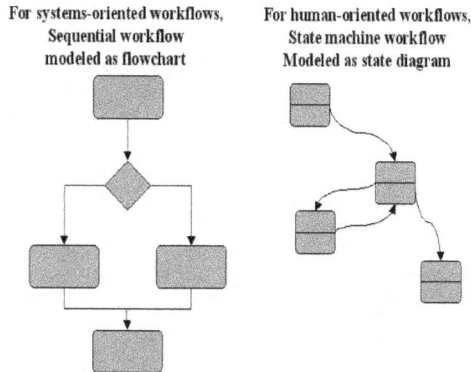

Figure 2: Sequential vs. state-machine oriented workflow modeling

With both techniques it was not easy and fast enough, to meet the needs of business people, and modeling all of the rules still required some business and/or software engineers. Business rules exist to resolve complex decision-making and neither approach (sequential nor state-machine) directly applies. For this reason, we separated business rule modeling from process design and filled the gap with a business like tool, which we named the Configuration Box (ConBox).

The Configuration Box (ConBox)

The ConBox is the tool at hand for defining, maintaining and deploying the active behavior of the processes at Migros Bank. It offers several advantages primarily at the conceptual level of process-oriented systems modeling. For example:

- A business-user-oriented model definition, because business rules are widely included in user requirements.
- Independence between the model definition and its implementation, indeed the specification of the rules, is a high level abstraction using business like semantics and a business like, natural language - English.
- Uniform representation of all rules. All of the different types of rules are described using the same formalism.

The ConBox uses the Event-Conditional-Action[2] (ECA[2]) paradigm, meaning:

- on event: { if (condition equals true) then {action-1} else {action-2} }.

Beside the rule management, all the other needed information to run a process is included as well. This includes property management, visibility and availability definition, layout definition, roles, rights and obligations management, as well as support of the different real-live work-styles reflected in the different frameworks underneath. In fact, the **ConBox** acts as the **glue** between the **process maps** created at design-time, the development environment that provides the source-code implementation of the **application frameworks,** and the **run-time engine**, which actually executes and manages the process instances within the people-to-people environment.

Markus Oschwald, Business Intelligence is responsible for the configuration of the processes with the ConBox: He states:

"With the ConBox it is possible to deploy a complex process in short time. The time to break in the use of the tool is very low because of its approach/configurations, which leads to a fast success. In addition, there is no programming know-how necessary. Migros Bank Workflow processes are not programmed but configured. The ConBox is generating the code and implementations occur easily and within minutes in the system. Also you can remove – at the push of a button – processes which are not in use anymore.

Case oriented approach

What makes Migros Bank Workflow both simple and effective is the core concept that lies behind of the system: coordination of process instances through a case approach. Every process becomes a case. Migros Bank Workflow ensures accountability, coordination, visibility, end-to-end tracking and feedback, a critical ensemble for delivering superior, speedy service at a reduced cost.

Pre-defined work styles

On top of the interaction model from Action Technologies Inc. we identified the patterns of best practice work-styles we normally use with the following result:

Delegate means the execution of one or more cases (including its tasks) to other persons, but keeping the overall ownership.

Consolidate is referred to as grouping different cases with its subtasks into one new major task, including new ownerships.

Forward is similar to delegation, but the ownership of the case moves to another user.

Revert gives the possibility to take back or cancel the case processing to the user currently having the ownership.

Validate implies the Go/No-Go decision making activities (i.e. approvals).

Escalate is needed for exceptional processing of cases including its tasks.

Suspend and resume gives the possibility to suspend and later resume the case processing.

Workflow Design using Patterns

Having these generic work styles at hand, it became possible to define design patterns reflecting people interaction and their best practice work-styles as the basic guidelines used for Migros Bank workflow design. The importance of patterns in crafting complex systems has been long recognized in other disciplines. Christopher Alexander and his colleagues were perhaps the first to propose the idea of using a pattern language to architect buildings and cities. His ideas and the contributions of others have now taken root in the process design community at Migros Bank. In short, the concept of the design pattern in workflow provides a key to helping business engineers leverage the expertise of other skilled business people. Furthermore it helps business people to manage the issue of knowing tools and notations in detail.

Migros Bank Workflow Implementation Building Blocks

The four elements described below implement the design patterns introduced above and are the basic building assemblies used for the workflow implementation at Migros Bank.

Main Case Processing Pattern

Every process implementation has one main processing thread. All of the different responsibilities will be managed on this level, including case initiation and creation, the ownership, and observers rights and obligations. Structured and unstructured data (text, attachments, audit trail) are managed on this level and will be made available to children thru inheritance.

Sub Case Processing Pattern

The main process thread can have many children, typically resulting from delegation activities. Sub case process threads themselves can be nested as deeply as required. Sub cases inherit from their parent the information needed and allowed. Through profiling, it is possible to restrict the view and/or manipulation of data included in the parent process.

Approval Processing Pattern

Most business relevant activities require some kind of approval. Especially in banking it is necessary to implement and follow many regulatory statutes like Basel II and others. Approval process patterns take the internal rights and responsibility policies into consideration and provide digital signature approval(s) depending on the case's context.

Notification Processing Pattern

This pattern is used to notify a person or a group of persons of a noteworthy business event, such as that a specific case has been approved or that case processing time has elapsed. Notifications are simple e-mails containing a hyperlink, which points to the case/sub-case instance and when clicked by the recipients will guide the user to the process instance.

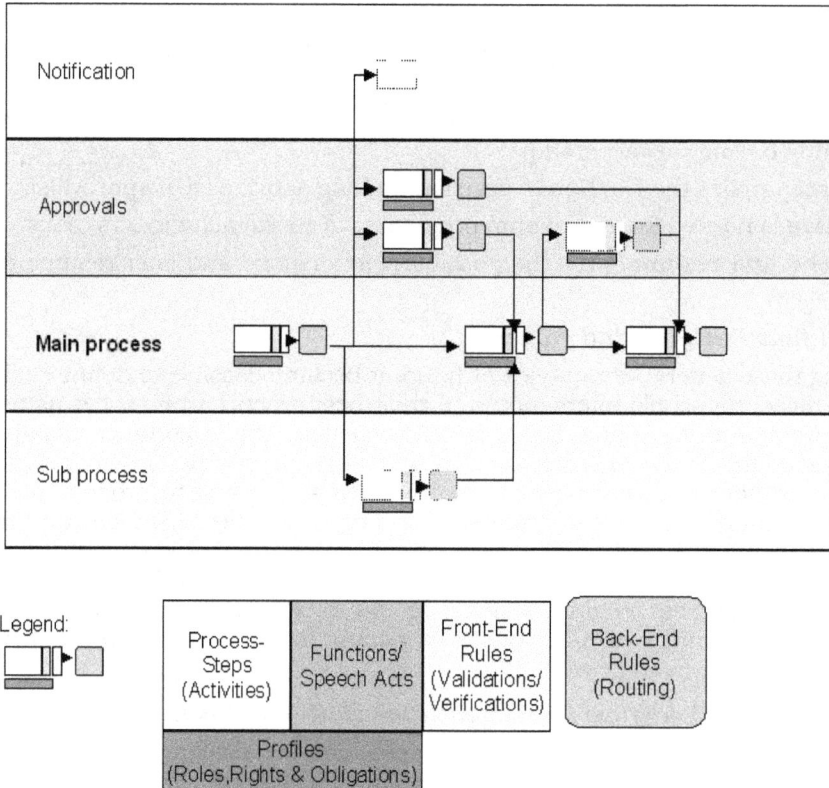

Figure 3: Overview of design pattern elements used for Migros Bank workflows

Statements of Andreas Staubli, Business Engineer and responsible Project Manager for Migros Bank Workflow:

"With Migros Bank Workflow we are able to implement fast new processes. Thereby it is possible to react effectively and with a low reaction time to changed business requirements. With the transparency over all organizational units within process execution, the process and auditing acceptability is higher then ever before. Through rule based processes control, effort could be decreased and quality of orders could be increased at the same time"

4.3 Organization

In the past the interactions around client requests were all coordinated via phone, email, fax, mail and face-to-face meetings. The propensity for misunderstandings and miscommunication was high. Moreover, there was no visibility into the process, no formal accountability for who had agreed to perform what work by when, and no consistent audit trail. Introducing the electronic people-to-people workflows was key to reorganizing the Migros Bank organization and to change the way people worked. First Migros Bank centralized mid- and back-office activities physically as well as organizationally. At the same time, front-office activities located in the branches distributed all over Switzerland have been reorganized and made nearly paperless. Channeling all of the different media (phone, fax, paper, electronic documents and mail) and streamlining the business requests from the front to the middle and back-offices thru a case approach has been provided by the Migros Bank workflow system.

Standardizing individual Processing thru Cases

The Migros Bank workflow system design meshes efficiency and effectiveness through the same interface. The case form provides the information needed for both extreme, efficient processing of standard service requests, such as moving funds from one account to another, and effective response to a non-routine request, such as locating information on implications of a foreign real estate purchase. A routine case is moved quickly and completely through the different processing steps. A non-routine case is moved quickly and completely through the approval and collaboration steps too. The case is always kept in view and all different kind of interactions are never left open. Every case has a complete process audit trail managed by the system and updated automatically. The audit-trail shows all of the activities within a case and thus strongly reduces the operational risk of violating rules and/or regulatory policies.

Altogether, this solves one of the single largest and most widespread problems in process coordination, the lack of 'visibility' into the processes. In traditional workflow systems no single person has an overall view of the system but only sees his or her own part of the process. As a workflow moves through the network of interactions and interdependencies, it disappears from view. There is no direct and simple way to tracking state, reviewing which workflows are pending, completed, due or delayed. There is no overall history attached to the workflow as it moves through the complete process swamp and no flexible feedback on it or its progress. There are no built-in metrics of the process as contrasted to the individual tasks and operations carried out within it.

Migros Bank Workflow remedies all of this. It is in this sense that it is a management system. It ensures that the steps for the process and responsibilities for carrying them out are handled in context of a case. The initiation of a case creates a set of interactions where every element is captured and coordinated.

Any user can check on pending, open and completed cases and tasks. The system even highlights or notifies users about cases soon to become overdue. Searches for cases, clients or task completion are provided and can be sorted e.g. by date and time. This feedback adds a valuable facility that is already generating new initiatives building on the Six Sigma approach to total quality management: root cause analysis of recurrent problem areas, deduction of new and better business rules and a spirit of continuous improvement.

Each night, all user and organizational changes are imported. When changes happen, screen and user interface will be adopted over night, depending on the new user's profile. Open cases are shipped automatically when critical changes, e.g. an employee has left the company, happened, to the supervisor, so that not a single case can be lost.

A single workbox is managing the open cases of a user. Different than in the e-mail inbox, they see immediately what they have to do, and what somebody else has to do for them.

Integrated time management is remembering cases. When a case is overdue in an employee's "to do list" and where somebody else has to do something for them.

5. USERS AND WHAT THEIR JOBS ENTAIL NOW, COMPARED TO PRE-INSTALLATION

The Front-Office

The Middle and Back-Office's direct "customer" is the Front-Office - people like Relationship Managers and their Assistants. The Relationship Manager acts on behalf of the Banking client and initiates a request; the Middle-Office ensures that the request is honored. That sounds simple. It has to look simple to be efficient and effective. The new cliché for the Migros Bank Workflow-based coordination link between Relationship Managers at the front end (the firing line), and the middle- and back-office is "Fire and forget." And, of course, an implicit adage is that clients must be able to fire and forget too; if they are ever made aware of the process it is because something has failed. Of course, making it all look simple and being able to fire off a request and be sure it will be fully handled is not at all simple.

Customer care in private as well as retail banking has to be provided in a business context that is extremely complex, time-dependent, global, varied and demanding in terms of operations speed, quality and efficiency. The Relationship Managers must access specialists on the client's behalf as needed when needed, in _any_ area of financial planning and services. Private and Retail banking involves very large portfolios of investments, including securities, real estate, trust funds, and loans.

Transactions often have many zeros at the end of the money amount. Relationship Managers gather information for clients on funds, countries, industry sectors, and international financial instruments. All this has to be done now and done right.

The staff in the Middle- and Back-Offices who process the Relationship Manager's requests flag _cases_ as either normal or high priority; normal ones require a two-hour re-sponse and high priority ones thirty minutes. While it may take days or even months to complete some of the client requests, the pressure is always on and kept on to make sure they are handled as quickly as possible.

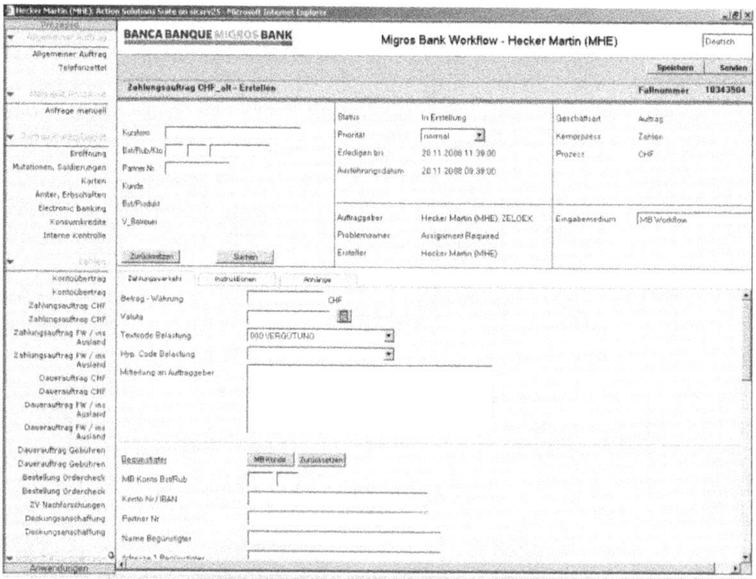

Figure 4: Front-Office view

The Middle- and Back-Office

Trust is the key word here: personal trust in the relationship, trust in the Relationship Manager's expertise, trust in the institution (Migros is one of the great names in this regard) and trust in the competence and reliability of the bank's operations. It is in this last area that the Middle- and Back-Office is absolutely critical to the bank-client relationship. Every day, around 800 new client requests for processing, information, approval, or transaction handling are sent to the Middle- and Back-Office by e-mail or fax, with about 2,000 phone calls that add another 800 requests. Every customer request becomes a *case*. It takes 180 staff to coordinate these "*cases*", with coordination the key word and the very foundation of the success of the Migros Bank Workflow initiative in making everything so "simple." These are not data entry clerks but a help desk of knowledgeable bankers, with years of experience within Migros Bank. Four years ago, when the Middle-Office was first established, paper, time and geography dominated service response times. Mail coming into the Middle-Office typically took three days to work its way from a branch office, with plenty of back and forth phone calls and telephone tag messages, before the instructions could be carried out. The Middle-Office managers are only now beginning to have the accumulation of time series and statistical data that Migros Bank Workflow gathers. This data will enable them to undertake a rapid and deep change in the organization of the Middle- and Back-Offices, its staffing and workload management and the embedding of business rules in the software. To date, their focus has been on the existing organization and to leverage how people do their work today. The larger opportunity is how to design the work of tomorrow.

The Implementation Team

The Migros Bank core project team consisted of six people: a project manager, three business analysts and two IT professionals (plus two developers from Systems Integration Center AG). Twenty pilot users and specialists from systems engineering and the data center also contributed to the project. Systems Integration Center AG and its experienced team of developers, armed with Action Technologies' business process management platform, the ActionWorks® Business Interaction Model were critical to the success of the project. Systems Integration Center AG conducted the project in phases. Contrary to standard practice, Systems Integration Center AG did not spend months mapping out requirements before they began developing the system. Instead, the team gathered requirements from Migros Bank business leaders in enough detail that allowed them to map a prototype of Migros Bank Workflow in just two days. This was only possible due to the patented ActionWorks® Business Interaction Model that acts as a universal translator between the language of business and the language of technology. This prototype became the starting point for weekly discussions between Systems Integration Center AG and Migros Bank's Management for additional system requirements and changes. In the week following every meeting, Systems Integration Center AG has implemented at least 80% of the change requests from the last meeting allowing them to quickly move forward towards a successful launch.

6. HURDLES OVERCOME

5.1 Management

There were no big management hurdles – rather a member of the executive board, coming from Credit Suisse, initiated the project. He knew about the success of the ServiceNet application (former award winning solution) at Credit Suisse and enriched this solution with his own ideas – the outcome is, that we have additional to ServiceNet (one generic process), rule based, individual processes, which we maintain by our own business people.

This member of the executive board and his team were charged with finding new ways of improving the middle- and back-offices effectiveness and efficiency. The reorganization had been established in 2006 to provide a central coordination point for all elements of the "middle" and "back" offices that service and leverage the front-end Relationship Managers.

It was evident, that for the successful implementation of all of this new processes a workflow system was required, that was proven and efficient like no other at that time.

5.2 Business

There was a strong body of opinion in the operations side of Migros Bank and the IT-Provider at that time, that, what was needed was a "better" technology system. This led to problems that held up the deployment of the Migros Bank concept of process, cases and service and led to a planning focus on replacing the technology platform rather than improving the process and service performance. 'Home-grown' development of a workflow system by the IT-Provider was planned with a process that ate up several years. But ActionWorks® was already available and able to deliver on this case-approach. Other vendors lacked the process mapping and modeling tools and methods to avoid "workarounds" and also could not meet the timetable. In the end, these problems were resolved through the weight of evidence. System Integration Center AG, using the ActionWorks® Business Interaction Model, was able to build a prototype quickly and met the key criterion for planning, design and systems operation; process design first and technology second. *"Only Action could handle collaboration in a clean way with no workarounds"* said Stephan Wick, an executive member of Migros Bank. Six months later, Migros Bank Workflow was up and running. Initially, users did not anticipate turning away from physical formulas to electronic ones. This attitude mainly occured because there was little process thinking beyond one's own organizational unit. Through continuous training and presentations at the branches acceptance increased.

The linking from the mail system with Migros Bank Workflow was another step towards acceptance (E-Mail Notification). But the key for changing minds was, in the end, improved functionality and performance. When a user has the subjective sensation that the application and live processes are good and positive things, then acceptance and adaption come faster.

5.3 Organization Adoption

The obstacles to the deployment and acceptance of the Migros Bank Workflow were not technical; rather they were cultural. There were two schools of thought among employees. The first group was comprised of early adopters, who found the system easy to use and immediately saw the benefits of a workflow system that allows them to manage their correspondence, orders and paperwork more efficiently. These employees not only embraced the workflow solution, but also provided valuable feedback to the solution's designers.

The second group was made up of very experienced individuals who questioned the need for a new system and the additional guidance it provided and were resistant to using the Migros Bank Workflow because they felt that it created more control and less "jester's license" in work. Because the majority of front office work had been paper intensive, it is natural that a certain number of employees would be reluctant to learn the new technology on top of their heavy schedule. Through continuous training and presentations at the branches, acceptance increased strongly. After working a few months with the new system, this group of people recognized that they could focus much more on front operations and client relationship management instead of paper work – thus gaining much more time and freedom to do what they really like to do - business.

Migros Bank Workflow Configuration

Hardware:
- 1 dual CPU App Server
- 1 dual CPU process manager
- 2 dual CPU database servers configured in a fail over cluster
- 1 test server for unit and integration testing
- 1 server for acceptance testing and a potential replacement server for disaster recovery as required by business continuity planning
- 1 development server

Software:
- Microsoft Windows 2003 Advanced Server
- Microsoft SQL Server 2000, Microsoft IIS Web Server
- ActionWorks® Metro 5.2
- ActionSolutions® Software Suite 1.0

Other systems:
- Oracle Information Warehouse (customer, staff and organizational data)
- Integration with Microsoft Outlook E-mail system
- Integration with Microsoft Office (Word, Excel)

7. BENEFITS

Until recently, process improvement implementations across all business areas were not affordable for mid-size companies. However, mid-size companies have to enforce compliance rules and have to fulfill legal requirements to the same degree as large companies. Most early process improvement attempts at mid-sized companies were dropped after facing high costs and lengthy lead times, resulting in not having a business case for most processes with lower volumes.

The same reasons drive large companies to implement the high volume - low value and very rigid processes first, struggling to produce good business cases for the remaining processes with lower volumes but often bearing high values. However the major part of operational risks can be easily shown to be associated with processes needing very high flexibility and covering high values (enforcing compliance rules in supporting collaboration of knowledge workers and decision makers with a complete audit trail).

7.1 Cost Savings

Throughout this report, benefits resulting from reduced rework, increased customer satisfaction, Six Sigma improvements, and organizational restructuring have been mentioned. None of these benefits are included in the calculations that follow. It is likely that, as documentation of these additional benefits is completed, an additional white paper will be submitted to the Workflow Management Coalition, documenting the above-mentioned economic benefits.

The business case presented here focuses entirely on economic benefits from cost savings in process design and implementation costs.

The Net present value (NPV) of the Migros Bank Workflow initiative amounts to two million CHF on a three years basis. It takes into consideration that Business Engineering has opportunity cost savings due to the fact that no additional staff/3rd party needs be hired/engaged to implement all of the 41 processes, which have been implemented over the last three years.

Net Present Value		2006	2007	2008
Investment	CHF	1'076'000	741'000	188'000

Opportunity cost savings	CHF	326'000	1'659'000	2'812'000
	CHF	-750'000	918'000	2'624'000
Present Values	CHF	-681'750	758'268	1'970'624

NPV 2006-2008   CHF   2'047'142

6.2 Time Reductions and Productivity Improvements
- Breakthrough in process implementation
- 23 processes implemented in 81 man days = $\varnothing$ 3.5 man days/process

8.   BEST PRACTICES, LEARNING POINTS AND PITFALLS

8.1 Best Practices and Learning Points

✓   The spirit of cooperation- the key to success is not simply 'computerize' existing activities, using machines to perform routine task more quickly. Rather it is to analyse how your business works and capture that knowledge in a working model. Then build solutions on top of that model to enhance both the efficiency and the effectiveness of your operations.

✓   Management buy-in- no enterprise-wide undertaking of process change can succeed without the solid support of top management. At the beginning of the project, it would be a good idea to have the senior manager of the team send a detailed memo of support to every individual in the organization who might be affected by the project.

✓   Early user education- once top-management has given the go-ahead, you should immediately begin educating users about the goals and implications of adopting the new system. People are often frightened of, and therefore resistant to, new technologies and systems. One thing to emphasize to users, whose working lives are about to be changed, is that the new system, unlike other automation experiences they may have had, is specifically designed to facilitate cooperation between people. It is not a process turning people into automatons, but rather a technology to facilitate the way they already work and to make them more productive.

✓   Evolutionary approach- avoid designing highly structured processes with complex rules for getting 'just' a model. Take the definitions available and try to implement them, but keep in mind that they are subject to change. Developers, especially, will need to accept that what they do rarely matches the business requirements the first time! Walk through with the users, do not just prototype. Develop processes in an evolutionary way, together with business people. Every iteration step (re-engineering of the process) should be visible/implemented within days, not weeks. Cultivate and formalize interactions with business people. Integrate selected key business people into the project team.

✓   High visibility- the department and the processes you begin with should have sufficient enterprise wide visibility and impact such that a success in its enhancement with the new workflow system will create an example other departments will wish to follow.

8.2 Pitfalls

✕ Do not analyse your entire business- it hardly makes sense to spend two years building a model of your operations, only to discover that the model is unworkable when you finally want to implement it! Rather we advocate a phased adoption strategy. Start with a select set of departments and apply the workflows to their operations. As you roll out into other departments, apply what you learned with the initial departments to achieve optimum results.

✕ Do not focus on routine operations first- Don't take a department with lots of well-understood routine forms, processes and rules that you can readily capture and automate. By contrast, departments like Research might not appear to be as good a choice because so much of its functioning depends on informal, unstructured interactions among research people. However, we advise starting exactly with departments like Research and their processes with a lot of unstructured data and interactions. Point your fingers on the real issues and solve them first, thus reducing the risk of failure with your project! Implementing later processes with a lot of routine operations will not be anymore a critical risk factor for your project.

✕ Dealing with patterns- pay particular attention to the applicability and consequences of making use of a pattern to ensure the pattern is right for your problem. Study the structure, participants and collaborations sections of the pattern's documentation in detail and make sure you understand how they relate to one another.

Use existing workflow implementations as pattern for the use of the patterns. Choose names for the patterns which are meaningful in the application context. If no pattern does fit your problem, take the time you need to create a new one. Pattern development takes time, but if you do it right, later on you will be able to re-use it in other processes and thus get back your time investment.

9. COMPETITIVE ADVANTAGES

We, have stepped ahead of our competition, not so much in terms of the technology, which is available to any of our competitors, but in our combination of the business focus on a relationship management-centric strategy, *Migros Bank Workflow* as the link between Relationship Managers and their clients and between the middle and back offices, and the process view of service and service design. The technological edge is that we've modernized our IT people-to-people platform and applications ahead of our main competitors.

The cost disadvantages faced by small and mid-scale organizations are eliminated, thus enabling Migros Bank to compete on service and specialization without incurring disadvantages of scale. Migros Bank is the first mid-scale company to benefit from these methods and inventions.

We have also reduced our operational risk by making sure that the internal guidelines and external regulatory requirements are fulfilled. Through the integrated rule management in the new people-to-people platform, Migros Bank adopts new requirements quickly and makes it easy for people to work together effectively. This is an advantage, which should not be underestimated in the advent of stringent regulatory requirements because the highest risk for banks today is rarely in routine operations, rather it is in informal, unstructured interactions among people working together.

As a result, Migros Bank is able to set the standard of service for our industry, grow our volumes and expand our client base without either eroding our margins or cutting back on service. It will be very difficult indeed for most of our competitors to achieve these same results.

10. TECHNOLOGY

All the applications have been built on the foundation of the ActionWorks® Process Engine from Action Technologies Inc. (Alameda CA) using the implementation framework developed by Action Solutions AG in Switzerland consisting of pre-built standard application components, repository, administration framework, a configuration framework and a rule engine.

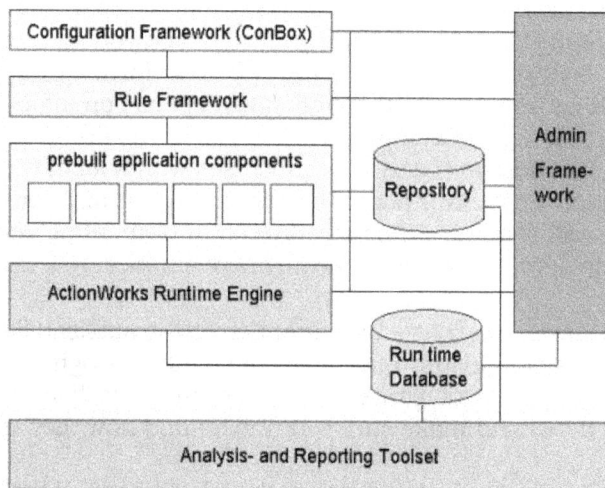

```
┌──────────────────────────────────────────┐        ┌─────────┐
│ Configuration Framework (ConBox)          │        │         │
├──────────────────────────────────────────┤        │         │
│            Rule Framework                  │        │         │
├──────────────────────────────────────────┤        │  Admin  │
│       prebuilt application components      │  ┌───┐ │ Frame-  │
│  ┌──┐ ┌──┐ ┌──┐ ┌──┐ ┌──┐                  │  │Rep│ │  work   │
│  └──┘ └──┘ └──┘ └──┘ └──┘                  │  └───┘ │         │
├──────────────────────────────────────────┤        │         │
│       ActionWorks Runtime Engine           │        │         │
└──────────────────────────────────────────┘        └─────────┘
                                          ┌──────────┐
                                          │ Run time │
                                          │ Database │
                                          └──────────┘
┌──────────────────────────────────────────────────┐
│         Analysis- and Reporting Toolset            │
└──────────────────────────────────────────────────┘
```

Figure 5: Migros Bank Workflow System frameworks overview

Migros Bank Workflow Frameworks

The behavior of the pre-built application components is held in the Repository. The developer is using the configuration framework and it's tool, the ConBox, to build the processes. The configuration framework is accessing the repository and shows to the developer the possible selections only to wire a process together using a user friendly GUI, driven by the repository. The definitions entered by the business user are checked in real time mode against the repository, thus avoiding erroneous definitions - reducing the error rate in building the process drastically. The defined process can be executed immediately after the definition in "test mode" and is then deployed after final acceptance to the production environment using a case definition language. The Rule Framework manages the GUI-content and the Process Flow based on the rules stored in the Repository. The pre-build application components consist of:

- Graphical user interface (GUI) components like search and identify corresponding bank, search and identify customer including validation rules for field content and field interdependency driven by the repository
- Data access and manipulation components
- Modular Process components reflecting common work-styles and their dynamics
- Document management components, including versioning, locking and accessibility management
- The Admin Framework allows managing the users and their roles, rights, responsibilities and the content of the Repository. All Runtime Data is stored in a Relational Database. Together with the definitions held in the Repository various user views and reports are easily produced such as (few examples):

- Work "to do" sorted and grouped by user selectable criteria's (i.e. business type, priority...)
- Work "due to me" sorted and grouped by user selectable criteria's (e.g. business type, priority...)
- Search on process items (cases) by various criteria's (e.g. customer, time window, business classification...)

All definitions of the re-useable components as well as their behavior and the corresponding rules are held and managed in the repository. Statistics on different case processing key performance indicators (KPIs) like standard variations (quantifiable difference between individual measurements) or standard deviations (average difference between any value in a series of values and the mean of all the values in that series) are available.

ActionWorks® Runtime Engine

Grounded in Theory, Successful in Practice: The ActionWorks® Business Interaction Model and Its Role in Migros Bank Workflow.

ActionWorks® coordinates commitments and interactions between an individual or group making a request (the *Customer*) and the recipient of that request (the *Performer*) in four phases.

All these interactions, nego-tiations, commitments, and decisions take place within the system leaving a detailed audit trail for tracking, auditing, root cause analysis, and continuous improvement purposes.

In the past Migros' interactions around client requests were all coordinated via phone, email, fax, mail and face-to-face meetings.

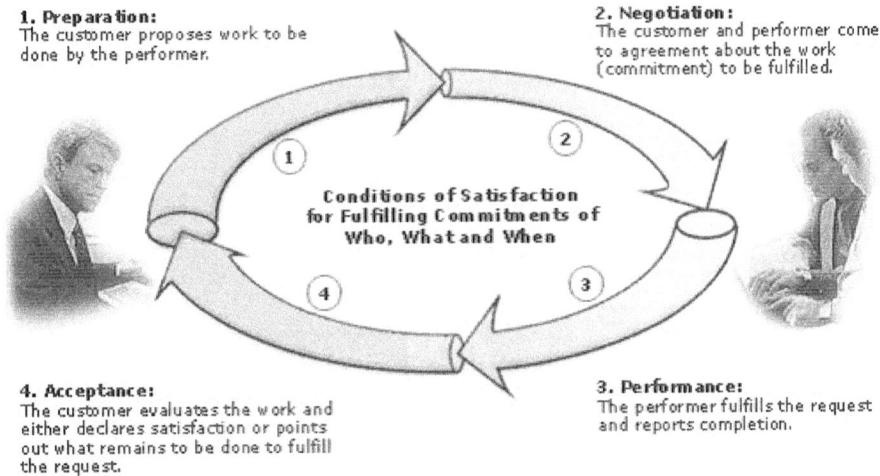

1. Preparation:
The customer proposes work to be done by the performer.

2. Negotiation:
The customer and performer come to agreement about the work (commitment) to be fulfilled.

Conditions of Satisfaction for Fulfilling Commitments of Who, What and When

4. Acceptance:
The customer evaluates the work and either declares satisfaction or points out what remains to be done to fulfill the request.

3. Performance:
The performer fulfills the request and reports completion.

Figure 6: ActionWorks® Business Interaction Model

The propensity for misunderstandings and miscommunication was high. Moreover, there was no visibility into the process, no formal accountability for who had agreed to perform what work by when, and no consistent audit trail.

Today, over 500 requests a day of varying complexity are coordinated through the Migros Bank Workflow System. And at the heart of every transaction lies the ActionWorks® Business Interaction Model.

11. THE TECHNOLOGY AND SERVICE PROVIDERS

Action Technologies Inc. has delivered for more than 20 years award-winning Business Process Management (BPM) software that reduces the time and cost of decision-driven processes by 40-60% and typically generates returns of more than 300%. The ActionWorks® Suite enables leading global customers to analyze, redesign, implement and continuously improve their operations through a patented system for managing negotiations and commitments.

(www.actiontech.com)

Action Solutions AG is responsible for the application building based on the Action Technology platform. The ActionSolutions® Suite is a unique Business Activity Software Suite consisting of different frameworks reflecting the way people work together. These frameworks and it's unique way of assembling workflows using generic work-style patterns were the base for the successful, rapid development and deployment at Migros Bank.

(www.actiontech.ch)

Systems Integration Center AG was the IT-Implementation partner for this project and it's experienced team of developers, armed with Actions' business process management platform and the ActionWorks® Business Interaction Model, were critical to the success of the project. Systems Integration Center AG conducted the project in all phases. Contrary to standard practice, Systems Integration Center AG did not spend months mapping out requirements before they began developing the system. Instead, the team gathered requirements from Migros Bank business leaders in enough detail that allowed them to map a prototype of Migros Bank Workflow in just two days. This was only possible due to the patented ActionWorks® Business Interaction Model that acts as a universal translator between the language of business and the language of technology.

(www.sicenter.com)

Techspace Aero, Belgium

Silver Award, Europe

Nominated by W4, France

EXECUTIVE SUMMARY / ABSTRACT

Techspace Aero designs, develops and produces modules, equipment and test cells for aircraft and space engines. The regulations in the domain require strict quality control of the products. The quality department, alongside the company's ambition to become the world leader in its areas of excellence, has decided to rationalize its applications for better department efficiency. At the same time, studies conducted by the IT department on the operation of the ERP used for quality management have demonstrated that a BPM solution could respond more effectively to the evolution requirements fixed by the company, and more specifically conform to the quality requirements within Techspace Aero.

The study presented here therefore relates more specifically to the Computer Aided Quality Management (CAQM) application *(in French: Gestion Qualité Assistée par Ordinateur – GQAO)*. The goal of this application is to better manage all quality incidents in order to make their administration and management more efficient, whether these are quality incidents linked to the Techspace Aero suppliers, or those discovered either during product manufacturing, or upon delivery of the end product to the customer.

OVERVIEW

Given its aim to become the market leader, Techspace Aero has decided to better understand its processes in order to optimize them and ultimately improve the quality of the products the company delivers to its clients.

This means offering the various company Departments appropriate IT tools to guarantee not only the management of vital company data , but also how this data is passed on between the various participants who are required to handle it, while respecting quality procedures and operational directives. After several months of analysis and an in-depth study of the market, at the end of 2006 Techspace Aero chose W4 BPM Suite as the corner stone of the implementation of a major IT project based around the company's processes.

Given the specific needs of the aircraft industry with regard to product quality requirements, the first processes to be described were those concerning quality applications linked to the manufacture and production of the sub-assemblies of aircraft and rocket engines. Up until then quality was managed by a set of heterogeneous and ageing applications, with redundant data and breaks in the processing. It relied on an intensive use of paper documents. The installation of a BPM Suite allowed the processing of all quality incidents to be grouped within a single application, offering greater flexibility in the processing sequences, and greater efficiency within the workshops and for the quality officers at all levels. The result is that the delivery of a final assembly to the client no longer requires any manual processing to search for closed quality incidents. The conformance certificate is generated automatically, after simple validation by the person responsible for its insurance. Previously this work could take several hours.

Now the different GQAO participants are aware of belonging to a global processing chain in the company. The borders between the various departments are fading away, the divisions are less marked and the company is beginning to take on board a culture of process implementation. That's how BPM-based projects within the IT department are leading to a constant increase in user and management satisfaction, thanks to the project team's ability to use all the modules of the BPM Suite.

BUSINESS CONTEXT

As a partner of the biggest worldwide aircraft manufacturers, Techspace Aero designs, develops and produces modules, equipment and test cells for aircraft and space engines. Thanks to its high technology products, Techspace Aero contributes to the success of many Airbus flights (A320, A330, A340 and A380), Boeing (B737, B747, B767, B777, B787) and Embraer (190) aircraft, as well as many others.

Product quality in the aircraft and space industry is governed by numerous regulations and standards (Techspace Aero is certified AS/EN/JISQ 9100, ISO 14001, EASA Part-21, EASA Part-145, FAR 145, and complies with AQAP 2110 certification). Any quality incident (Nonconforming product) must be tracked, the suppliers must be approved and the staff must be trained and certified in order to guarantee the safety of the aircraft and space engines.

With this in mind a single application that enables the management of all the administrative aspects and quality requirements relating to a product can only make the activities of the quality department staff easier.

For example, it is important to understand that before delivering part of an aircraft engine to its customers, namely an assembly of several dozen components, numerous file elements had to be validated at the end of the manufacturing process. The file is constituted notably of all papers issued by the quality department in order to track the slightest quality incident. This verification is now realized automatically by the application, which indicates to the quality technician any quality incidents that have not yet been validated, in order to focalize his/her energy on just the documents needing to be finalized.

THE KEY INNOVATIONS

The key change consists of making the management of quality incidents more flexible. After processing a quality incident, one or more interdependent files need to be opened in order to correct a product defect. Before the application was used all the files had to be closed when a decision was made on the last one. Now the files are automatically closed by the application as a decision is made on each file. The result is a reduction in the number of simultaneous actions (making it easier to monitor operations and making corrective tasks more efficient) and of summary operations at delivery time.

Techspace Aero
Groupe SAFRAN

GQAO

Rapport de traitement

Figure 1: Computer Aided Quality Management application banner
GQAO in French stands for Gestion Qualité Assistée par Ordinateur

Business

The currently installed ERP assures the traceability of parts, and the GQAO application handles the quality aspects of the parts by drawing on the ERP data, such as the definition of assembly or machining ranges, or the serial numbers of the different components used in engine sub-assemblies delivered to the customer.

The specifications of GQAO application were issued in April 2006, and the project implementation began at the beginning of 2007, along with the definition of processes (14 in batch 1) and the installation of the tools and components needed to take into account TechSpace's IT system in the application. Batch 1 went into production in January 2008, batch 2 in August of the same year, and batch 3 is currently being put into production. 20 processes for the GQAO application are deployed at the moment, representing for the 200 users (out of a total of 1,300 in the company) 7500 files processed since the go-live.

Process

GQAO is based on processes that are interdependent but autonomous, and the concept of modularity is reproduced in its formulation. Here the processes are those of the quality world, adapted to the specific constraints of the aircraft and space industry. The following is a subset of the more important ones, corresponding to more than 5000 files:

1. Nonconformance Handling: [RT: rapports de traitement]

2. Component Handling: [TC: traitements de composant]

3. Supplier Return Report (parts/informations): [RF: retours fournisseur (pièces/informations)]

4. Product Permit (Customer or Provider): [PP: permis de produire]

5. Acceptability List: [PP: Catalogue d'acceptabilité]

6. Touch up/Repair: [RR: retouches/reparations]

7. Concession request: [DD: demandes de dérogation]

8. Restrictive Conditions: [CR: conditions restrictives]

9. Anticipated Release: [PL: pré-libérations]

Figure 2: Implemented Workflow Processes

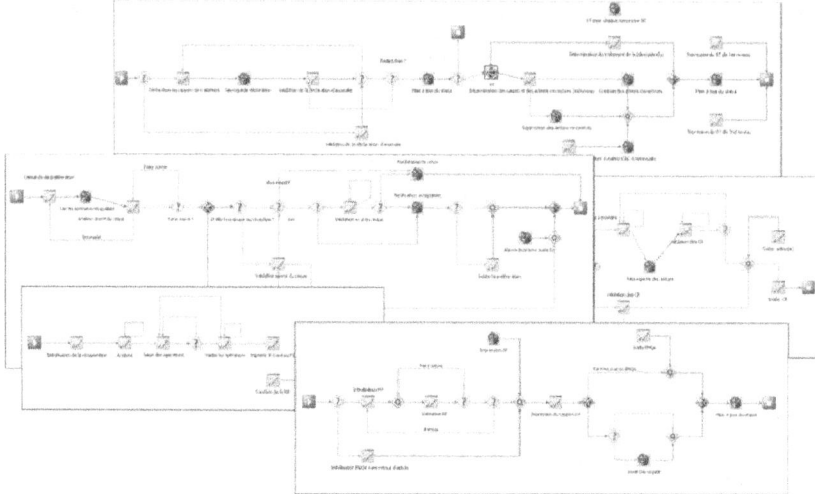

Each quality incident is supported by a process, and when this process ends it closes the incident and defines what the next processing will be and its consequences. Given the complexity of the process sequences, the mechanism will be illustrated using a specific scenario: The processing of an anomaly (quality incident) detected in production. For this reason not all flows developed in GQAO are visible.

An assembly component is detected as non-compliant during manufacture. A processing report is issued on the assembly (in order to trace that component X was put in assembly Y) with a "Component Handling (2)" decision. The system closes the "Nonconformance Handling (1)" of the assembly automatically and opens a "Component Handling (2)" file and a "Nonconformance Handling" on the component.

Figure 3: The simplified GQAO processing

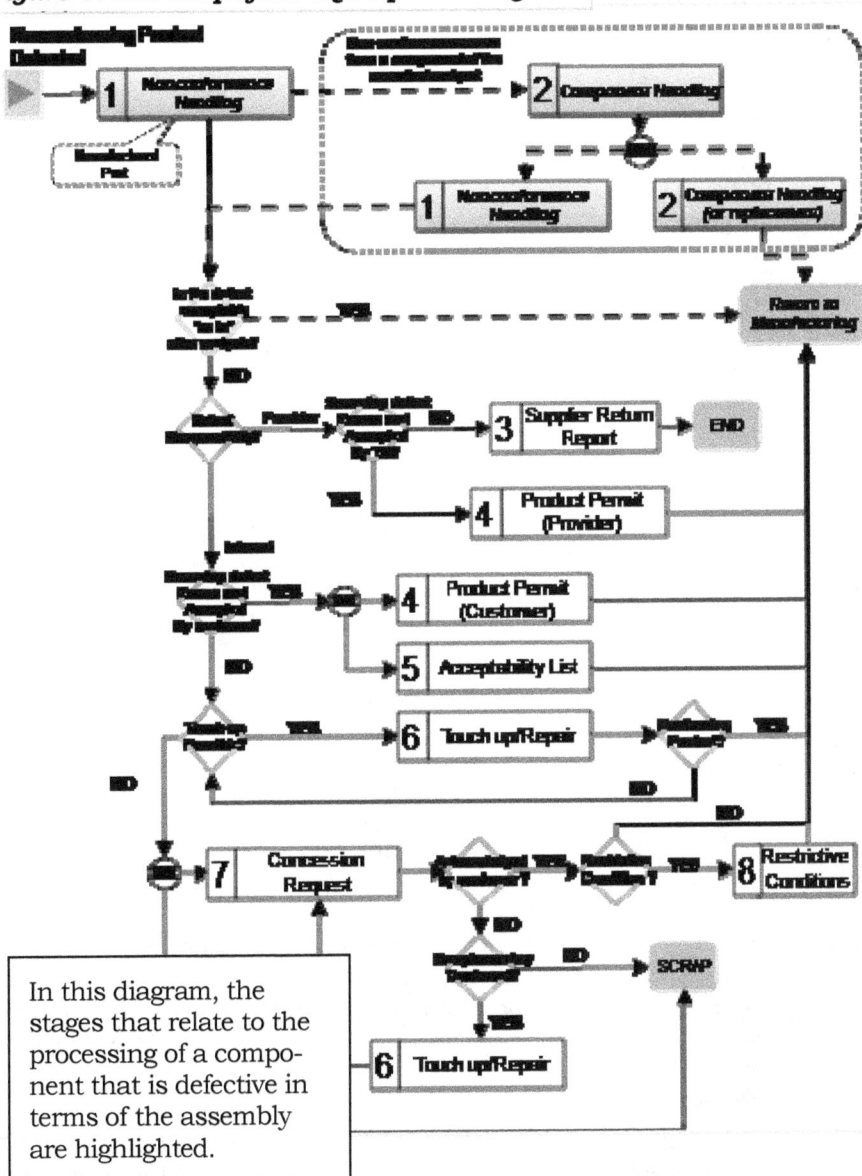

In this diagram, the stages that relate to the processing of a component that is defective in terms of the assembly are highlighted.

This operation offers the advantage of either correcting the component defect before reintegrating it into its original assembly, or, for logistical reasons, directly replacing the non-compliant component in the assembly (retaining the trace of this modification) and being able to correct the original component defect at the same time so that the repaired component can be integrated later into another assembly.

The GQAO has been created from the evolutions that would have been necessary if the ERP had evolved, with the use of a standard design tool for the modeling, which is then mapped with and implemented by the BPM solution.

Figure 4: Nonconformance Handling

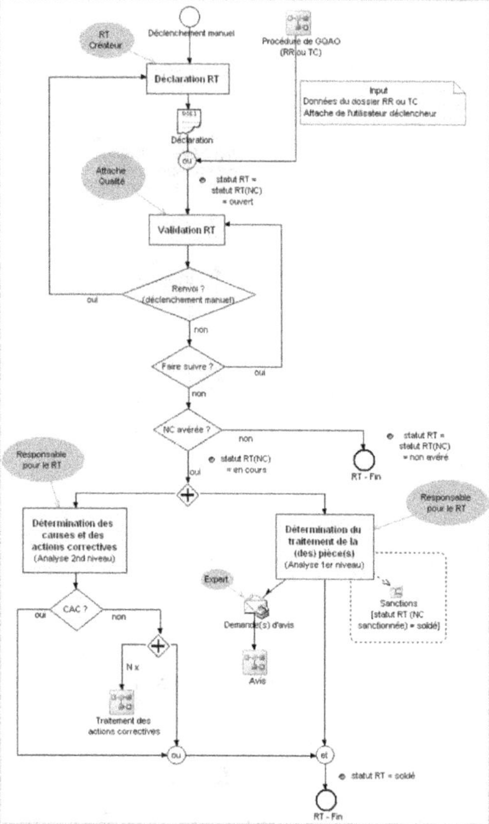

Figure 5: Component Handling

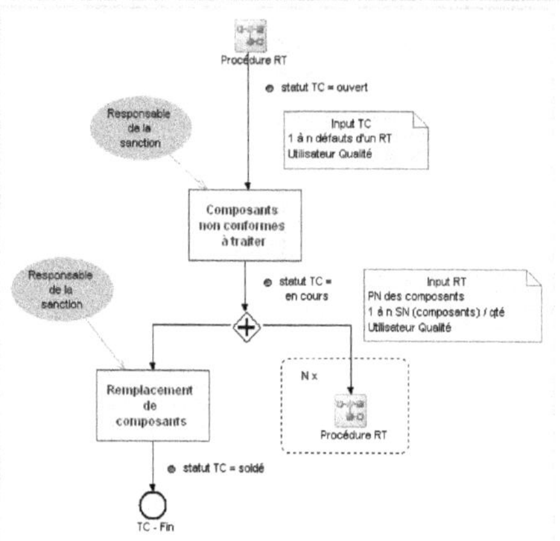

Figure 6: GQAO application: Activity screen

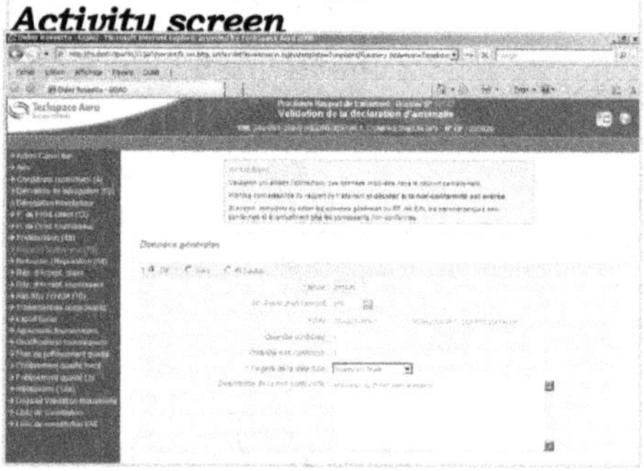

The automatic updates are therefore performed without the users having to interact with different applications (as was the case before), thus eliminating the risks of errors or oversight. However, for the moment, the updates to the ERP remain manual, with the user interface nevertheless providing direct access to the right screen. In a future version of the application, the updates will be performed automatically since the users feel more confident using GQAO.

As part of the overall project it was a key requirement that the process-based applications could access the ERP data in the same way as the other applications. The IT Department's work resulted in a description of this access in the form of services which are directly accessible in read-only mode from the processes. For updates, the data is presented to the user by the application, which can open the ERP on the relevant screen, allowing the user to input and manage the information in an appropriate format according to the particular context of each file.

Organization

The new GQAO application has led to a number of changes for the relevant people. For the workshop staff, operators and quality officers, it is first and foremost a more user-friendly application compared with the various applications that were available to them previously. Alongside the graphics charter that now complies with group directives, the ergonomics have been greatly improved, notably thanks to the to-do list approach and the automation of the data-dependent activities of the outstanding quality incident.

Paper has disappeared from the workshops and it is no longer necessary to input in the 'Legacy' applications (see fig 8).

Figure 7: GQAO to-do list

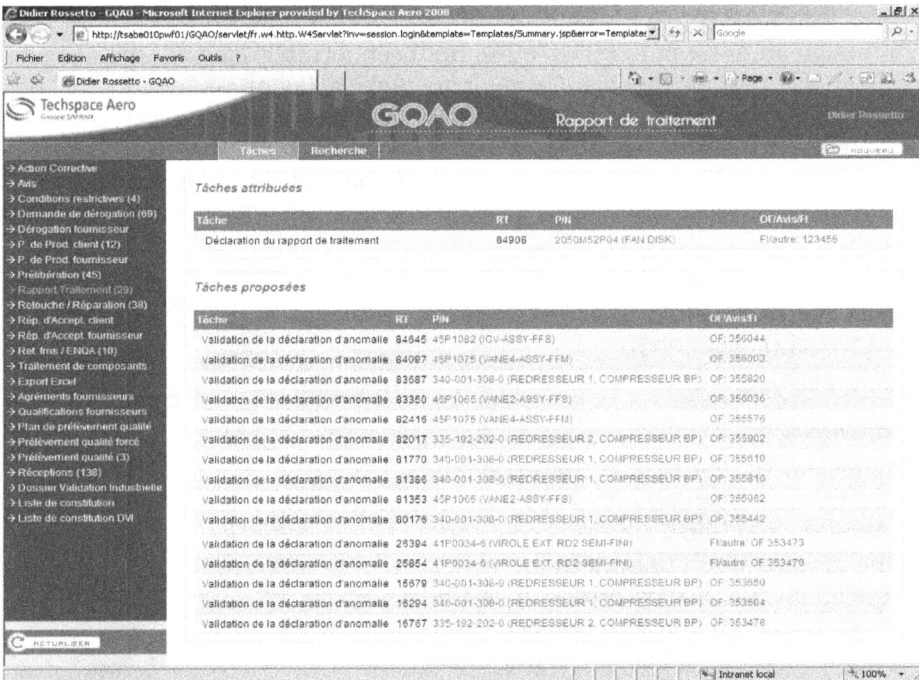

The harmonization is also a significant step forward: All the functions that were previously distributed between different applications have been brought together within a single interface, and the practices themselves have been rethought so as to no longer be specific to a single production workshop.

Figure 4: former applications

Now, when a file leaves a production workshop to be processed either by another workshop or by the supply chain, the operators retain visibility over its progress and thanks to the process description, which can be viewed at any moment, can better locate and understand any obstacles. After an initial phase of adaptation, the quality operators can now see the advantage of the new solution and are more positive, and the culture of process implementation is beginning to save time for the company and its impact goes beyond the quality aspect.

The divisions between the different company entities are beginning to fade, with everyone becoming aware of his or her role in a global process.

Even though a Centre of Excellence has not been formally created, there is a clear desire on the part of the management to have a better understanding of the processes. As was the case for GQAO, the project manager is the key point in the system, and each entity describes its processes and insures they are followed. The dematerialization that is being carried out at the same time is accelerating the structuring of the processes, notably by redefining the activities and the respective roles of each participant.

In addition, in each of the departments there are key users and centers of competence for the principal IT applications (ERP / CAD-CAM...) which guarantee the correct use of IT resources.

HURDLES OVERCOME

Management

For management, the biggest challenge has been to take on board the process dimension. Indeed, it is important to accept that it is the process that guarantees the result and systematically avoids errors. It is the result of an analysis of best practices and defines the order in which tasks are to be carried out and the associated responsibilities. This is in contrast with the manual processing where each file was an individual case and where the task order was decided according to what seemed the most logical, the most effective for the given case.

Lastly, although standardized, the processes integrate the team know-how and offer security and flexibility to the company enabling it to address the challenges of an ageing population and mobility in the teams, dictated by flexibility of production.

Business

The users have been a little disconcerted by the highly operational side of BPM: A task which is completed cannot be replayed or "saved" by the next office. Users have had to change their work habits and become more responsible. Training enabled them to take on board the benefits of working as part of a process, and now everyone thinks of the next users by verifying that all the necessary information has indeed been entered before signing off their tasks.

At the same time, the processes and the application have been improved to make things easier for the users, such as for example the ability to redirect a case from one team to another if a case has been sent to the wrong team.

Organization Adoption

During the processes definition phase, exchanges were analyzed, and in some cases tasks had to be distributed differently, sometimes with reallocations to different roles, or even several tasks grouped together into one.

Now these processes are in production, it's important to make sure that the old reflexes do not re-emerge, and that the new optimized procedures apply. To this end, participants have been trained and everybody else's actions explained to them in detail. They now understand why certain interactions have changed and that part of the information is now automatically dealt with by the application. Lastly, there was a multi-phase approach to process optimization to enable the operational organization to evolve accordingly.

BENEFITS

Production has less down-time because the operators in the manufacturing workshops benefit directly from a reduction in the time spent on the administrative processing of quality incidents. The time saved can be up to one week, thanks to the fact that paper documents are no longer exchanged and that the GQAO application provides better visibility.

Quality participants' efficiency has been improved: the time saved on administrative tasks has enabled members of the quality to spend more time on technical tasks with more added-value.

At the end of the production process, the conformance certificate that must leave with the part is obtained automatically once the system has checked that all quality incidents have been closed, whereas before this was done manually on paper and using several different applications. As a result hours have been saved, allowing for a faster and less pressurized customer delivery process. This aspect is all the more measurable when the manufacturing is complex.

GQAO provides a guaranteed check of the internal risk linked to the closure of a case at product delivery time.

The ROI is deemed satisfactory by Techspace Aero, aware that the underlying BPM platform will be exploited for other applications in order to capitalize on the investments that have been made.

Techspace Aero
Groupe SAFRAN

→ Action Corrective
→ Avis
→ Conditions restrictives (4)
→ Demande de dérogation (69)
→ Dérogation fournisseur
→ P. de Prod. client (12)
→ P. de Prod. fournisseur
→ Prélibération (45)
→ Rapport Traitement (29)
→ Retouche / Réparation (38)
→ Rép. d'Accept. client
→ Rép. d'Accept. fournisseur
→ Ret. frns / ENQA (10)
→ Traitement de composants
→ Export Excel
→ Agréments fournisseurs
→ Qualifications fournisseurs
→ Plan de prélèvement qualité
→ Prélèvement qualité forcé
→ Prélèvement qualité (3)
→ Réceptions (138)
→ Dossier Validation Industrielle
→ Liste de constitution
→ Liste de constitution DVI

BEST PRACTICES, LEARNING POINTS AND PITFALLS

During interactions with users

✓ *Involve users right from the application design phase. This requires a project manager experienced in this type of exercise*

✓ *Earn users' trust through effective supervision and good feedback*

✓ *Discuss the details of users' needs in order to create the screens they want. This significantly facilitates the adoption of the application*

✓ *During processes definition*

✓ *Adapt the specifications to the business process logic, obtain descriptions of the processes in addition to the data*

✓ *Ensure participants agree with each other about the processes before beginning to implement them*

✓ *Always keep in mind typical cases while defining processes, considering individual cases as exceptions*

✓ *In order for described process to be automated, it must have been designed with this in mind.*

✓ *At the organization level*

✓ *Encourage awareness of the real organization so it can evolve more fluid exchanges*

✓ *Make business users aware of the process approach and the benefits this can offer*

✓ *Take a step back and keep in mind how the intrinsic functionality of a BPM system can lead to simplification, and gain full knowledge of the target platform which may offer additional functions*

Pitfalls

✗ *Starting to deploy processes without the support of a person with strong experience of the subject*

✗ *Let users model the first processes alone, but provide them with support in how to describe them*

COMPETITIVE ADVANTAGES

The aircraft industry is driven by the quality of the products it manufactures. In this context, improving the administrative side of quality management has a particular impact on the internal organization. Given this, these improvements have the advantage of enabling seamless exchanges between the different departments of Techspace Aero, and also with its suppliers, and particularly at customer delivery time.

At the group level each individual feeds off the others in terms of creativity and innovation. This GQAO project follows this approach and is now the most advanced BPM application in the quality domain.

For the future, there is a plan in the short term to connect the system to that of the client and to relay the information produced by GQAO directly into this system. On a wider level Techspace Aero is enabling itself to accept the constraints dictated by its clients, and to offer its suppliers quality-related pages in the B2B platform with automated and more efficient exchanges.

The approach which is being promoted of understanding and controlling the processes is further accelerated by the document dematerialization project, which will naturally result in a simplification of the processes and time saving.

Finally, other projects have been started following the successful launch of the GQAO application, here is a sample:

• Purchase Order (non-aero) dematerialization (100+ users)

• Provider Invoice Dematerialization (40.000/year – 80+ users)

- Mission Requests Dematerialization (all the staff – 1.400 users)

TECHNOLOGY

Technical standards

- W4 BPM Suite
- Windows Server 2003 operating system
- Apache Web Server
- Tomcat application server
- SMTP mail server (Lotus Notes 6.5.4)
- Java/JSP/Ajax/Javascript/HTML
- Oracle database
- Access to ERP BaaN IV version ICv4

Architecture

The implemented application uses standard 3-layer architecture.

- Presentation Layer
  Intended for display in an Internet browser, the visible part of the application is developed in HTML. Certain logic is also relocated to the user's workstation through Javascript controls and Ajax calls.

- Business Layer
  In this layer, we find human workflow/technical flow and business area control and also management rules. The business process logic is based on W4 BPM Suite, and the business area logic is based on specific Java classes.

- Data Access Layer
  The handling of business area data is carried out using a Java framework developed in-house.

Figure 6: functional view of the process (Nonconformance Report)

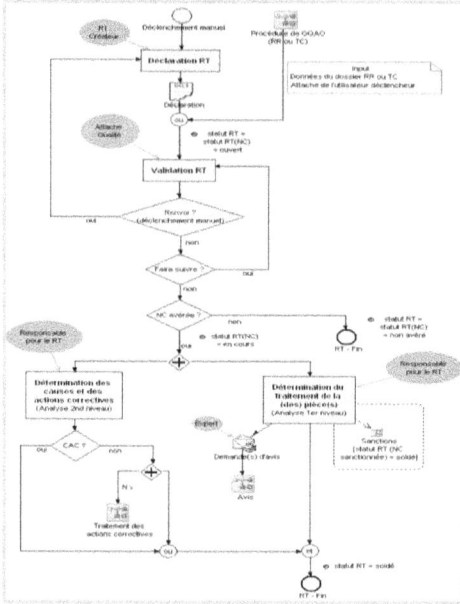

To improve the ergonomics of the application it has been decided to combine the representations of the functional processes, hiding the complexity of the underlying implemented processes, combining user steps and the use of different technical flows.

Figure 7: Technical flow

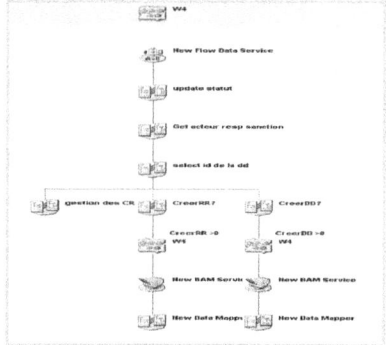

Figure 8:

Implemented process, with technical flow calls

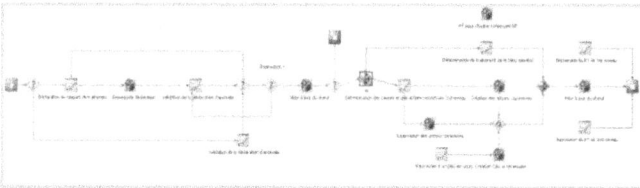

Each functional view of a process is backed by an implemented process.

When convenient, technical flows can be triggered by workflows. On return, a workflow can be triggered by a technical flow.

The whole combination makes the application run.

Mapping and re-engineering of the business processes with Win'Design for W4 BPM Suite

In two years Techspace Aero's development support team, a team attached to the IT department, has helped to map dozens of business processes.

Among the identified processes, Techspace Aero's directors have designated the priority processes which have been or will be subject to IT implementation. These are rethought, optimized and often simplified before being delivered to the development teams.

The default modeled processes show an obvious complexity which results from a raw harvesting of the know-how of the various company participants.

Figure 9: Process definition and optimization before implementation

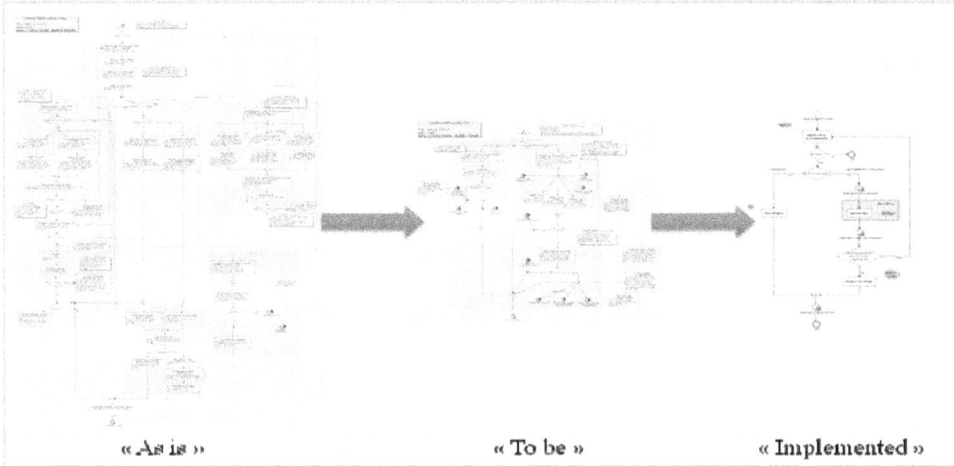

«As is»   «To be»   «Implemented»

Modeling and execution of Business Processes with W4 Studio and WW4 BPM Engine

Each workflow is implemented using W4 Studio before being injected into W4 Engine. The sequences of technical tasks (generation of documents, sending of emails, automatic triggers, etc.) are entrusted to the SystemFlow module of W4 BPM Suite. The GUIs are accessible via an Internet browser.

Figure 10: From technical modeling to the application supported by W4 BPM Engine

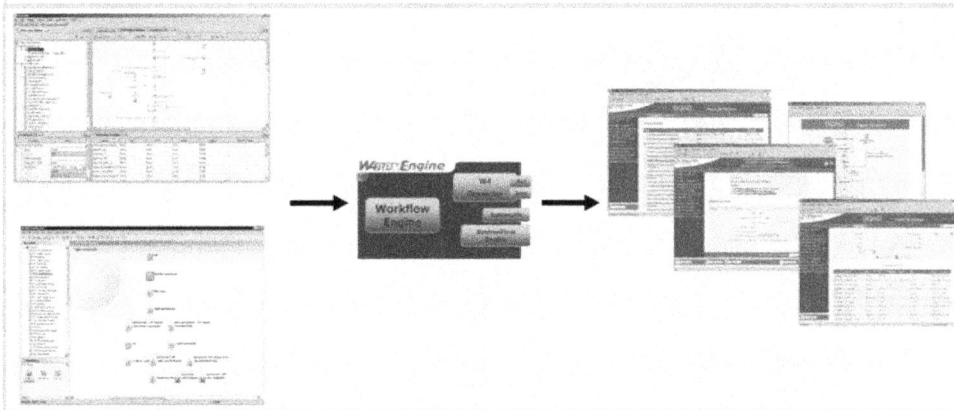

Monitoring of the processes with W4 Control Center

For each implemented application, users have expressed the need to have key performance indicators: A list of the files to be processed, people responsible for processing, state of progress in the processes, key dates (start, end, deadline…).

These needs are covered "out-of-the-box" by the Control Center module of W4 BPM Suite.

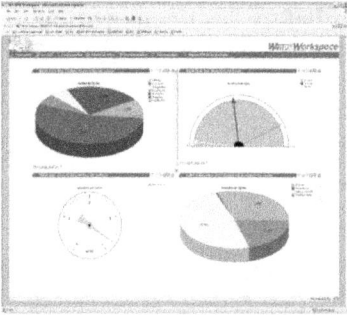

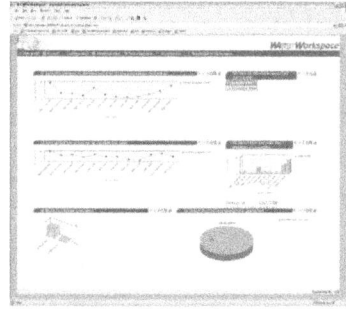

THE TECHNOLOGY AND SERVICE PROVIDERS

To successfully manage this huge IT project, the ISD (Information Systems Department) chose to bring together a mixed team and to be supported by an experienced W4 BPM Suite integrator. NSI IT Software & Services, certified W4 partner since the early days (1998), was chosen for its experience with the product and its ability to take charge of all the different aspects relating to the realization of such projects.

www.nsi-sa.be   www.w4global.com

Section 2

Middle East-Africa

PruHealth, South Africa

Gold Award, Middle East and Africa

Nominated by TIBCO, France

1. EXECUTIVE SUMMARY / ABSTRACT

PruHealth is a leading health insurance company which rewards members for adopting a healthy lifestyle. Launched in October 2004, PruHealth is a joint venture between Prudential and Discovery, the South African health insurance leader. Its model is based on a successful concept launched in South Africa.

Prudential is a leading financial services company founded in 1848 with over 21 million customers and 28,000 employees worldwide.

PruHealth is using a business process management approach on top of a service oriented architecture to create a more agile IT infrastructure – one that enables them to adapt their processes to business opportunities and bring products to market more quickly in the highly competitive health insurance market in the UK. PruHealth acquired the BPMS software in August 2007 and had already started to deploy processes on a service oriented architecture by April 2008, a significant achievement in a short space of time. PruHealth's IT team and back office and systems support is located in Johannesburg, South Africa.

2. OVERVIEW

There were three key business drivers which led PruHealth to embark upon their BPM journey:
- A requirement for customer centricity
- A desire for ongoing product and service innovation
- A requirement for efficiency improvements

PruHealth has accomplished their goals in each of these three areas for process improvement and has reaped significant business benefits within the first year of the change management program.

PruHealth has eliminated costly manual and paper-based processes by automating highly complex business processes relating to new customer acquisition, claims management, managing appointments with screening partners, tracking usage and preparing corporate bills. The automated processes interface with channel partners via B2B communications. The automation of these key processes has enabled PruHealth to manage exceptional levels of growth in their business, namely an increase of 67% in insured lives in 2008.

PruHealth conducted in parallel a project focused on adopting a services oriented approach, leveraging existing legacy system components and a business process management implementation. PruHealth needed to improve responsiveness to change, reduce time to market for new product and services introduction and further enable the multiple business partners and channels to market. The two separate initiatives were highly complementary as the SOA project provided reusable, documented services which could be reused by the newly automated business processes.

PruHealth was able to recoup their initial investment in the BPM and SOA projects within the first year and has enjoyed much improved visibility of their end-to-end processes and confidence in their ability to meet increasing market demand for their services. PruHealth overcame some challenges during the implementation, including spending more time up front on the initial process design than they had done with their previous development approach and slow adoption of the new processes by the business analyst and end user communities.

3. BUSINESS CONTEXT

PruHealth was set up as a joint venture in 2004 for the UK private healthcare market which is an increasingly competitive marketplace. PruHealth has 2.5% market share and competes with much larger players such as BUPA and PPP. The healthcare market is increasingly reliant on the internet as a primary vehicle for interfacing with corporate and private customers and as a vehicle for exchanging vital information with business partners in the healthcare supply chain. The driving motivation behind the change program was a requirement for greater organisational agility, to bring new products and services to market more rapidly and to gain operational efficiencies.

4. THE KEY INNOVATIONS

4.2 Business

PruHealth has realigned itself to become significantly more customer centric and has developed rich portals, paying a lot of attention to the customer experience. The portals are the main vehicle for communication with customers and business partners. A new process for managing appointments with screening partners has been introduced, tracking usage and preparing corporate bills.

PruHealth repackaged its Vitality product in 2008 which encourages customers to self assess their dietary and exercise regimes and to adopt a healthier lifestyle. Since the introduction of this revitalised portal, customer engagement on the website has increased fourfold with no additional marketing effort as a result of process improvements.

4.3 Process

The ten business processes deployed by PruHealth include onboarding new customers and administering check ups for customers with partner organisations; these were previously manual processes and could involve as many as 100 separate actions being initiated. New processes also track usage of services provided in the Vitality programme and prepare corporate bills. Prior to automation, processes were untracked and susceptible to human error with, for example, errors in the routing of outstanding actions between pools of back-office staff.

[see Figure 1 in appendix for a process map for a specific process example).

The development and operational teams used a 6 Sigma approach to process design and modelled the processes in a standards-based modelling environment (TIBCO Business Studio™). All of the newly automated processes live within the process repository, which is the master repository for all processes at PruHealth, and are documented and maintained in synch at the design level and the operational level. The process design can be adapted directly by modifying the process definition and flows and by taking it through all the required change management steps and rigorous testing before deploying the new version to the production environment.

In parallel to business process transformation, a number of legacy components from existing applications were packaged and exposed as services to the enterprise service bus. Some new services were also developed, keeping custom coding to an absolute minimum. These services are reused by the business processes and are catalogued in the services repository. The enterprise service bus manages all inter-application updates and has eliminated all point-to-point interfaces. The enterprise service bus provides rich information about processing exceptions and failures.

4.4 Organization

The impact on the employees is best characterised by a reduction in the complexity of their tasks. Previously there were multiple manual processes, some of them highly complex, no automated tracking of progress and limited flexibility to change processes. Not only does PruHealth enjoy greater visibility of their end-to-end processes but they are also able to meet stringent audit regulations with very little additional effort due to the rich tracking and reporting information available to them through the BPMS.

With the introduction of BPMS, PruHealth has been able to reduce dependencies on some key individuals by capturing their domain expertise and applying it through business rules.

5. HURDLES OVERCOME

Management

Some of the biggest challenges were aligning staff to process and customer requirements and ensuring that there was sufficient internal education and communication. From a systems delivery perspective, it was a challenge to understand the impact of systems changes and to implement these changes. The availability of a common process and services repository helped anticipate the impact of systems changes.

At the outset, PruHealth was keen to adopt agile methods and acquire new tools and technologies while retaining rigour in testing and live deployment. The management team decided to start their analysis from the bottom up and quickly solve some operational issues through the automation of key processes. The BPM project took longer than expected as there had been less of a focus on upfront process design previously. PruHealth now has a greater understanding of the importance of detailed process design prior to deployment and appreciates the ability to preview resource requirements through process simulations and SLAs before deployment.

Business

From a business perspective, PruHealth was resource constrained rather than financially constrained. Once staff are trained on specific technologies for which there is a demand in the South African market, it becomes more difficult to retain them. PruHealth has initiated a knowledge management program in order to optimise use of their internal resources.

Organization Adoption

End users and business analysts were not overly enthusiastic about the improved processes. An increased focus on rigorous design up front generated more work for business analysts. Although improved business processes derive significant benefits for the organisation, comprehensive processes do not excite individuals.

6. BENEFITS

6.1 Cost Savings

The automation of core business processes reduced the training time for new users and optimised resource utilisation by routing work based on skillset. PruHealth is able to benefit from a much improved ratio of lives insured per person.

6.2 Time Reductions

"There were many things we liked about this project", says Dos Santos. "Development time was one third of the original estimate, because components are resilient out of the box, coding is minimal, and testing is easy".

BPMS tools allow users to configure, simulate, deploy and manage processes with far reduced IT involvement which saves significant time and involvement from IT. Less time is spent on training new users thanks to the automation of tasks.

6.3 Increased Revenues

Membership at PruHealth is growing very fast, in fact it is twice the growth rate of Discovery, one of PruHealth's parent companies. Improvements in efficiencies directly attributable to business process implementation have resulted in more lives being insured with a minimal headcount increase in 2008.

See Figure 2 for growth rate of PruHealth compared to Discovery.

6.4 Productivity Improvements

The detailed documentation and traceability enabled by the new approach to business process management has enabled PruHealth to demonstrate compliance to stringent regulations such as the Financial Promotions Act in the UK.

The key challenge for 2008 was to increase efficiency to deal with the company's rapid growth. Membership was projected to grow 67% with only 5.8% increase in headcount. Efficiency was achieved through a combination of automation, product simplification, optimization and process improvement. Processes have been segmented according to skillset and tasks can now be routed to individuals with the right skills to manage processes.

7. BEST PRACTICES, LEARNING POINTS AND PITFALLS

7.1 Best Practices and Learning Points

- ✓ *Applied BPM tools and methodologies*
- ✓ *Agile methods*
- ✓ *Removed dependencies on key individuals*
- ✓ *Distributed workload*
- ✓ *Optimised resource utilisation by routing work based on skillset*
- ✓ *Enabled process improvement*
- ✓ *Using Business Studio to plan and simulate process improvements resulted in better SLA compliance*
- ✓ *Greater sub-process reuse on subsequent projects*
- ✓ *Invested in tools and change management to evangelize the new approach to development and business processes*

7.2 Pitfalls

- ✗ *Set expectations incorrectly for the Return on Investment for the first project*
- ✗ *Underestimated additional effort required in process design phase to get the process design and flow right*

8. COMPETITIVE ADVANTAGES

"TIBCO's software gives us a competitive advantage against larger competitors (with larger IT teams) by providing an agile infrastructure that reduces development time and provides rapid return on investment."

Paulo Dos Santos, CIO, PruHealth

9. TECHNOLOGY

TIBCO iProcess™ Suite is an open and standards-based BPM solution that extends from process design to process optimization. TIBCO iProcess™ Engine is the foundation of the suite and provides a powerful platform built to handle the most complex and demanding processes in any organization. It includes complete support for load balancing, multiple background processing, and real-time process monitoring to ensure highly available (24/7) system uptime.

TIBCO Business Studio™ software is the modeling and simulation environment for the iProcess Suite. It unifies key elements of BPM – modeling, management, simulation, and implementation – in one design environment. Different views of the same process model allow business and IT to collaborate seamlessly to create executable business process models.

TIBCO ActiveMatrix BusinessWorks™ software is a standards-based integration backbone that includes an enterprise service bus (ESB) and web services platform to connect disparate applications and data with little to no programming. It provides an integrated services environment (ISE) for creating web services and orchestrating process flows to improve the consistency and adaptability of both IT and business operations.

10. THE TECHNOLOGY AND SERVICE PROVIDERS

Software vendor: TIBCO Software

TIBCO technology digitized Wall Street in the '80s with the event-driven Information Bus® software, which helped make real-time business a strategic differentiator in the '90s. Today, TIBCO's infrastructure software gives customers the ability to constantly innovate by connecting applications and data in a service-oriented architecture, streamlining activities through business process management, and giving people the information and intelligence tools they need to make faster and smarter decisions, what we call The Power of Now®. TIBCO serves more than 3,000 customers around the world with offices in more than 20 countries and an ecosystem of over 200 partners. Learn more at www.tibco.com.

TIBCO Professional Services in South Africa were also involved in this project at PruHealth.

11. APPENDIX FOR PRUHEALTH AWARD SUBMISSION

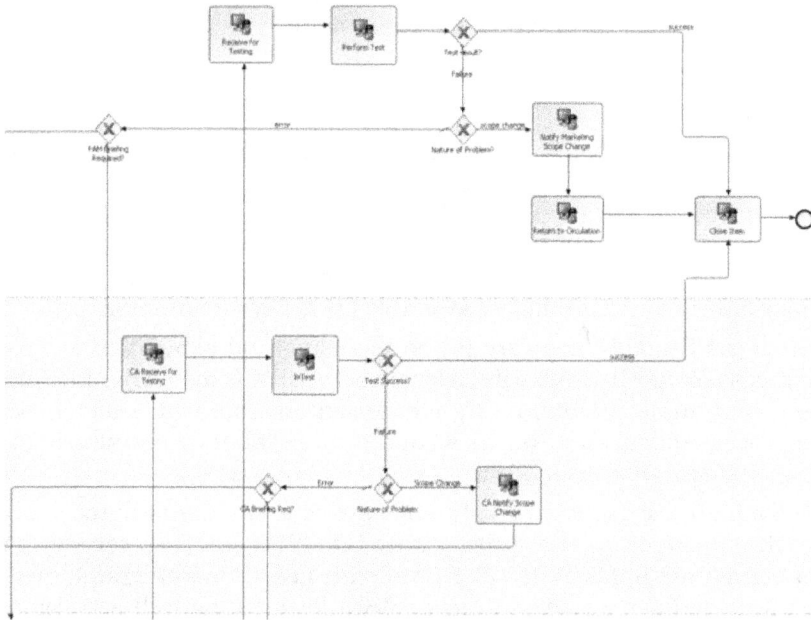

Figure 1: Process for managing appointment with screening partners, tracking usage, and preparing corporate bills.

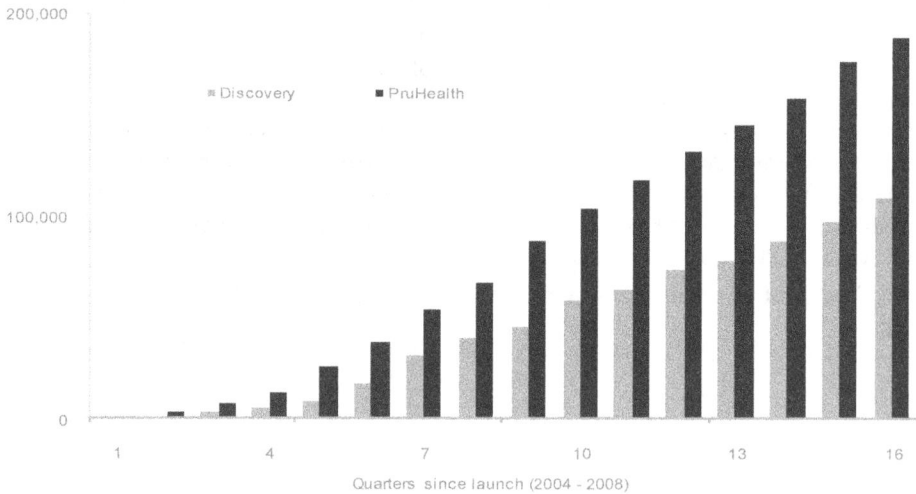

Figure 2: Membership growth of PruHealth vs Discovery

Section 3

North America

City of Edmonton, Alberta, Canada

Finalist, North America

Nominated by Computronix, Canada

1. EXECUTIVE SUMMARY / ABSTRACT[1]

We describe the basic concepts, workflow design and robust implementation of an electronic circulation system using the POSSE® Business Process Management tool suite. A key business process for the City of Edmonton is the consultation of internal and external stakeholders on applications for new licenses, permits, by-law amendments and certain key City-wide initiatives. In the past, documents were circulated by sending paper copies to stakeholders who then returned the annotated copies. The comments from the various stakeholders were manually collated into a single document for the subsequent decision process. This paper based circulation process was slow and fairly labour intensive. In 2006, we developed and implemented a leading edge POSSE® Web-based Land Development Application (LDA) system that allowed the applicant to submit electronic copies of application documents. The LDA included a rudimentary web based circulation subsystem that enabled the circulation of LDA application documents electronically to some of the stakeholders for comments. The LDA system has been used to successfully process over 1000 applications since its inception in August 2006.

Building on our experience with the circulation subsystem of the LDA and use feedback, we designed and built a new web based circulation system with the following three key goals:

1. Significantly simplify and improve the user interface;

2. Create a stand-alone generic version of web based circulation that can be used with other business processes with similar circulation needs, and

3. Enable external stakeholder groups to self administer their own user accounts, create simple workflow and dynamically report on outstanding requests.

We also document key process innovations used during this project – (a) separating the decision making process from the circulation process; (b) effective direct involvement of external and internal stakeholders for workflow design, and (c) use of the user interface model to jump start the workflow design process.

2. OVERVIEW

In this award submission document, we describe the concept, design and POSSE® based implementation project for Electronic Circulation at the City of Edmonton. The City of Edmonton is a municipal government body in a metropolitan area of more than a million people. As the local government, the City is responsible for issuing a variety of permits and licenses and amending its bylaws. The City frequently consults internal and external stakeholders on license and permit applications or key City projects as part of a larger decision making and regulatory process. This consultation process includes the circulation of docu-

---

[1] Segments of this document are being submitted as a paper to the 2009 BPM and Workflow Handbook (http://www.bpmf.org/books/2009_call_for_papers.htm)

ments such as engineering drawings, draft copies of bylaws and reference materials e.g. surveys and research information. See Figure 1 for a conceptual diagram of the workflow for circulation.

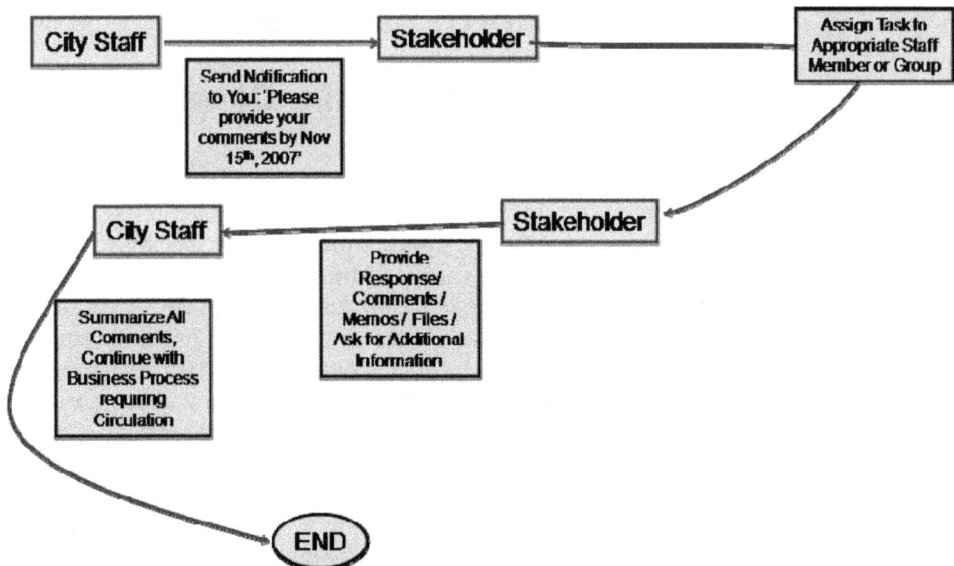

Figure 1. Basic Circulation Process

As shown in Figure 1, the City staff member initiating the circulation sends a notification to a contact person in the stakeholder organization. Stakeholders include internal City departments and external agencies such as utilities and departments in other orders of government. The contact person at the agency then assigns the task to the appropriate staff member or sub-group. The agency staff member reviews the documents provided and submits a response. The city staff member then collates the comments into a single summary report for input into the subsequent decision making process.

3. BUSINESS CONTEXT

In the past, the circulation process described in Figure 1 was paper based and each step involved mailing hard copies of documents. Paper based circulation has two significant gaps from a business perspective: scalability and the fact that agencies cannot collaborate on a circulation. There is a linear relationship between the number of stakeholders and the effort required to create, circulate, and track physical copies of documents as well as collate the resulting comments. Collaboration between stakeholders is limited as they are not able to see each other's comments until a collated set of circulation comments is created and recirculated. Both of these issues result in an extended duration for the circulation process often contributing weeks or months to the overall decision process time frames.

Collaboration between stakeholders is critical to the process. For example, a stakeholder, such as a power utility company, may need to read the comments posted by another stakeholder, such as a utility regulator, before responding to a specific request for comments. Using paper, this would require multiple circulations for a single application. The first circulation for regulatory agencies such as utility regulators and other orders of government and then the second circulation for secondary agencies such as utility companies and community organizations.

An electronic collaborative web based circulation eliminates this requirement as all comments submitted by one stakeholder are instantly viewable by all other stakeholders. There are a few use cases where the collaboration is undesirable and the system can provide the flexibility to turn off this feature.

In 2006, the City of Edmonton implemented a web based Land Development Application (LDA) system that allowed an applicant to submit electronic copies of application documents. Applicants would create a new LDA and upload required documents such as draft plans and amendment proposals through the LDA web page.

The LDA system included a basic electronic circulation subsystem that was used to circulate the electronic documents submitted by the applicant. A City employee would add any required covering notes or additional documents before initiating the electronic circulation process. The LDA circulation subsystem would email a link to a web page that had specific circulation details to all the required stakeholders. The email specified a circulation end date after which the link would no longer be available. After the stakeholders reviewed the documents online, they were able to submit their comments either by typing them into a text field on the web page or by uploading a separate document. The upload feature was also used to submit scanned copies of manually annotated documents. The LDA system automatically collated the comments for the summary report. While the LDA circulation subsystem functionally implemented the same process model described in Figure 1, it was integrated into the business system that managed the land development approval lifecycle. This tight integration of the system meant that it could not be re-used for other circulation processes.

4. THE KEY INNOVATIONS

Collaborative web based circulation systems solve two critical problems with paper based circulation: stakeholders are able to view each other's comments immediately; and, the summary of stakeholder comments is auto-generated at the end of the circulation process thereby eliminating the manual process of collating comments.

The LDA system, described previously, has been used to successfully process over 800 applications since August 2006. The LDA circulation subsystem was a rudimentary system, customized to work with the LDA business process. The technical implementation could not be easily re-used for circulations for other business processes. Responding to customer demand and building on our experience with the LDA circulation subsystem, we designed and built a new generic electronic circulation system to achieve the following key goals:
- Simplify and improve the web user interface,
- Create an independent implementation of a web based circulation that can be used with other City business processes with similar needs, and
- Enable external stakeholder groups to self administer their own user accounts, create simple workflow and report on outstanding requests.

The key innovations introduced in this project are:

4.1 Business

Development of a common business vocabulary for process outcomes

Figure 2 illustrates the resulting workflow model for the generic electronic circulation system developed using the POSSE® workflow engine. Some of the terminology is specific to POSSE, but can be easily translated to other workflow development engines. A 'job' is used to refer to a workflow container object that contains a collection of process steps (tasks) and the process workflow. A 'status' is used to provide a quick overview of the overall progress of the processes and is used for reporting. A status is set by an event such as the completion of a task or a specific trigger. Triggers can be based on many criteria including dates, milestones or number of views. Tasks are completed by selecting an 'outcome'. Outcomes are used to direct workflow by initiating the next process. Outcomes may also trigger a status change on the job.

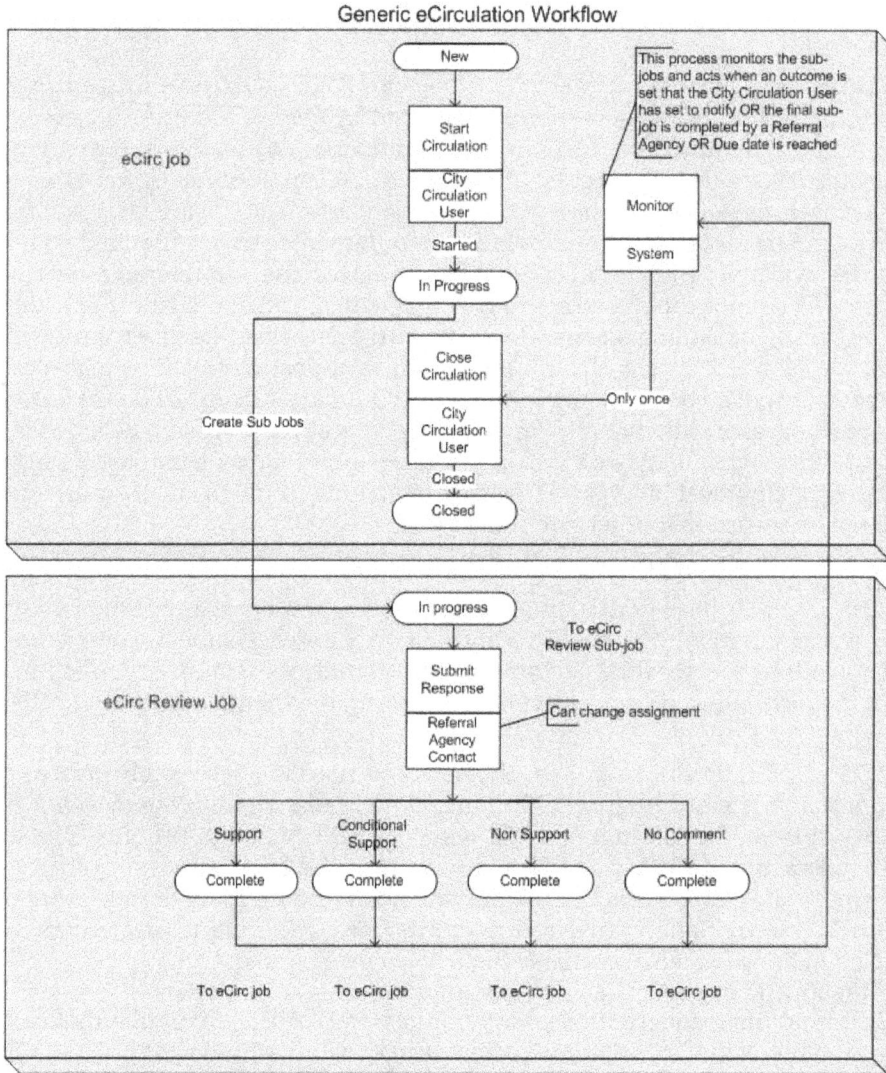

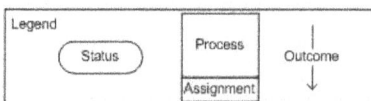

Figure 2. POSSE® workflow model for electronic circulation

The circulation process involves three basic tasks – (i) start circulation, (ii) submit a response, (iii) close the circulation. We configured the system to implement the conceptual workflow model from Figure 1. The 'start circulation' task is initiated by the City staff member responsible for the overall decision process. The 'start circulation' task then becomes independent of the overall decision process that requested the circulation process. In other words, the circulation process for a permit looks identical to that of a plan amendment. The 'submit response' step has one of four outcomes – (i) Support, (ii) Conditional Support, (iii) Non Support, and (iv) No Comment. The interpretation of each outcome is unique for different decision processes and does not affect the circulation process. The 'no comment' outcome enables the stakeholder to acknowledge receipt of the circulation without selecting a position. Using a standard set of outcomes and leaving the interpretation to the overall decision process maintains the generic nature of the electronic circulation system.

4.2 Process

Use of the User Interface mock-up to kick-start workflow design

The typical starting point for developing a workflow system is a sample workflow document. End user focus groups or workshops refine the final workflow. The system interface is usually created after the workflow has been fully defined. For this project, we reversed the process. We mocked up the user interface and presented it to the stakeholders in a series of workshops. Figure 3-Figure 6 illustrates our mock-up of the electronic circulation system. On these slides we referred to stakeholders as 'agencies' to accommodate terminology that is understood by most attendees in the workshops. Figure 3 illustrates the default first page for the electronic circulation system. It shows a list of requests that are assigned to the currently logged in user. Figure 4 shows a sample response for a circulation. The response is either provided as plain text in the field marked 'response' or in an uploaded document using the document upload feature. Figure 5 illustrates some key additional features of the circulation system such as the ability to view contact information for the individuals responsible for the circulation request. It also provides a quick link to a page with other completed circulation comments. Figure 6 illustrates the ability to view comments from other stakeholders without waiting for a summary document. The 'Print Friendly' link at the top left also provides a real-time snapshot of the circulation summary report.

With these mock-ups in hand, we engaged the stakeholders and gave them the task of helping us re-design the user interface without worrying about the workflow. In this process, the stakeholders validated some of our assumptions and refined others. Indirectly, they also asked for useful website features that clarified the back-end workflow required to enable the feature. For example, they wanted to view requests assigned to other individuals in their group – this meant that we had to implement a workflow step to facilitate assignment of review tasks to individual users. In general, the feedback from these sessions helped clarify how the majority of stakeholders would interact and manage their use of the system. These comments were then translated into workflow by our business analysts. This workflow was then vetted by a small subgroup of stakeholders. We found that the people in our stakeholder group were much more likely to give us feedback on the styling and functionality of a webpage than on a complex business process or workflow model. We leveraged this to our advantage and designed a system that worked for our stakeholders. Giving the external customers a 'say' in the system development has also assisted in early adoption and even anticipation of the delivery. These screenshots and comments from stakeholder workshops were critical components for the POSSE® workflow model in Figure 2.

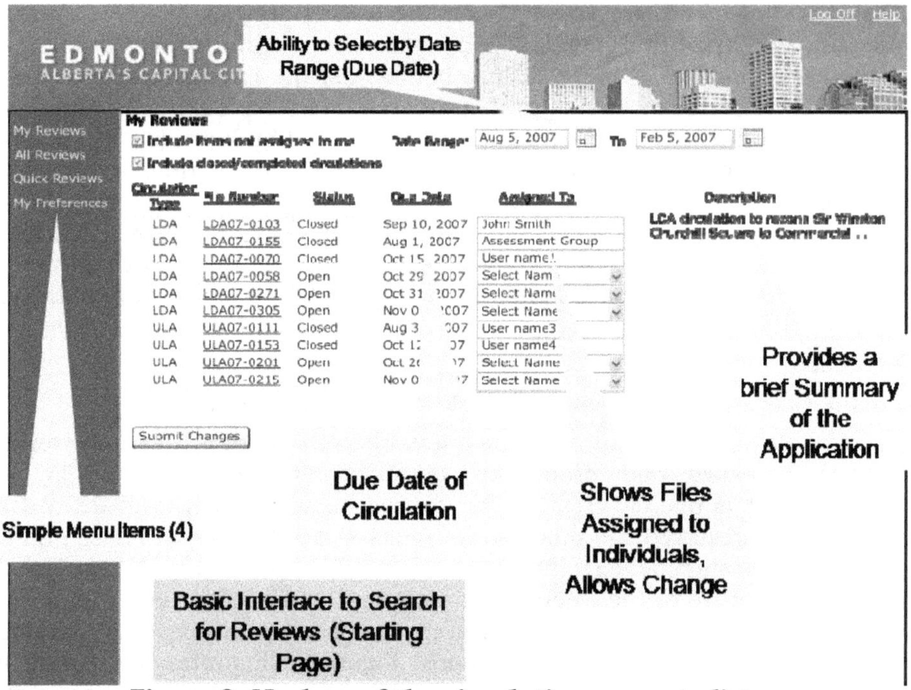

Figure 3. Mockup of the circulation requests list page.

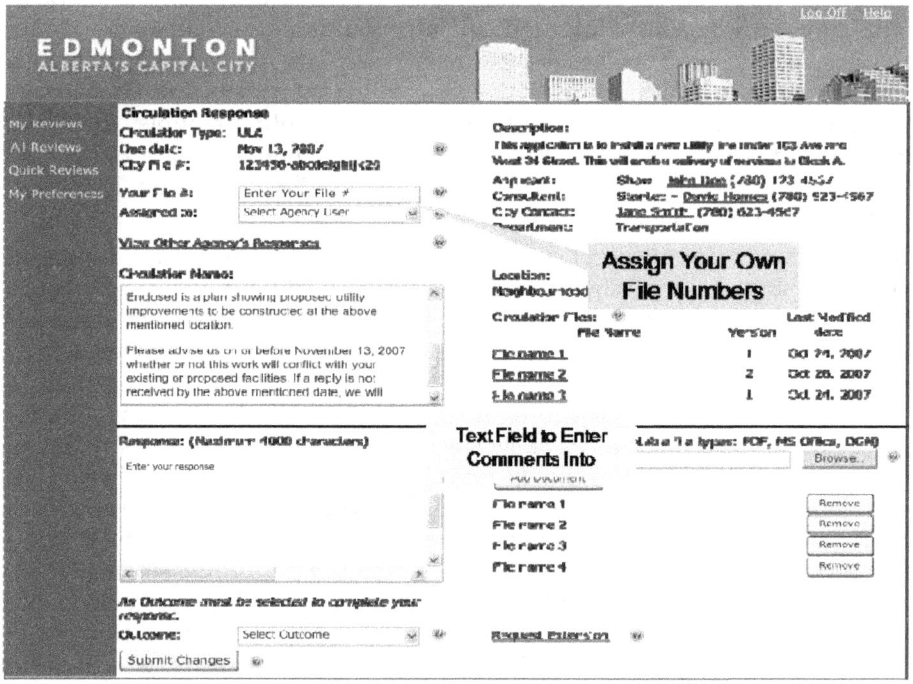

Figure 4. Mockup of the Circulation Response page

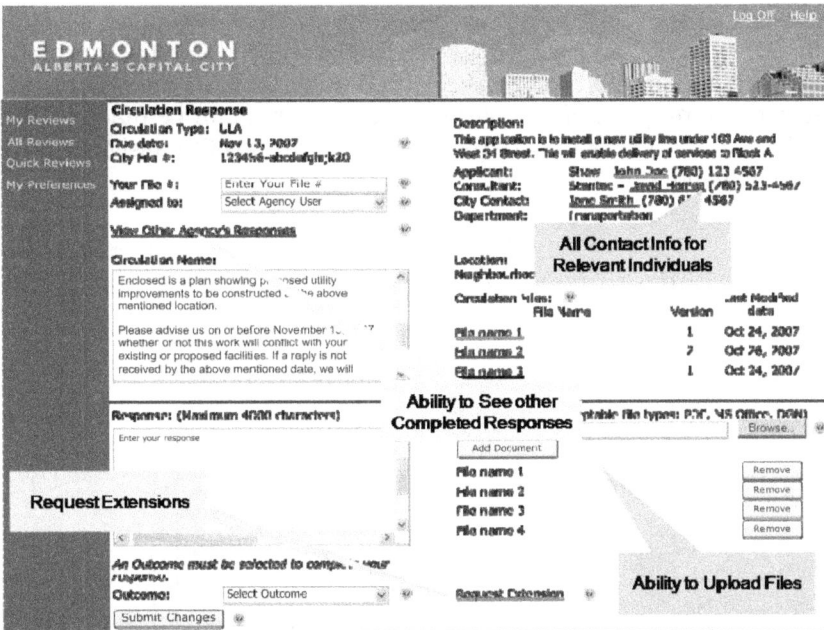

Figure 5. Mockup of the circulation response page illustrating features

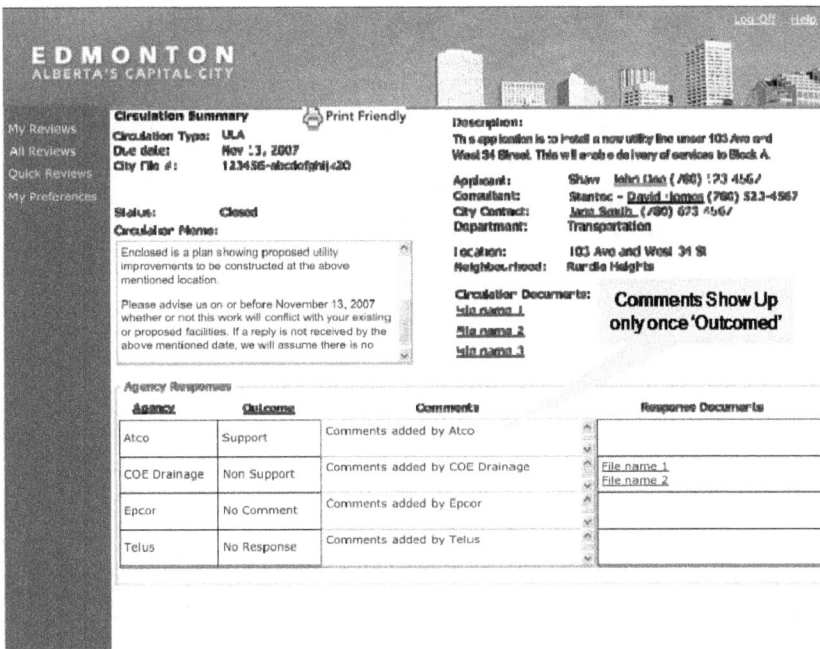

Figure 6. Mockup of page viewing other circulation responses

d) Enabling end user account self management

Figure 7 illustrates the use cases for the electronic circulation system. The agency contact is the agency staff member that receives the request and assigns the request to the appropriate personnel. The agency user is the individual that responds to circulation requests and the agency administrator administers the user accounts. The concept of a group was developed to facilitate mass assignment of requests. For example, an agency with fifty users could create five groups with ten members each to identify the five specialized subgroups in the organization that respond to different types of circulations. Assignments can be made at the group level so that all the users in a particular subgroup see the assignment and the first one to respond removes it from the list.

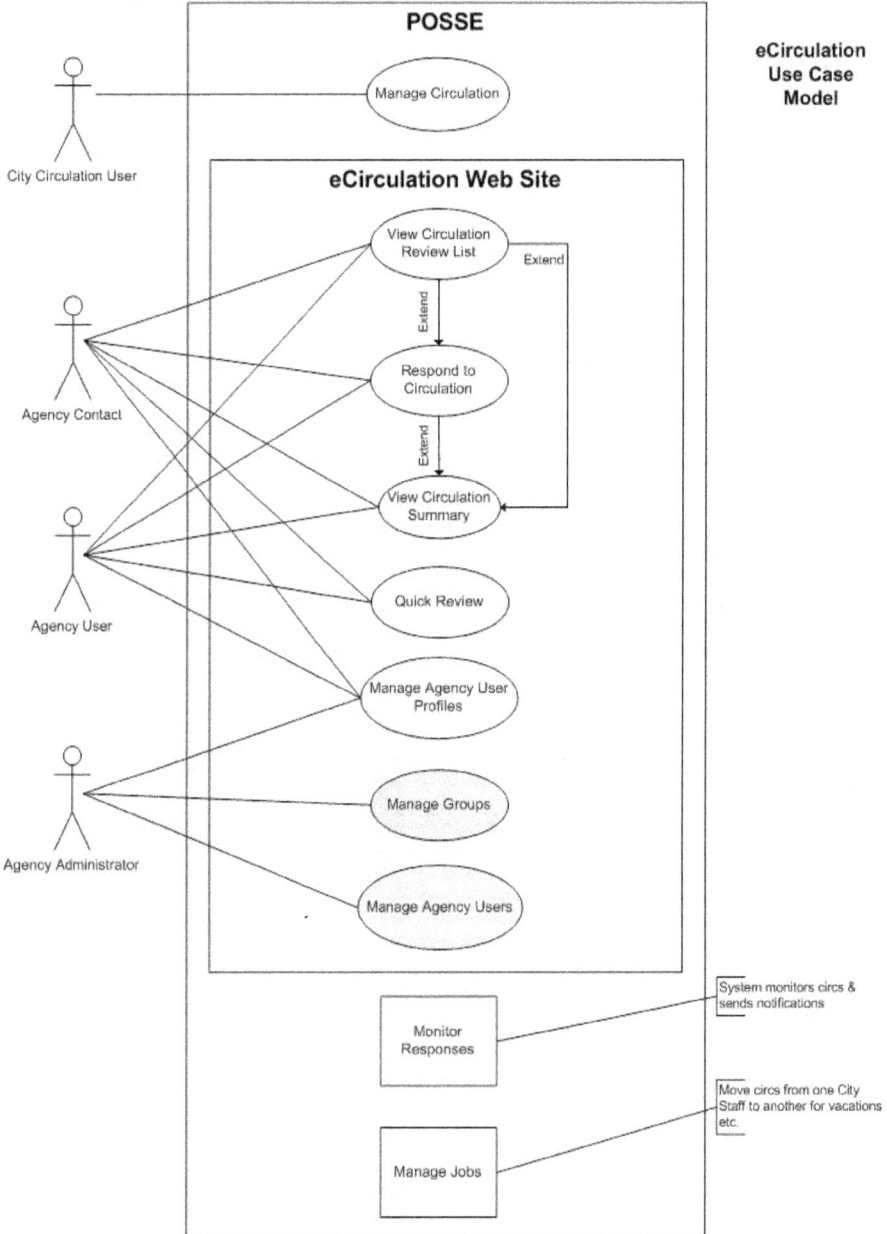

POSSE

eCirculation
Use Case
Model

Manage Circulation

City Circulation User

eCirculation Web Site

View Circulation
Review List — Extend

Extend

Respond to
Circulation

Extend

View Circulation
Summary

Quick Review

Manage Agency User
Profiles

Agency Contact

Agency User

Manage Groups

Agency Administrator

Manage Agency Users

Monitor
Responses — System monitors circs &
sends notifications

Manage Jobs — Move circs from one City
Staff to another for vacations
etc.

Figure 7. Use case concept model for electronic circulation

Two separate web modules were created to accommodate these use cases. The first module was a series of web interfaces for viewing and responding to circulations. This module closely matched the screen mock-ups in Figure 3-Figure 6.

The second module provided a series of interfaces for user maintenance and administration functions defined in Figure 8.

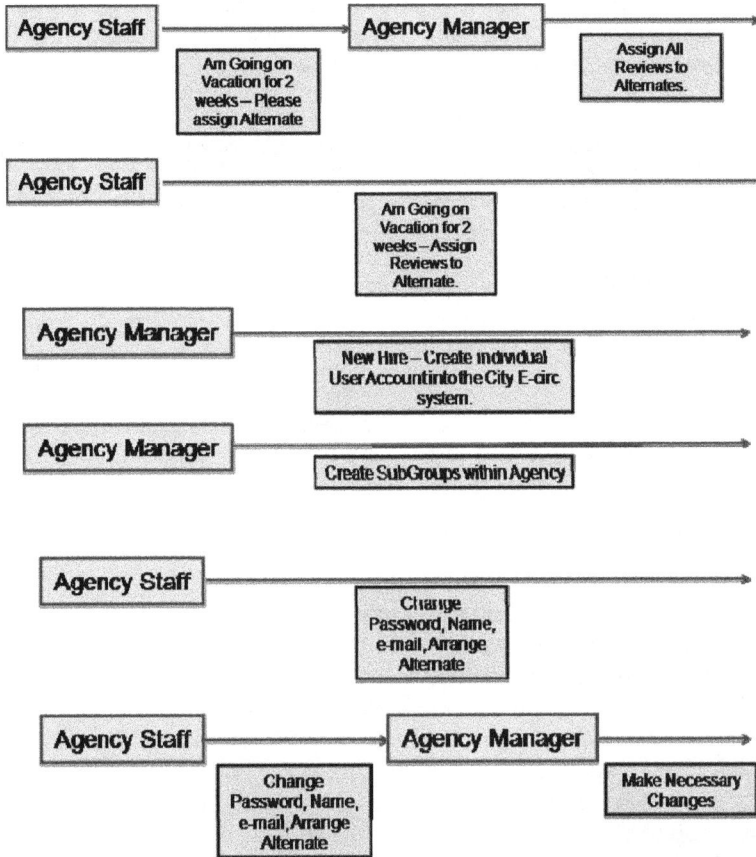

Figure 8. Basic functions of the user administration module

Each module was developed separately understanding the required integration. A detailed explanation of the workflow steps and corresponding design process can be found in the Appendix.

4.3 Organization

Separation of the circulation process from the decision process

Workflow for regulatory approvals can be fairly complex. As circulation is generally a minor activity in the overall decision process, circulation systems are customized to the type of consultation and designed into the engine processing the decision workflow. A permit approval system would implement a separate circulation subsystem from a plan or bylaw amendment system. This creates a problem as recipients of circulations from different City business processes are often the same stakeholders. This meant that the stakeholders needed to be familiar with multiple systems that had similar functional workflow. As an initial step in this project, we isolated the common activities in the circulation sub-process for a variety of business processes. We had to remove all the decision activities from the circulation process, as decision activities are not the same across different business processes. This effectively limited our definition of circulation to be a relatively simple process of sending documents to stakeholders, receiving comments and producing a summary of all comments as illustrated in Figure 1. In our process audit, we found many City processes that were amenable to this process decomposition. As an example, Figure 9 illustrates an excerpt from the LDA business process that shows some of the key processes for electronic circulation. Our redefinition of circulation as a standalone system with a standard defined set of actors (city staff members, stakeholders, etc.) helped simplify the workflow as shown in Figure 1.

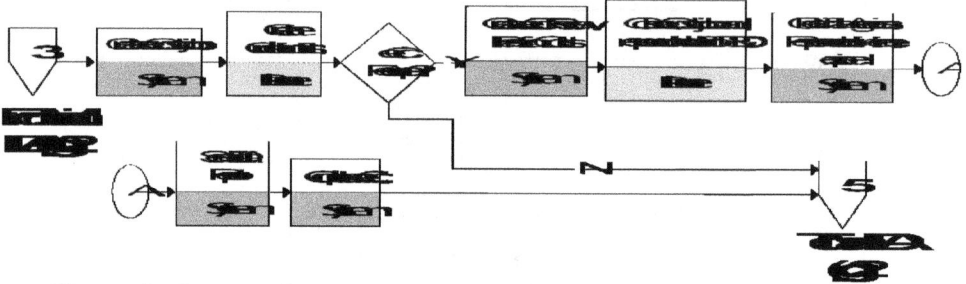

Figure 9. Excerpt from the LDA Business Process Document indicating the Customized LDA E-circ implementation.

5. HURDLES OVERCOME

Management

The project clearly benefits multiple business processes and fits within our overall corporate goal of better integration with the stakeholder community. However, without the decomposition and extraction of the circulation process, it would have been very difficult for separate business areas to envision this shared system implementation of a common business process. After we made the case for shared implementation, our sponsors, the Planning and Development and Transportation departments, were able to co-sponsor the project. We did not face the hurdle of business adoption as these departments are involved in a significant percentage of stakeholder consultation processes and have a critical mass of business processes that would benefit from the use of this system. The partners in the project realized that they were building for the benefit of the entire organization, not just their immediate needs and made a conscious decision to invest in the future.

Business

The business agreed to accept the implementation in phases and to interim alterations of their processes during the development of the new electronic circulation system.

Organization Adoption

Once fully implemented, all departments that have the need for an electronic circulation process can elect to switch their existing processes. Since the system is designed to be independent, the decision process does not need to be automated to take advantage of electronic circulation. The method employed for the development of this system helped to build goodwill with the external agencies. It is important for us to keep them 'on side', since their participation is key to the success of the project.

6. BENEFITS

6.1 Cost Savings

As electronic circulation is adopted by business units, each business unit can expect savings in mailing, couriering and staff time costs to the extent that it replaces their old process. This may also potentially reduce our paper consumption and reduce our environmental footprint.

6.2 Time Reductions

Reduce cycle time and number of cycles

The electronic circulation system allows collaboration between stakeholders and early visibility of comments. This reduces the time required for the circulation and the number of re-circulations.

Faster distribution of documents

Documents can be quickly distributed to a broad spectrum of stakeholders with a minimum amount of effort. There is minimal time lag between the notification and document availability as the documents are available online. The online system also allows version control thereby enabling minor changes to documents even when the circulation is in progress.

Reduced training time

Creating a simple, single interface for agencies to use reduces the amount of time required for staff training for multiple systems.

User self-management

Since agencies are able to create and manage their own users, they no longer have to call the City for administrative tasks. Additionally, since account creation is no longer done by City staff members, this time can be used on other tasks.

6.3 Increased Revenues

No direct revenue growth is expected other than what is gained from a slight improvement in the cash flow for fees and taxes due to potentially faster processing of applications. The primary motivation of the project is not to increase revenues, however. The system also results in an overall improvement in the City's perceived image if we are able to fully open up and web-enable the public involvement phase of multiple regulatory processes.

6.4 Productivity Improvements

User Interface improvements

The outcomes for multiple circulations can be set at the same time using the web list view page. Stakeholders and view short blurbs about routine circulations and submit outcomes quickly without viewing all the documents associated with the circulation.

7. BEST PRACTICES, LEARNING POINTS AND PITFALLS

7.1 Best Practices and Learning Points

- ✓ *Validating assumptions with stakeholders*
- ✓ *Using the user interface to help develop workflow and use cases*
- ✓ *Engaging target groups at an early stage of development*
- ✓ *Keeping the interface simple*
- ✓ *Helping business to think beyond their silo and realize the organizational benefits of development*

✓ *Recommending that any business unit wanting to use a electronic circulation system should also look at building a web based application system so that documents can be received electronically.*

7.2 Pitfalls

✗ *Starting a design process for workflow for a web based system using a workflow model instead of the user interface.*

✗ *Building in any decision making step into the workflow for circulation.*

8. COMPETITIVE ADVANTAGES

While there are no direct competitive advantages to building an electronic circulation system, speeding up the development or regulatory approval processes by speeding up stakeholder consultation makes the City an attractive place for business. There is a perceived competitive advantage to a government that leverages web technologies to speed up otherwise slow business processes.

9. TECHNOLOGY

The solution uses the POSSE® suite of tools running on an Oracle® database. POSSE® has a business rule based user configurable workflow engine. For this project the tools used include POSSE STAGE, the configuration utility, POSSE OUTRIDER, the web application server and the POSSE user GUI. POSSE is a rapid application development platform specializing in workflow based applications. With POSSE's rapid prototyping and development capabilities, we were able to develop the circulation system with much less effort and resources as compared to building a web application from scratch. POSSE also enabled us to create a fully web enabled interface with only minor web development work. The web interface also implies that no client software installation is required for stakeholders. Overall, we highly recommend POSSE as an application platform for the stakeholder consultation process.

10. THE TECHNOLOGY AND SERVICE PROVIDERS

Computronix is the vendor of the product who also supplied consultants to work on the project for the City. POSSE® is a BPM engine tailored to government workflow. It simplifies the application prototyping and development process by providing a rapid application development environment. Selecting POSSE as our application platform has enabled a fast implementation of the electronic circulation process. www.posse.info

11. REFERENCES

http://permits.edmonton.ca/?appArea=Subdivisions

Dickinson Financial Corp., USA

Finalist, North America

Nominated by Adobe Systems Inc., USA

1. EXECUTIVE SUMMARY / ABSTRACT

Motivated by competitive pressure to improve its customer service, standardize its forms and increase potential future growth, Dickinson Financial Corporation (DFC) had the opportunity to implement new solutions that would ultimately reduce internal costs, improve scalability and customer services, generate ROI, ensure compliance with bank processes and attain better risk management. DFC chose to put into action automated document processes based on Adobe technologies in an effort to achieve its business goals of increased customer satisfaction and a "paperless bank."

2. OVERVIEW

For DFC, one obstacle toward effective customer service was the company's reliance on paper to initiate and process customer service requests for new accounts, account changes, stop payments, and other activities. With its new solution, DFC was able to turn each workflow and external system into paperless processes by integrating Web services in an SOA platform. With Adobe LiveCycle Forms ES, Adobe LiveCycle Process Management ES and Adobe Portable Document Format (PDF), employees gained countless hours for more profitable interaction with customers and an increased capacity to take on additional workload.

DFC has seen significant results since the implementation of Adobe solutions, realizing 1,408 percent ROI over the course of three years and a number of positive qualitative and quantitative results (detailed below).

3. BUSINESS CONTEXT

Prior to the new system, customer service staff depended on paper forms to address customer requests at various branches. The forms typically had to be routed manually to DFC's central office for processing, sometimes taking up to three weeks to complete. This was even the case for something as simple as sending a debit card to a customer, and with 70 percent of DFC's customer base in the Armed Forces, quick banking was essential and long delays were unacceptable. Also, identifying and correcting human errors caused additional delays and increased administrative costs.

Josh Laire, project lead and application development integration manager at DFC, realized that these outdated processes were preventing company efficiency and growth. At the time, DFC had plans to add another $3 billion in assets and grow from 100 branches to more than 200, which time-intensive manual processing threatened to slow down. The company knew that a change was needed to improve its customer service, standardize its forms, reduce internal costs and ensure compliance with bank processes.

4. THE KEY INNOVATIONS

4.2 Business

Thanks to the new dynamic online service for debit card applications, DFC accelerated card approval and delivery to customers by 300 percent, from 15 days to five. Employees now have more time each year to talk to customers about their needs and explore cross-selling and up-selling opportunities – allowing for productive and increased customer interaction and service.

- The customers also are also able to see transactions on their account immediately or within just a few seconds versus waiting for a couple of days to get this done. This is extremely important on items that the customer doesn't want to pay for, such as when a Stop Payment is processed.
- By allowing the customer server person to spend less time looking at the computer and more time interacting with the customer, DFC can provide enhanced customer experiences in person as well.

4.3 Process

Prior to the new system, employees conducted most processes manually. For example, for any given form, an employee would retrieve and fill out a document from DFC's intranet, obtain information verification, sign the form, and conduct extensive data entry. Only after this laborious process would a customer order be placed – sometimes taking up to three weeks from start to finish. DFC staff even had trouble with simple customer tasks, and human errors were common.

The new system eliminates minor human mistakes, and enhances employee productivity. Additionally, DFC chose to utilize Web services to communicate between core systems in order to effectively automate several customer notification forms.

Process architecture.

The process architecture involves key stakeholders from across 6 banking institutions that cover 23 states. The Customer Service Representative (CSR) works with the customer in getting the correct information from the Mainframe into the transaction form for that particular customer. Once the form is submitted, it goes to the Back Office group at the company headquarters for approval, if the approval is needed. When the changes or approvals are complete, the information is loaded into our Core Mainframe system via Web Services. The final form is loaded into DFC's Document Repository system for retrieval at upon request.

Currently the processes are only designed for internal use. However, the process can be opened to the internet to allow for a Self-Service option to the customers of our banks.

One of the main considerations when choosing our platform and deciding about the architecture was to make sure that it was designed in a way that the individual processes could be used from multiple access points. The Web Services are created in a generic (plain) manner that allows each point of access the ability to manipulate it on the fly to retrieve the desired information or to perform the desired functions.

With its new solution, DFC was able to turn each workflow and external system into paperless processes by integrating Web services in an SOA platform using Adobe technologies.

4.4 Organization

Today, DFC uses dynamic digital documents to initiate the automatic processing of a number of customer account activities and requests. This has impacted DFC staff considerably. DFC staff can now enter a few details about existing customers or requested services, and backend systems instantly validate and pre-populate the appropriate forms with data – quickly and conveniently. For example, dates are entered in the correct format and accurate social security numbers are dynamically entered. Also, this automatic process virtually eliminates illegible and incomplete forms that were a major source of delays, saving several days or even a few weeks of processing time.

When a form is complete, the new system initiates a consistent process that automates approvals routing, data entry, and finally sends notification to the customer.

5. HURDLES OVERCOME

The primary issue that was faced when working to move from Manual processes to Automated was overcoming some human fears. The biggest fear was that the system wouldn't work or that it would have incorrect data submitted. To overcome this, DFC created several sets of reports that the end-user management has access to that show the data that was used and the start and end time for the processes. This shows that the items are moving faster without as much human interaction and builds trust in the system, by verifying the correct information was used.

In addition to overcoming human fears, DFC enhancing its customer service to address competitive goals, standardized its forms, procedures and workflows throughout the entire organization.

Management

Management was involved in this project at all levels. Analysis, communication and compromise were necessary for establishing a common ground upon which DFC could make assessments and implement change. Management focused on the same gains and was willing to think outside the box to work towards a common goal. Establishing realistic expectations and timelines were challenges that were faced. Focusing on functionality, performance and benefits helped with setting realistic goals and timelines.

Business

In an attempt to gain the confidence of the business, Laire, along with the implementation team, gradually deployed the debit card application one institution at a time. This way, they could successfully identify any potential issues and better manage the implementation.

Organization Adoption

Because of DFC's strategy for implementation, as well as extensive training for its employees, the execution went smoothly and bolstered end user's confidence and faith in the application. DFC provided support and assistance to employees throughout the process, and set best-practice standards for other form projects.

6. BENEFITS

6.1 Cost Savings

- Savings of more than $2.4 million across Dickinson subsidiaries
- Successfully executed CIO charter by using technology to grow banking services
- Through productivity gains and operational cost reductions on the debit card processing solution alone, DFC realized total project benefits of $632,880—a 71 percent ROI over a three-year analysis horizon.

6.2 Time Reductions

- Slashed time to process debit card requests by 95 percent.
- Due Diligence Forms handled 76 percent faster; Address Change Forms 50 percent faster; Account Closing Forms 43 percent faster
- Dramatically accelerated processing time for banking forms—90 percent of benefits realized began in first year
- With a dynamic online service for debit card applications based on LiveCycle forms, DFC accelerated card approval and delivery to customers by 300 percent, from 15 days to five.
- Time spent on manual review was slashed from approximately 15,960 staff hours annually to just 85 hours. Now, employees have more time each year to talk to customers about their needs and explore cross-selling and up-selling opportunities.

6.3 Increased Revenues

DFC has seen significant results since the implementation of Adobe solutions, realizing 1,408 percent ROI over the course of three years. A specific break down of these benefits includes:

- The time spent processing address change forms dropped by 50 percent, which resulted in annual benefits of $108,000
- Time spent processing account closing forms was reduced by 43 percent, which resulted in annual benefits of $187,260
- $2.4 million in savings was gained across Dickinson subsidiaries
- Through productivity gains and operational cost reductions on the debit card processing solution alone, DFC realized total project benefits of $632,880—a 71 percent ROI over a three year analysis horizon.

6.4 Productivity Improvements

- Accelerated time-to-revenue with faster service delivery
- Slashed time to process debit card requests by 95 percent
- Due Diligence Forms handled 76 percent faster; Address Change Forms 50 percent faster; Account Closing Forms 43 percent faster
- Enabled bank to serve more customers without increasing staff

7. BEST PRACTICES, LEARNING POINTS AND PITFALLS

7.1 Best Practices and Learning Points

- ✓ Work small to big – use smaller projects to build the buy-in to the system.
- ✓ Build expertise in the environment
- ✓ Make sure that your infrastructure is designed to handle the expected workload and additional growth

7.2 Pitfalls

- ✗ Know the abilities of your team and the amount of work that can be handled – once success is seen, everyone wants to join in

8. COMPETITIVE ADVANTAGES

"In this industry, we must win our customers' loyalty through service excellence," says Laire. "If we're slow to respond to their needs, we risk losing them."

Time-to-respond is essential in the financial industry, and fast-reacting financial organizations have a big competitive advantage. DFC has enhanced its customer service over its competitors by reducing internal costs, improving scalability and customer services, generating ROI, ensuring compliance with bank processes and attaining better risk management.

In the future, DFC plans to make a number of additional implementations including the migration of 161 forms from their current environment (paper or electronic) into a workflow system, the inclusion of signature pads and integration with Web service / API management system. DFC is also starting to focus on giving incentives to consumers, such as a savings account "change back" program.

With Adobe LiveCycle ES, the company can now automate document completion, delivery and processing, moving forms cross-country instantly, turning a 10-15 business-day process to 10-15 minute process all while significantly increasing saving costs, operational efficiency and customer loyalty.

Laire says, "The automation supported by Adobe LiveCycle solutions is helping us to meet our customers' needs more quickly and accurately—and that, in turn, is helping us meet our targets for growth and profitability."

9. TECHNOLOGY

To help meet its business goals and increase its advantage over competitors, DFC turned to Adobe LiveCycle Forms ES and Adobe LiveCycle Process Management ES, speeding the completion and processing of forms as platform- and application-independent Adobe Portable Document Format (PDF) files.

By choosing these products, DFC has met its goal of effective customer service and has eliminated the company's reliance on paper by using dynamic digital documents for a number of its account processing activities.

LiveCycle Forms ES reduces training costs and increases user adoption by leveraging PDF to maintain the look of paper forms yet with increased functionality. With the ease-of-use of PDF documents, employees and customers can simply complete forms – all while engaging in a dynamic experience. Adobe LiveCycle Process Management ES software offers DFC visibility and control over its business processes, allowing the bank to streamline its end-to-end process, including dashboards to view business operations in real time and significant management tools to address day-to-day activities.

DFC has seen significant results since the implementation of Adobe solutions, realizing over a thousand percent ROI over the course of three years, in addition to increased customer and employee satisfaction.

10. THE TECHNOLOGY AND SERVICE PROVIDERS

Adobe Systems Incorporated (http://www.adobe.com):
- Adobe LiveCycle Forms ES
- Adobe LiveCycle Process Management ES
- Adobe Portable Document Format (PDF)

Office of the Under Secretary of Defense (OUSD) for Acquisition, Technology & Logistics (A T & L), USA

Finalist, North America
Nominated by Oracle Corp., USA

1. Executive Summary / Abstract

The OUSD AT&L Enterprise Architecture must support an inspired, high-performing, boundary-less organization that delivers. We must be an agile, motivated, collaborative, and creative organization with new ideas and new ways of doing business.

OUSD AT&L chose to deploy a very agile and collaborative driven solution leveraging the latest technologies and methodologies in Business Process Management and Enterprise 2.0. With a focus on quickly delivering capabilities to the field OUSD has focused on BPM and Enterprise 2.0 for secure and scalable solutions.

2. OVERVIEW

Over 7,000 US Department of Defense's end-users across over 60 communities and over 1,000 Collaboration Projects are deriving benefits from the use of this agile collaborative EA initiative leveraging BPM and Enterprise 2.0.

Four major categories of users exist across the user base: Internal IT project and support staff, end-users requesting support and training, external end-users (including contractors), and financial / governance users.

Access by all levels of users is strictly governed by OUSD AT&L security policies and procedures. The solution is fully vetted and compliant with OUSD AT&L Enterprise Architecture policies including user access control. Users can access the system via the intranet and through the firewall via the internet, but are strictly checked for access privileges via Department of Defense (DoD) Common Access Cards (CAC) and passwords. Access is separated across both Secret Internet Protocol Router (SIPR) and Non-Secure Internet Protocol Router (NIPR) Networks and integrated with Public Key Infrastructure (PKI).

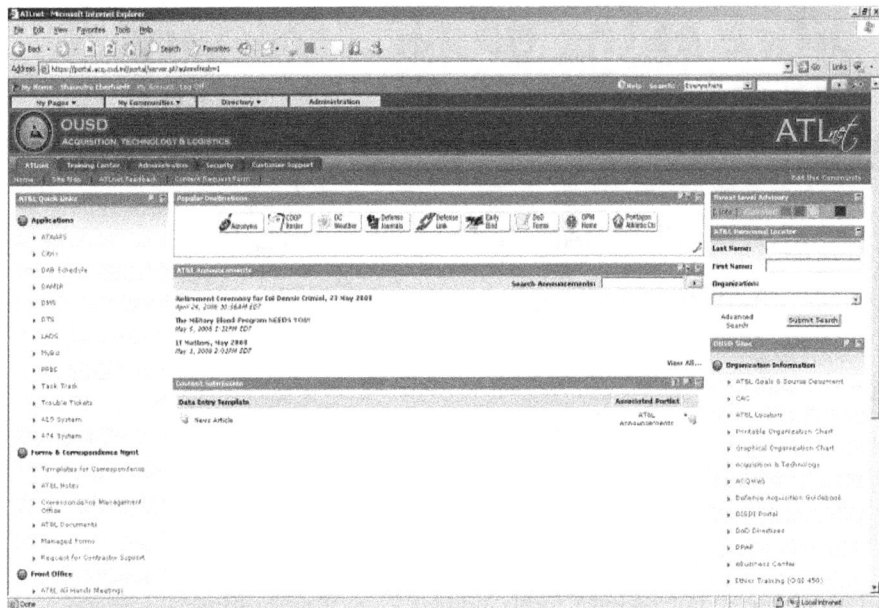

Figure 2.1 Access via ATL net

Secure access to all processes and content is provided through single-sign-on (SSO) based on the profile of the end-user. Access to communities, content, data, and other information is automatically given to each end-user based on this common profile with integration with both Active Directory and the Information Technology Database (ITMDB). This provides an easy and secure single point of access for all end-users, easily manageable, that is updated in real-time.

OUSD AT&L found BPM and Enterprise 2.0 solutions to meet the need for a secure, EA approved way of transforming their organization so they could deliver agile capabilities for their stakeholders. Four process implementations are in production with more enhancements and new projects underway.

3. BUSINESS CONTEXT

Over 7,000 US Department of Defense's end-users across over 60 communities with four major categories of users exist across the user base: Internal IT project and support staff, end-users requesting support and training, external end-users (including contractors), and financial / governance users required secure access to processes that at first were paper driven, inefficient and prone to error. Of special note was the heightened security and inherent risk of security breaches that could be caused by these inefficient and hard to audit manual processes.

Upon analysis OUSD's motivation for change fell into 3 categories (Efficiency, Control, and Agility) and was mapped out in Figure 3.1.

Figure 3.1: Key areas of motivation for introducing BPM and E2.0

4. THE KEY INNOVATIONS

The OUSD ATLnet solution is truly an innovative use of the latest technologies and methodologies focused on real measureable results for the stakeholders. Reducing costs and cycle time for over 7,000 end-users with a small support staff while maintaining a high rating is amazing considering the diverse set of end-users (over 60 communities) and the rapid deployment of capabilities (3 months). OUSD also maintained its ideal of an open standards based heterogeneous EA, being able to incorporate both existing .NET and Java technologies in its solutions. The solution is also not only fully vetted and compliant with OUSD AT&L EA, but also incorporates DoD CAC and encryption technologies. OUSD AT&L is continuing to deploy new capabilities to support its mission and vision.

4.2 BUSINESS

The Office of the Under Secretary of Defense (OUSD) for Acquisition, Technology & Logistics (AT&L):

- Innovate and collaborate to support mission requirements
- Lead the enterprise and drive business success.
- Operate as a collaborative neighborhood, developing people to strengthen the community.
- Align with and support the Department's transformation priorities.

OUSD AT&L foresaw BPM and Enterprise 2.0 solutions as key to transform their organization into one that was agile enough to support the rapidly changing requirements of the diverse organization while meeting strict security and EA requirements.

Logical Architecture BPM and Enterprise 2.0

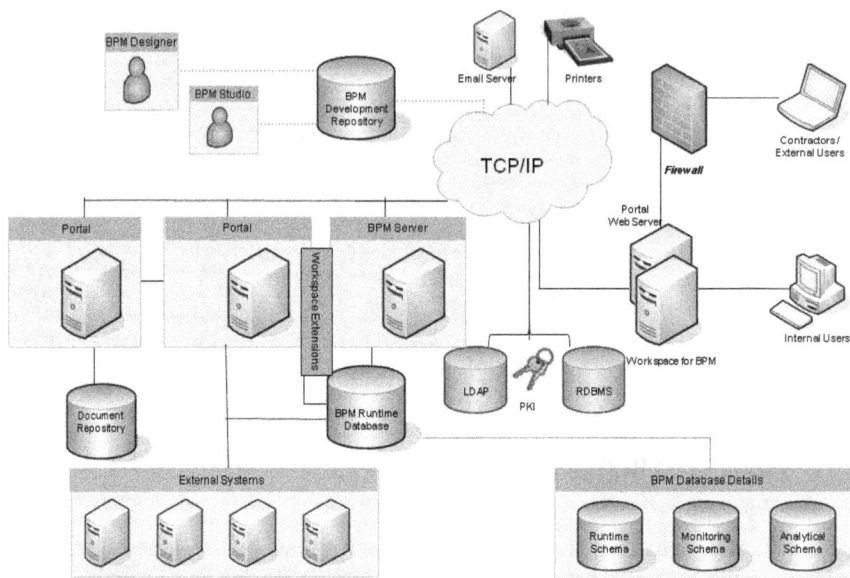

Figure 3.1 (Generalized Logical Architecture)
* Note that this is generalized and redacted for security purposes and this infrastructure is in place for both NIPR and SIPR Networks.

4.3 PROCESSES

Over 7,000 users are allowed seamless access to electronic content from policies, and procedures, documents, maps, to organizational maps based on their security profile. Large cost savings were seen due to less paper printing and the centralized versioning of documents and other content. Additionally, real time updates to content are fully available including threat level status integrated with the homeland security system. Finally, OUSD deployed new Web 2.0 technologies into the enterprise with: User-created mashup applications and web content, Blogs, wikis, RSS, Web services, Role-based security, Developer-driven mashups and web application management, Reusable widgets, SSO, usage tracking and Perimeter security and authorization.

The OUSD's system was first launched in June 2007. Consequentially, several development spirals (capability releases) have been implemented in 3 months increments. From its first production release ATL net has achieved significant benefits for the end users. Currently, over 4 successful implementations are in production with enhancements and additional projects in the works.

1. Over 10 training requests occur each month. OUSD ATLnet allows end-users to find, request, qualify for, and receive confirmation of their request automatically.

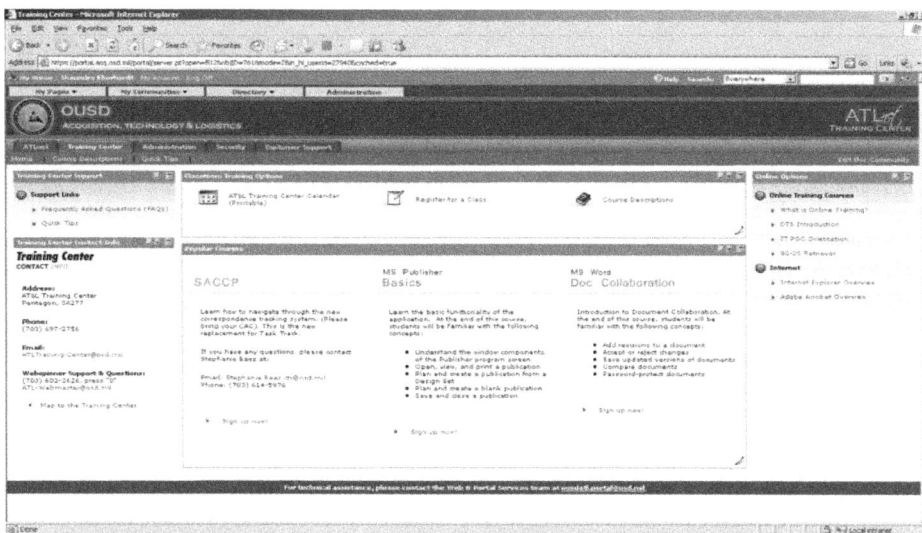

2. The BPMS provides an integrated support community allowing on-line IT ticketing and support.

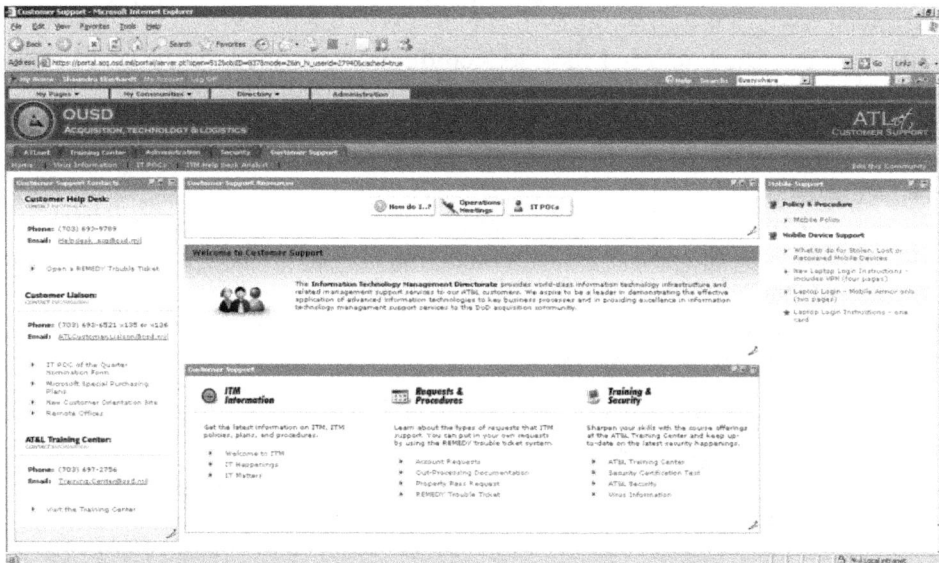

Over 150 support requests are processed a month. Originally, support requests took over 2 weeks on average to be resolved. Now support requests usually take days. Additionally, the management and control of support requests are now not only more manageable, but also more aligned to strategic OUSD initiatives. In implementing a rules based process, the requests can be categorized into those that are less than 80 hours to those that require initiation of a project initiative.

3. Over 50 External Visit Requests a month are processed. Originally, these requests take over 2 weeks and now they can be completed within 1 day.

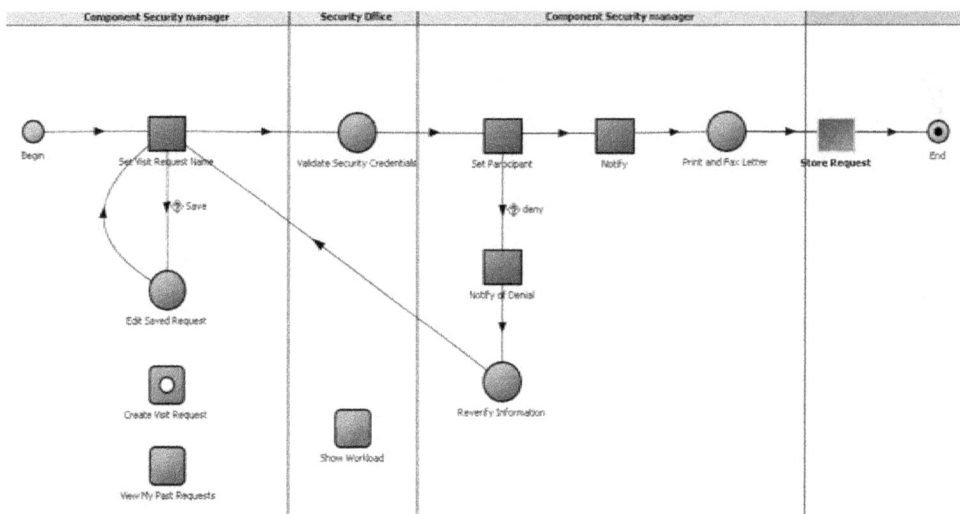

- Intro to VAR
- Facilitates the preparation of Visit Authorization Letters for AT&L employees who need to visit other secure Department of Defense work locations
- Current Process Frustrations
  - Too much manual effort for coordination between Security Offices. As a result, submissions can be lost and sometimes incorrect.
  - End to end creation of VAR letter takes days, even weeks
- VAR BPM Process
- Focused on Improving:
  - Overall Time for VAR lifecycle
  - Reduce Manual effort with emailing/faxing/phone calls. Ex. Eliminate needless emails, faxes, and phone calls
  - Increase communication. Ex. Only notify roles when there is work ready for them to process
- Transparency for the client across the whole process
  - Real time knowledge of VAR status throughout the process
- Reduced workflow lifecycle
- Reduced Visit Authorization letters by an average of 2 weeks
- Real time notification via email, one click access to activities

4. Hundreds of erroneous accounts are produced a year, which is solved by the new External Account Creation System (EACS). Even one security breach can causes severe repercussions. The new system implements the control, auditing, and governance capability to reduce these to near zero.

Full graphical access and look-up of the OUSD organizational structure for such a complex organization was impossible prior to the implementation of this system. The system also handled the movement of personnel between departments and among external contractors.

- Introduction to EACS
  - The process for creating external user accounts in Active Directory and the AT&L profile user repository Information Technology Management Database (ITMDB).
  - Accounts must be created in order to gain access to AT&L applications
- Current Process Frustrations
  - Manual submission of information created in excel spreadsheet and imported into AD and ITMDB via batch processing
  - Hundreds of erroneous accounts are produced
  - Many accounts are never used due to validation of end user
  - Contractors returning to AT&L have duplicate accounts
  - As a result, End User repositories are cluttered
- AT&L's External Account Creation System BPM Process
  - Focused on Improving:
    - Reducing erroneous accounts in AD and ITMDB
    - Validating account information before creation
  - Ex. Jane Doe switches from gov't employee to contractor, as a result, don't create another user account, just change profile data.
  - Track changed and new accounts

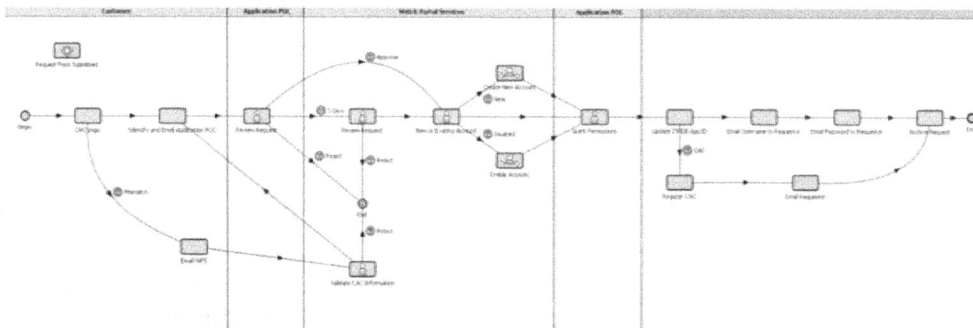

5. Common Access Card Location Finder:

The common access card is the standard identification card for Department of Defense and is the primary means to gain access to all computer networks and systems.

The use of Business Process Management and Portal technologies and methodologies has allowed agile development and implementation of capabilities that would not be possible otherwise.

6. Acquisition Information Management System (AIMS) is the most current process being implemented. This process will be used to manage milestone information for Major Defense Acquisition Programs. There will be multiple phases of this project and we are working on the initial phase automates their document review and coordination process and pull data from another repository. AIMS will be a part of the SOA architecture being established for AT&L so the future phases will import data from multiple sources, provide data analysis, time driven activities, etc.

4.4 ORGANIZATION

With a small project staff supporting over 7,000 users over such a diverse set of communities applying EA discipline and engaging the stakeholders was extremely important to the on-going success of the solution. OUSD implemented Portal, Business Process Management, Web 2.0, SOA, and SOA Governance solutions.

The solution was architected to be based on open standards and heterogeneous. Its implementation included leveraging both existing .NET and Java technologies proving both openness and reusability of EA components.

The staff consists of both IT and subject matter experts (SMEs) formed as a Center of Excellence (CoE) and at times includes external stakeholders so capabilities are directly tied to the mission. Additionally, several pre and post implementation techniques were used to increase project acceptance and reduce risk. For each development spiral several iterative analysis sessions were scheduled with key stakeholders. Two or more ATL net preview sessions per spiral were also enacted with end-user feedback modifying the current solution prior to roll-out. During the launch of new capabilities, on-line and in person training are available, as well as follow-up sessions. Finally, on-line after action reviews (AARs) with questionnaires in the portal were used to not only get immediate feedback, but also affect the next project. The solution has over a 98% positive feedback rating with the other 2% feedback being introduced into following capability spirals.

5. HURDLES OVERCOME

Any introduction of a new system has to overcome barriers both in IT and across the business. As BPM and E2.0 technologies are so new and transformational this made the challenge even greater. But, positioned correctly, with the right stakeholder involvement and expectation / change management BPM and E2.0 creates even greater opportunities for successes.

Management

Key to their success was a proper chain-of-command with clear lines of authority and responsibility. Forming the CoE with core staff and representation from the all stakeholders was the next step. Regularly briefing the chain of command on progress was another key factor for success. Finally, a proper change management and governance structure enabled them to control change, risk, and scope.

Business

The business was used to accomplishing things a certain way, mostly driven by historical precedence. Holding briefings, training, and as well as including key business stakeholders in the CoE were all essential aspects of ensuring buy-in from the business.

Organization Adoption

"Small & Simple with Big Impact"

Presenting change in small bite sized components go along way in smoothing stakeholder acceptance. Keep it Simple Stupid (KISS) is axiom to live by. Also, we made sure to have continued engagement and a true change management processes, knowing that we wouldn't get it right 100% the first time. This is why we ran customer surveys to measure the usability of the new processes. The feedback allowed focus on the customer and change features as required.

Benefits

6.1 COST SAVINGS

Cost savings of the system were due to decreased paper, fax, and phone usage. We have not conducted a quantified analysis. However, here are some qualitative facts:

- 7,000+ users
- Forming:

- 60+ communities. Allowing collaboration, document control (versioning), messaging, etc. This significantly cuts down the document version conflicts, paper, and phone costs.
- 6,000+ collaboration projects: Project based collaboration and management. Significant cost savings across paper, phone, meetings, and fax.
- Visit Authorization Request (VAR): Over 600 / year with over 5 pieces of paperwork, numerous calls, and faxes required otherwise.
- Training request (Over 70 year): now on-line. No paper packages.

6.2 TIME REDUCTIONS

Across the 6 production processes there are a lot of reductions in wait and execution times. Two estimated examples are:

*150 support requests / month * 12 months * 9 days (from 2 weeks to 1 day)*	*= 16,200 person/days*
*50 External Visit Requests / month * 12 months * 9 days (from 2 weeks to 1 day)*	*= 5,400 person/days*

All the other processes also produce significant user time reductions to accessing content.

6.3 INCREASED REVENUES

OUSD AT&L does not measure increased revenue due to projects. However, we do measure stakeholder satisfaction (meeting the needs of the customer and therefore better usage of the system). We also measure against our core mission.

The solution has over a 98% positive feedback rating with the other 2% feedback being introduced into following capability spirals.

The OUSD AT&L team must align with and support the Department's transformation priorities.

✓ *Innovate and collaborate to support mission requirements*
✓ *Lead the enterprise and drive business success.*
✓
✓ *Operate as a collaborative neighborhood, developing people to strengthen the community.*

Our BPM and Enterprise 2.0 solution implementation was vetted both technically and strategically as part of our Enterprise Architecture (EA). Our program is seen to support AT&L's transformational priorities (checked above). Note that transformation is an on-going process and even after the success of our first 4 processes in production we now have several projects on going and fully funded. This proves our capability to produce value and is equivalent to a business-increasing revenue.

6.4 PRODUCTIVITY IMPROVEMENTS

Overall: Development Spirals decreased to 3 months from 1 year. Essential when you have such a small project team.

All 7,000 users have instant access to content based on their profile. This allows our stakeholders a self service environment.

Additionally, increased safety and security are especially important for AT&L. The management, auditing of internal and external (e.g. contractor) access to both facilities and systems are sometimes of paramount importance. Several processes allow AT&L to manage these accounts based not only on profile, but also role, position, and time. The value of this can not be underestimated.

BEST PRACTICES, LEARNING POINTS AND PITFALLS

7.1 Best Practices and Learning Points

- ✓ *Think Big, Start Small, Move Fast*
- ✓ *Keep it Simple Stupid (KISS)*
- ✓ *Establish a clear Chain-of-Command, with appropriate sponsorship levels*
- ✓ *Establish a Center of Excellence (CoE) with a core team that includes SMEs from the customer(s) when possible*
- ✓ *Governance across the project and services is essential*
- ✓ *Know your "As is"*
- ✓ *Get Buy-In (IT & Business & Leadership – Executive)*
- ✓ *Foster Business Desire for Change*
- ✓ *Constant marketing*
- ✓ *Adhere to a Reference Architecture*
- ✓ *Take a phased approach to its implementation*
- ✓ *Maintain project management discipline*

7.2 Pitfalls

- ✗ *Don't underestimate the "that's how it was done" inertia*
- ✗ *Don't have a build and they will come philosophy*
- ✗ *Don't underestimate challenge of changing thoughts from IT infrastructure to providing Business Services*

8. COMPETITIVE ADVANTAGES

The ATL net solution is truly an innovative use of the latest technologies and methodologies focused on real measureable results for the stakeholders. Currently, the solution has over a 98% positive rating. Reducing costs and cycle time for over 7,000 end-users with a small support staff while maintaining this high a rating is amazing considering the diverse set of end-users (over 60 communities) and the rapid deployment of capabilities). OUSD also maintained its ideal of an open standards based heterogeneous EA, being able to incorporate both existing .NET and Java technologies in its solutions. The solution is also not only fully vetted and compliant with OUSD AT&LEA, but also incorporates DoD CAC and encryption technologies. OUSD ATL is continuing to deploy new capabilities to support its mission and vision.

9. TECHNOLOGY

OUSD AT&L implemented a BPM / E2.0 Enterprise Architecture (see Figure 9.1) that included Oracle Business Process Management Suite, Oracle WebCenter (Portal). This BPM / E2.0 solution integrated with various internal and external systems including PKI, Active Directory, Database, .NET and Java Applications and Forms.

Logical Architecture BPM and Enterprise 2.0

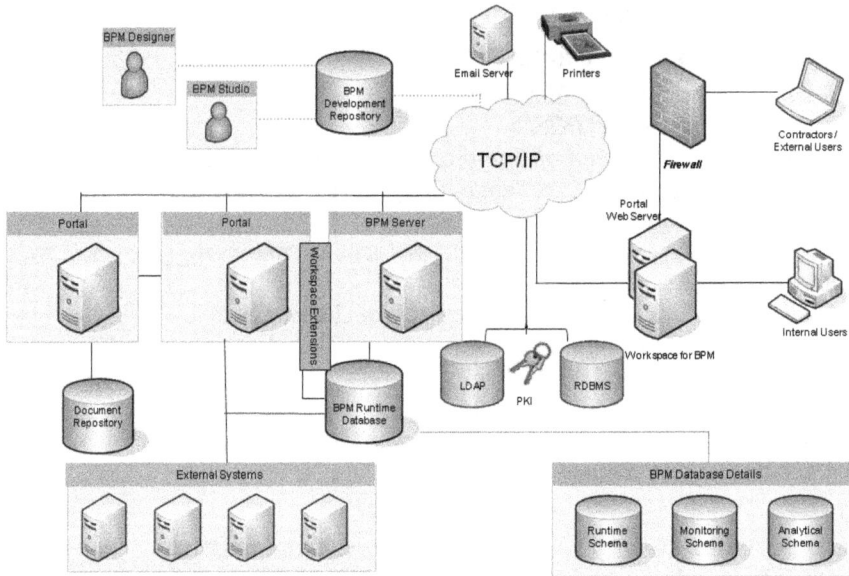

Figure 9.1 (Generalized Logical Architecture)

* Note that this is generalized and redacted for security purposes and this infrastructure is in place for both NIPR and SIPR Networks.

10. THE TECHNOLOGY AND SERVICE PROVIDERS

Oracle Software was used in this implementation: www.oracle.com

Tribunal High Court of Justice of the State of Hidalgo, Mexico

Silver Award, North America

Nominated by PECTRA Technology, USA

1.   EXECUTIVE SUMMARY / ABSTRACT

Within the framework of e-governance developed by the Government of Mexico – with the purpose of improving the quality and transparency in management and increasing the efficiency in public services – the High Court of the State of Hidalgo implemented an Integral Program of Processes Systematization. The project included the integration of tasks of 51 first instance courts and their second instance courts, each one of them with numerous individual, complex, and manual processes. In addition, all the value chain participants – both internal and external - were integrated: Organization (Courts, Courtrooms); citizens (Lawyers, parties involved in the trial), and the Government.

The implementation, which was granted the Award to Innovation and Quality 2007, allowed saving unproductive time linked to jurisdictional and administrative paperwork, reducing the average time of legal actions resolution, increasing drastically the transparency in management and getting traceability and total control of the process.

OVERVIEW

The Integral Program of Processes Systematization (BPM) - implemented by the High Court of Justice of the State of Hidalgo, Mexico – arose as an answer to the constant need of citizens for more immediate and agile means for the support and solution of disputes, within the framework of the e-government strategy developed by the National Government. The project development was guided by the following strategic goal: ***to promote and monitor, through a BPM platform, the unlimited compliance as required by law respecting the rights and freedoms directly fighting lack of transparency and impunity.***

The project included the integration of tasks of 51 first instance courts and their second instance courts and consisted of migrating all the processes inherent to each court to a single and centralized process applicable to each institution of the 17 cities making up the State of Hidalgo.

Apart from unification and automation of the different processes and manual tasks, the project integrated all the value chain participants: Organization (Courts, Courtrooms); citizens (Lawyers, parties involved in the trial), and the Government. For each one of them there are different benefits and functionalities described throughout the document, amongst which are: transparency portal, online file control, judicial funds management; among the main ones.

The implementation was granted the Award to Innovation and Quality 2007, prize awarding the best practices of technological innovation and government innovation in public management; it aims at strengthening knowledge management and creative participation of public officers as regards modernization and quality of the services offered.

The solution administers an annual average of 40,000 legal actions and leads to the following main benefits:

- Time saving of administrative paperwork: 90%.
- Time saving of jurisdictional paperwork: 60%.
- Reduction in the average length of a trial. Before the process implementation, trials lasted 2 years or more; after the process automation and unification, this period was reduced to 1 year.
- Time reduction when submitting records; from 30 seconds before the implementation to 1 second after the implementation.
- This time saving as regards downtime goes up to 10,000 hours per year for citizens and staff. This is a consequence of the online traceability of files and status which considerably reduces the visits to the places where the documents are found.
- Goal fulfillment of management transparency, through government indicators which measure technological innovation and quality.
- Traceability of the process and employee control.

2. BUSINESS CONTEXT

In an effort to offer an answer to the citizens' needs of having transparent public management and, with the purpose of being protagonists in the knowledge society, the Mexican government has developed an e-government strategy which frames its actions. To do this, it was crucial to make a change in mentality, in methodology and in perspective, which is translated into a change of the public service concept for citizens. Mexican public institutions have been forced to reformulate their guidelines and their methods to apply in service provision as well as in the costs administration derived from them and to improve communication with the citizens in a simple and effective way.

In this context, the High Court of Justice developed the Integral Program of Processes Systematization (BPM), offering a faster, more dynamic and more transparent legal management.

In this sense, the implementation of a work platform based in Processes (BPM) was not limited to certain courts nor to any areas considered strategic by the Judicial Power, but it was conceived as an **Integral Program** which unifies the jurisdictional and administrative processes to integrate them in an unique language to follow the activities applicable to each Court, Lower Court and Administrative Areas.

To do this, it was necessary to integrate the tasks of the following areas which make up the organization: 51 first instance courts and second instance courts, each one with numerous individual, complex, and manual processes.

Courts of first instance: Their function is to administer and solve lawsuits in civil, family, business and criminal matters. This function includes analyzing the claims and statements of the parties, receiving the evidence presented for the case and passing sentence. The project includes 51 courts distributed as follows: 15 for criminal matters, 8 mixed, 2 lower mixed, 3 for family matters, 6 for civil matters, 15 for civil and family courts and 2 specialized in justice for teenagers.

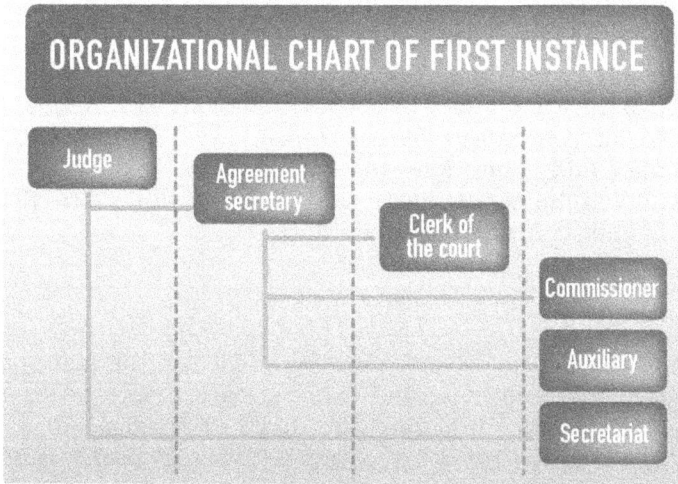

Second instance courts: their function is to learn and solve the appeals, which allows making a new revision of the court resolutions challenged. These courts have the following structure:

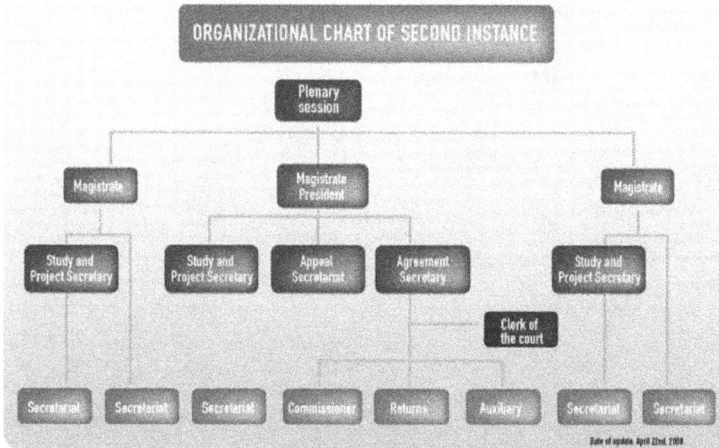

In relation to the problems caused by the irregular and manual management performed, Alma Carolina Viggiano Austria –President of the High Court of Justice of the State of Hidalgo- *hereby states that: "Citizens complained a lot about the times and delays in judicial proceedings. And we could not find out which part of the process was stopped. Every trial has a different time, but lawyers and litigants have certain deadlines to prepare and answer a lawsuit, to present evidence, etc. Officers also have terms which we could not make them fulfill or know if they were fulfilling these terms."*

At an internal level states that: "At first, we noticed that our technicians did not understand our lawyers and vice versa. Besides, our lexicons were very complicated. Thus, we created a kind of symbiosis between both professionals and started a mapping work to identify the stages of the process. Obviously, this was not simple since, for example, in civil matters, there are countless processes; however, it allowed us to have better visibility of the situation state."

In this context, the project was started with the goal of guiding the actions of the Judicial Power of the State of Hidalgo, assigning people in charge, times and short, medium and long term goals to offer a more effective public service and to strengthen the Judicial Power at the institutional level:

- To promote and monitor, **through a BPM platform**, the unlimited compliance of the Rule of Law as a basic condition for a harmonic, collaborative and peaceful social coexistence, in which actions by people, authorities and institutions as required by law to offer legal certainty and safety to the population, respecting the rights and freedoms, and directly fighting corruption and impunity.

3. THE KEY INNOVATIONS

Business

The development of the project has a strong impact on the main participants of the value chain, linking internal and external participants to the organization, geographically distributed throughout the State of Hidalgo, Mexico, including: Organization (Courts, Courtrooms); citizens (Lawyers, parties involved in the trial) and the Government.

To illustrate the relationship of the value chain through the solution, the graphic below is shown: Every process starts with a "promotion" at the Filing Office. At this stage, the type of trial (matter), court and location is distributed according to criteria. Once the court receives the requirement, all the activities linked to the First Instance processes are activated and – in case of appeal- the Second Instance court activities are started. All this is controlled by the government and by an on-line follow-up by the citizens.

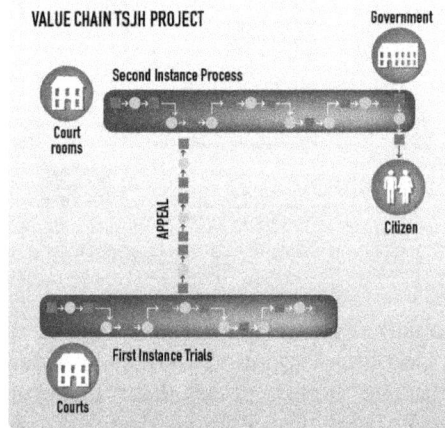

4.1.1 Benefits and functionalities for the members of the High Court of Justice.

At the level of the organization's participants, three main benefits are presented: traceability and on-line follow-up, judicial funds management, information security with access in accordance to profiles, and *Business Intelligence* tools.

Traceability and online follow-up.

After implementing the project, public officers can have detailed information of the process stage in which the legal action is, as regards the status and physical location of the file. Sentences corresponding to each event can also be accessed to on-line.

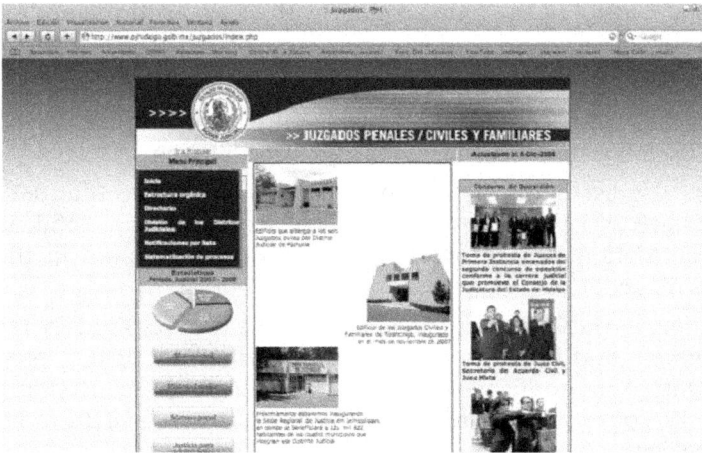

Judicial funds management:

The process also includes the ***Judicial funds management***, which consists of handling values on consignment to the court when, in some cases, one of the parties makes payment deposits. This is so; for example, when a father pays alimony for his children to the court while the trial is in process and until the legal custody is determined. The judicial fund gives the money to the mother when the process is finished and it ensures law enforcement.

Value handling by the judicial fund is an extremely careful and priority task. Through the BPM solution inclusion, it was possible to establish clearly the value handling within the court, which also allowed tracking its location both in the courts and in the fund itself, offering **total transparency in the process**.

Access to information in accordance with profiles.

The third key point that manifests the impact of the implementation at business level in the internal participants of the organization is the access to information in accordance with user profiles, which ensures its security and confidentiality. Profiles internally considered are the following:

First and second instance	
Internal	At the court:
	-Judge (1st instance) / Magistrate (2nd instance)
	- Agreement secretary.
	-Clerk of the court.
	- Commissioner.
	At the institution:
	-Judicial Fund.
	- Administration.
	- Accounts office.
	- Presidency.

Business Intelligence Tools.

Having access to centralized management information to make decisions and to plan the public administration is another of the central contributions of the solution. This allows having quantitative and qualitative information of the execution of defined processes, bottle necks and budget execution. It also allows the total control of the management with clear, accurate and objective metrics.

4.1.2 Citizens.

The solution also allows providing a high added value service for citizens: control and on-line follow-up of legal actions and files statuses.

It is done by the list notification system published on the Internet in the portal: http://148.245.145.212/notificaciones/frm_busqueda_notificaciones.aspx, where an information service which benefits lawyers involved in the trials and the parties is offered.

The notification is published **automatically** once a resolution in relation to an event is achieved, and it allows informing the parties about the "process status" and "the result". This notification is automated for all the courts participating in the project: 17 courts in 17 cities geographically distributed in judicial districts mentioned below:

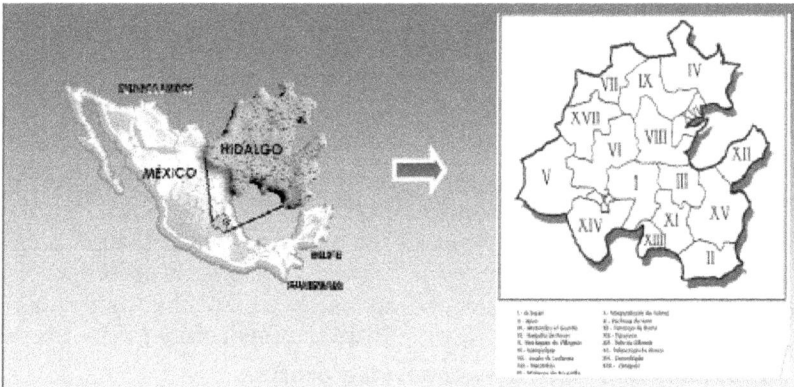

In the portal, the main functionalities offered to the citizens are:

- To consult the notifications by entity
- To consult the court to which he/she was assigned
- To assign several search filters (e.g. file number or date on which the notification was issued)

The notification system can be accessed from Internet 24/7.

4.1.3 State and Federal Government.

There are two main contributions offered by the solution in the integration of participants belonging to the government: transparency in management and information security.

Transparency portal.

At government level, the main benefit offered by the solution is the transparency portal, which can be accessed by the following URL: http:// www.pjhidalgo. gob.mx/trans/index.php. Transparency, apart from being the core of the Program for Institutional Strengthening, is an obligation on the part of the Federal and State Government and all their institutions.

This transparency portal allows users to:

- Review all the documentation related to transparency regulations.
- Consult information request statistics in real time.
- Review the transparency publications in all the corresponding instances.

- Request detailed information about salaries, wages, commissions, legal operation, among others.
- Link with INFOMEX system through the website to request non-restricted information for the citizens: (http:// infomex.hidalgo. gob.mx/infomexhidalgo/).
- Settle an accountability culture.

Apart from accountability and information transparency, the system is linked through the process to the publication of sentences of each matter dealt both in the first and second instance processes and for civil, criminal and family matters.

Information security: access by profiles.

Also in the case of external users belonging to National and State Government, the solution proposes an information access scheme through profiles, which ensures confidential information security. Profiles considered are the following:

First and Second Instance Trials Profiles	
External	The Government:
	• Instituto Federal de acceso a la información Pública (Federal Institute of access to Public information).
	• State Government.
	• Record, statistics and universities institutions.

PROCESS

4.2.1 *Situation previous to process automation*

Before the project development, the High Court of Justice had a context controlled by the following factors:

- Important delays in Trials: According to Viggiano Austria: "in courts, like in many tribunals in the country, we use 16 manual records books. In a book, we record the initial processes, that is, the lawsuits. In others: the petitions, the documents filed, values received (such as promissory notes). Each one of these procedures took us 30 seconds. So, if we counted the approximate
- 400 procedures that all the officers did every day, we had an average of 3 hours."
- Need for a more transparent management. Citizens requested initiatives which could offer visibility of the public management and its results. Besides, this was also included within the e-government strategy developed by the Mexican Government with the main goal of making the public administration more transparent in the entire Federal Government.
- Manual activities. "Before, when officers did not go to work, the process was stopped since the files stayed on their desks; this was a factor to be solved", says Alma Carolina.
- Inconsistent data. The organization had some kind of what, according to Gartner consulting, is called "spaghetti network" with isolated systems, not connected among them, which provided irregular, isolated and not always consistent data.
- Irregular criteria. Every court making up the High Court of Justice had their own manual processes, each one proceeding individually, with their own criteria and, as a general result, the Court lacked consistency in its processes, activities and in its way of performing them.

4.2.2 *Implemented process*

The process implemented consists of an automated administration model, as a solution of process integration for the management and justice administration of the Judicial Power of the State of Hidalgo. One innovation of the project was the creation of a **unique process of civil, criminal and family matters**; this is why all the courts of the 17 judicial districts must comply with these processes, reducing the discrepancy of criteria and procedures in each one of the courts.

The processes implemented in First Instance Courts are shown below, both in criminal and family matters (both images explain exactly the graphic of the processes implemented; the images are a screenshot of the processes). In case it is required, there is a full size image of each process available.

First Instance in criminal matters:

Proceso en primera instancia en materia Penal (Penales Pachuca)

Process in first instance in Family matters:

Proceso en Primera Instancia en Materia Familiar (Pachuca)

4.2.3 Architecture

The implementation of the project was based in the following architecture:.

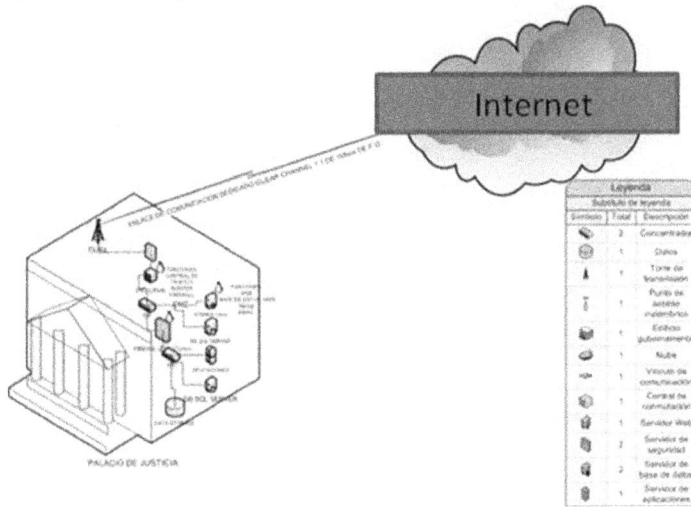

Computer Networks and wireless networks implemented in each judicial building allow computer systems to store information directly in the server, so that the local server data are validated and consulted in real time.

PECTRA BPM Suite functioned as the basis on which all the processes are executed, integrating databases and intranet applications for different functionalities, such as file traceability.

At **platform** level, it is important to mention that we count with:

- PECTRA Server: A HP Proliant Server (2 processors, 8GB RAM, 3 HD 145 GB each).
- WEB Server: A HP Proliant Server (2 processors, 8GB RAM, 3 HD 145 GB each).
- DB Server: A HP Proliant Server (4 processors, 16 GB RAM, 10 HD 145 GB each).

At **integration** level, vertical applications have been developed (web applications) in Microsoft .Net 2003 (Visual Basic) and a Microsoft SQL 2000 database is used, developed under the guidelines of the implemented processes and internal policies of the organization.

ORGANIZATION

For the development, implementation and maintenance of the project a special area in the System Department has been created; this area is aligned with and specialized in the Process Management philosophy. It includes different profiles, which go from project leader to functional analysts and developers.

This team works in a transdisciplinary manner with the teams of the "owner" areas of the processes which were automated, including judges specialized in criminal and civil-family matters and officers involved in the tasks to be developed.

Impact at the organization level has been really important since it implied changing substantially the organizational culture, with strong actions by Change Management and areas and departments integration described in the following section.

4. Hurdles Overcome

The main drawbacks when implementing the project were human factors at the organizational culture level. "We knew that if we adopted new technologies, there would be a natural resistance from personnel. In this respect, we have carried out different actions to make our personnel aware of the advantages that a new system could offer", says the President of the High Court of Justice. Because of that and, to perform the mapping, 2 people were added to the technical team: a judge specialized in criminal matters and another one, specialized in civil and family matters. Both have contributed to identify the mapping stages and to enter thecodes to the system. Both became involved and committed their teams from the beginning of the project.

Currently, the personnel have a different integration with the various areas which make up the organization and have considerably increased their productivity (see benefits section). *"We had to organize group activities and work on personal development topics". Even if we had the best IT platform, everything would have been impossible if the project leader was not convinced about it. I know many justice courts which have been trying to implement something like this for many years and they have not succeeded. The problem is neither money nor technology, it is a matter of organizational culture"*, says Viggiano Austria. These barriers have been overcome with actions taken in Change Management, making the current success of the project implementation possible.

5. Benefits

As an introduction, we present the main metrics of the High Court of Justice activities and the processes implemented, to then detail the benefits in accordance with the 4 axes requested: cost reduction, time reduction, profit increase, productivity increase.

Impact of the processes in the Trials (Instances) carried out by platform in 2007- 2008.

During 2007, of almost the 40,000 matters settled in all the courts of the State of Hidalgo, 59% corresponded to the Civil and Business Matters. The rest to the Family and Criminal areas had 31% and 10% respectively.

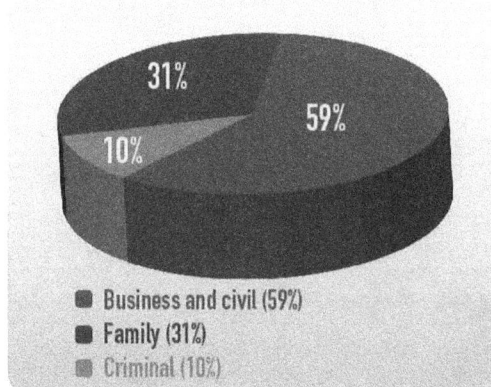

In the graphic, the ratio of trials carried out in 1 year can be observed. The project focused in automating the information flow and processes of these three types of trials, starting with the Business and Civil matters.

Main results:

- Real time statistics of trials, their ratio and progress status in the legal process chain.
- Resolution publication on the Internet, reducing:

- The number of requests by lawyers or parties on trials' status and their resolution.
- File search time.
- Travel expenses (even outside the city) since it is possible to consult the trials' status on the Internet.

In Criminal Matters, a total of 3,021 orders of arrest were recorded during 2007. Of which, 56% were released, 15% were of appearance, 13% were of re-arrest and 11% were denied.

Main results:

- Real time statistics of trials, their ratio and progress status in the criminal legal process.
- The internal control of the orders of arrest allows to:
- Reduce the time and cost of the trial.
- Keep a statistics close to the orders pending to be executed and their deadlines.
- Work together with other institutions such as the Justice Attorney
- General's Office for the prompt execution of the orders of arrest.

5.1 Cost Savings

Cost Savings	
Organization	Savings in stationary and printing costs.
	Savings in costs due to lack of process traceability.
Citizens	Savings in travel expenses and lawyers and parties' time due to the possibility of consulting the process status and the result by the online notification.

5.2 Time Reductions

Time reductions	
Organization	Time saving in administrative paperwork: 90%.
	Time saving in jurisdictional paperwork: 60%.
	Reduction in the average length of a trial. Before the process implementation, trials lasted 2 years or more; after the process automation and unification, this period was reduced to 1 year.
	Reduction in the record time; previous to the implementation of the project it took 30 seconds;

	currently, it takes 1 second per record.
	Reduction of time for promotions over 50% by ensuring their reception by citizens in less than an average of 15 minutes.
	This time saving as regards downtime goes up to 10,000 hours per year for citizens and staff. This is a consequence of the online traceability of files and status which considerably reduces the visits to the places where the documents are found.

5.3 Increased revenues

As this is a non-profit government organization, in this section we show the benefits the solution offer to citizens:

Benefits to citizens	
Citizens	Availability of online information 24 hours.
	Transparency in management and access to public information.
	Reduction of trial costs.
	Speeding up of paperwork.

5.4 Productivity improvements

Productivity Improvements	
Organization	Availability of online information
	Productivity increase of 90% due to reduction of unproductive time.
	Incorporation of management skills of the new IT solution.
	Removal of unnecessary bureaucratic processes.

6. BEST PRACTICES

The development and implementation of the project was based on the methodology of Pectra Technology, which counts with 10 years of quality certified under ISO 9000:2000 standards. From the implementation of this successful solution, we can highlight as Best Practices & Learning Points:

- Follow-up of implementation methodology certified by global standards
- Thorough evaluation of the business context and the customer's needs, both current and future
- Thorough documentation of processes and data gathering
- Execution and monitoring of the project together with the customer, with milestones and deliverables defined at the beginning of the implementation.

- Use of risk and diverts management methodology.
- Satisfaction of all needs presented by value chain participants in the market to which the solution aims.
- Thorough market studies for the detailed gathering of these needs
- Methodological framework:

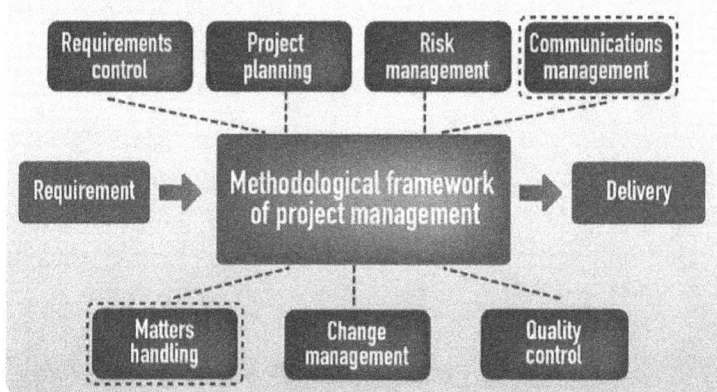

Implementation

To plan the development and application of this technological platform made necessary the prioritization of those areas which require immediate implementation of this information management scheme. To this end, a 6-month work scheme was defined. Its goal was to gather the civil, family and criminal trial processes, connectivity, training and release of 5 pilot applications in the same number of courts corresponding to civil, criminal, family, and mixed and lower mixed legal matters.

Once the functionality goals and expectations were achieved, after the first 6 months, a three-month period of program repetition in the rest of the Judicial Districts was started to operate in all the courts.

Awards for best practices.

In the framework of the best practices and competitive advantages, the institution was granted the award to Innovation and Quality in 2007 by the Government of the State of Hidalgo to the most innovative institutions of the Public Sector. Thanks to this award, the organization was positioned both at social and political level for its innovation and quality.

7. COMPETITIVE ADVANTAGES

The implementation of Information Technologies – BPM – to achieve a better and more efficient management, allows the High Court of Justice of the State of Hidalgo to count with the main competitive advantages described below:

- **Efficient management processes:** They integrate workflows to create fast, productive and highly organized management processes.
- **Service quality:** It provides the tools necessary to become an administration oriented towards providing quality services to the citizens.
- **Strategic information:** The solution provides key information to make crucial decisions, allowing planning and accurate control of resources and costs.
- **Advanced functionalities:** They allow managing the strategy, investments, human resources, records and relations with the citizens, providing the necessary technology to create modern and simple services.

- **Policies and government plans measurement:** It allows having quantifiable results for a responsible use of budgets.
- **Security:** To facilitate the compliance of legal issues in relation to information security and protection.

Currently, this program is used in Civil, Family and Criminal Courts of the Judicial District of Pachuca, Civil and Family Courts of the Regional Headquarters of Justice of Tulancingo, and Courts of the Regional Headquarters of Justice of Huichapan. The expansion to the rest of the Courts is under process and the next step to implement it in the Regional Headquarters of Justice of Ixmiquilpan.

8.   TECHNOLOGY

At the integration level of the solution, 2 vertical applications were developed, one for civil and family processes and another one for the criminal process. Both vertical applications were customized for each one of the 7 profiles (a judge, two agreement secretaries, two clerks of the court, two commissioners, a judge's secretary and a party officer) required by each court. The vertical applications cover the whole process (civil-family and criminal), starting with the activities related to the filing officer and ending with the activities in charge of the judge.

The vertical applications related to the civil and family processes were developed as WEB applications and have, approximately, the automation of 80 activities and their corresponding screens, per each process. Whereas the vertical applications for the criminal process automated, approximately, 60 activities and their corresponding screens.

It is worth mentioning that 40 sensors or traffic lights were programmed by criminal lower court and 15 sensors by civil or family lower court, totaling about 220 sensors which contribute to the metrics offered by the Business Intelligence tools of the solution.

The infrastructure supporting the solution and its integrations are described in the graphic below:

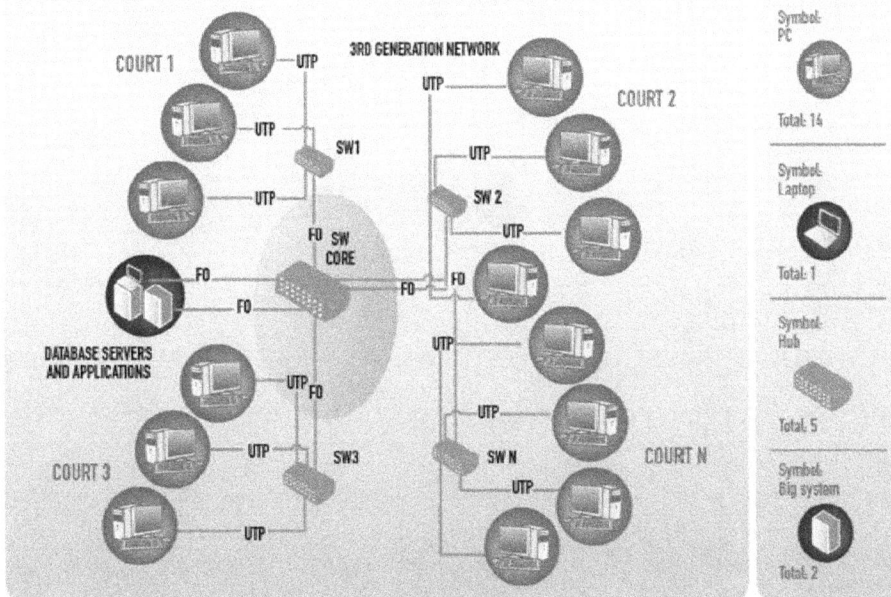

9.   TECHNOLOGY AND SERVICE PROVIDERS

The project was developed by PECTRA Technology together with its specialized partner in Mexico. ACERTI (Asesoría y Certificación SC).

PECTRA Technology is a company specialized in Process Management, with more than 12 years of experience on the market and 200 successful implementations in the USA, Argentina, Mexico, Colombia, Spain and Chile. We have an extensive network of partners in the entire Latin American region and we offer services to more than 50,000 end users who, in turn, serve more than 6,000,000 users/customers. For more information, please visit: www.pectra.com.

ACERTI

PECTRA Technology's IT Department along with its Marketing Department has accomplished this important document. Juan Chacón, PECTRA Technology's Marketing Manager and Vanina Marcote, PECTRA Technology's Marketing Coordinator, planned the data searching and writing.

Different techniques were used to collect the information. Interviews to the people in charge of the solution's design and implementation were carried out (in an average of two hours each); and also a performance evaluation was carried out in the entire company to respond appropriately to the requirements demanded by the Global Excellence in Workflow Awards for innovation and excellence in workflow implementations.

U.S. Xpress Enterprises, Inc., USA

Silver Award, North America

Nominated by Cordys Ltd., UK

EXECUTIVE SUMMARY / ABSTRACT
"Automating the Value Chain"

U.S. Xpress Enterprises stands today as one of the premier transportation companies in North America. Founded in 1985, U.S. Xpress is the third-largest privately-owned truckload carrier with over 8,500 trucks and 26,000 trailers. U.S. Xpress has reshaped the landscape of transportation by developing revolutionary innovations that continually deliver unmatched levels of customer satisfaction.

With the demand for trucking services closely tied to the economy and fulgurations in fuel prices, margins can be low and U.S. Xpress is continually looking to increase the efficiency of its operations to ensure bottom line corporate success. In 2008 U.S. Xpress faced the additional challenge of acquiring several other companies and bringing together the disparate systems of these sister companies. The company therefore introduced a new effort to "automate the value chain." This program is focused on bringing greater operational efficiency to its IT systems and greater visibility of disparate processes across four distinct operations. It aims to build a process infrastructure that will enable it to not only continue its successful business strategy of acquiring partial ownership in synergistic companies, but to make its process infrastructure a factor in accelerating profit and growth through aligned support of that strategy. This alignment was realized through delivering more agile process incorporation of existing and new business systems, more flexibility in incorporating and leveraging disparate systems across multiple organizations, and improvements in gaining process-metric and business-metric visibility in existing and new processes.

With the growth model of merger and acquisitions motivating this change, the

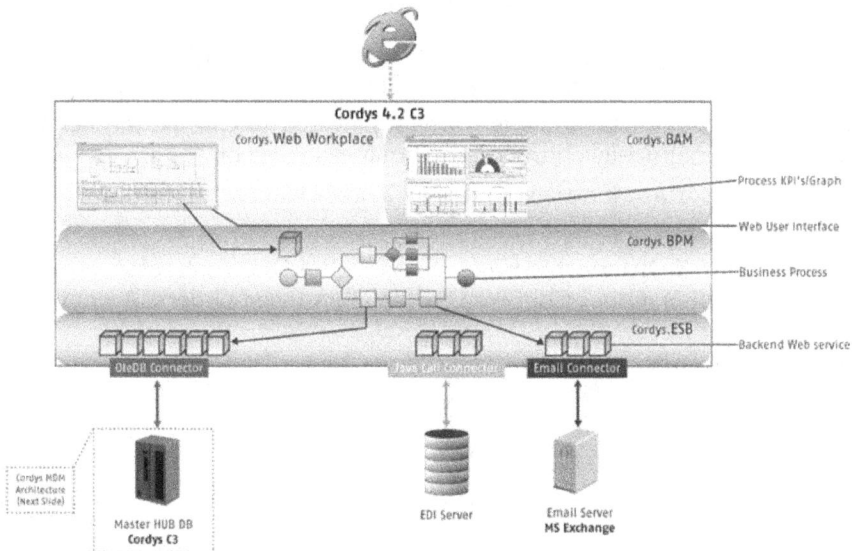

specific project goal was two fold: 1) As U.S. Xpress continues to acquire more trucking entities, it is imperative to get a better exposure of all the orders that are being submitted and processed by U.S. Xpress umbrella entities; 2) Gain a maximum operational efficiency in terms of processing and pricing orders by allowing each trucking entities within U.S. Xpress umbrella to bid for each other's orders.

The implementation objective of the project, named the "Load/Bid Board Project," was to develop an integrated solution that enables various independent trucking entities within a broader U.S. Xpress umbrella to expose and bid for each other's orders. The approach was to design and implement a seamless scalable solution where the organization can easily incorporate new trucking entities into the Load/Bid Board application with minimal effort. U.S. Xpress opted for a process centric, loosely coupled layered architecture using a Master Data Management (MDM) model, dynamic processes and business rules, Business Activity Monitoring (BAM), and a web based user interface that empowers business users, IT support.

OVERVIEW

In addition to the need to bring together the disparate systems of its acquired companies, which would remain on their own Transportation Management Systems (TMS), U.S. Xpress was also challenged with manual, labor-intensive load sharing processes. These processes introduced large room for error for loads to be rejected - where there was really capacity which would result in lost revenue. Additionally, with future acquisitions, U.S. Xpress wanted a solution that was scalable and flexible. In response, U.S. Xpress created the "Load/Bid Board Project," a business process centric solution where each trucking entities can expose a set of orders to others trucking entities within a wider U.S. Xpress umbrella organization. Depending upon the nature of orders and availability of equipment, any trucking entity can accept one or more exposed orders or counter bid an order. The final decision to award an order remains within the control of original trucking entity that has exposed the order.

The "Load/Bid Board Project" is based on a process centric, loosely coupled layered architecture. In the first step, U.S. Xpress used a Master Data Management (MDM) model to create virtual view of all the orders in various legacy systems. On the top of the MDM Layer, U.S. Xpress build a set of dynamic processes and business rules to process orders. They also provided visibility into these processes through a dashboard using Business Activity Monitoring (BAM). A web based user interface was developed to provide a single view of orders across LBB umbrella entities. Business users were empowered to change the behavior of the processes by dynamically changing the business rules on the fly, IT support.

Some of the important matrices that U.S. Xpress wanted to keep track were:

- The Average time between Order Exposed to Order Acceptance
- Number of Orders at various states within Order processing such Available Orders, Order Counter Bid, Total Exposed Orders, Accepted Orders or Order Declined
- Average Order processing time

Finally, there was a set of dynamic business rules that the application administrator has full control to modify dynamically anytime during/before/after order(s) is/are processed. For example:

- Price tolerance when an order is accepted
- Rule associated with rate calculations

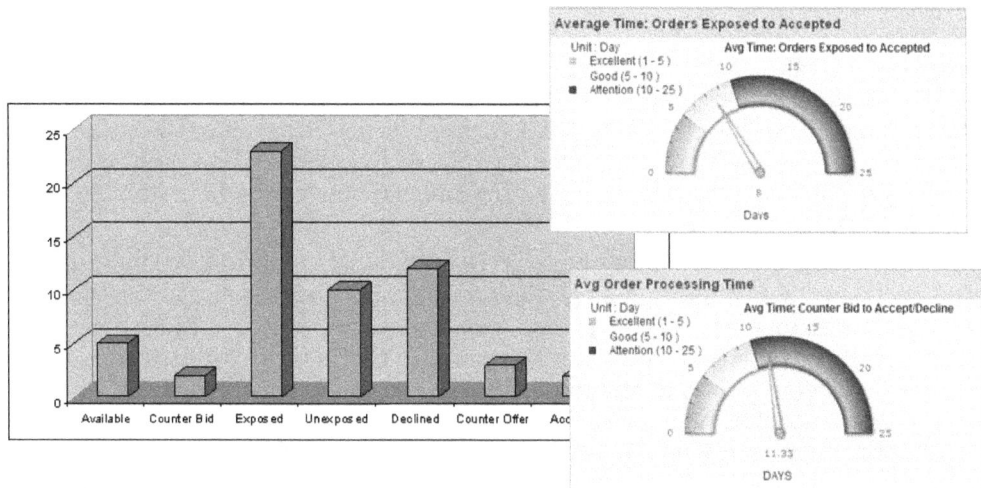

Business Context

The U.S. Xpress business model allows each trucking entity within the wider umbrella to operate independently. When a trucking entity is not able to fulfill an order, it can e-mail/call/fax the order detail to other trucking entities. This causes a number of orders to go unaccounted and there is no auditing mechanism to insure each order is indeed processed within a given SLA.

The driving motivation of the U.S. Xpress initiative was to automate and stream line order exposing, bidding and acceptance processes to support future growth through M&A. Therefore it was critical that any solution must not only support current trucking entities but also facilitate future growth. Finally, operating in a very competitive market place with very thin profit margins, it was critical that the solution has lower TCO and was developed on a platform that supports rapid development.

The Key Innovations

The business impact of the U.S. Xpress project allows its trucking entities to have a Single View of Exposed Orders in near real-time - hence greatly reducing the average order processing time. As importantly, it provides a complete auditing and tracking capability to insure all orders are indeed processed or declined with valid reasons.

The existing process before the U.S. Xpress project was labor intensive with limited scalability to support growth. For example, if Arnold (one of the trucking entities) did not have the capacity to fulfill an order, it would typically call U.S. Xpress to inquire if they could process the order, and what it would cost. At times, Arnold would simply leave a voice mail to the U.S. Xpress administrator or send e-mail. In case the U.S. Xpress administrator was either on vacation or away, the order inquiry would remain in his/her inbox until he/she got back. The same process applied to when an order was counter bid by U.S. Xpress. Overall, there was a potential of dropping an order or processing it after a deadline had already been passed.

After studying the current state, a set of high level key processes were identified such as:

- Expose Orders
- Accept Orders
- Submit Counter Offers

Using the top down design approach, the initial focus of the design was to define both "as is" and "to be" processes. The goal here was to lay down all the steps in each process regardless of manual or system activity. Once the process was finalized, a list of web Services were identified, both the existing and new ones that are required to execute each process. The process model also dictated backend system integration points.

Once the required components were web Services enabled and exposed on top of an Enterprise Service Bus using standard connectors, each activity on the process was mapped to a web service (backend order look up, EDI processing, Rate tolerance business rule, user approval, etc). Once the activities were mapped, the process was simulated to benchmark to insure it still met the business criteria and SLA. Additionally activities related to exception handling, escalation steps and transactional integrity were added as needed.

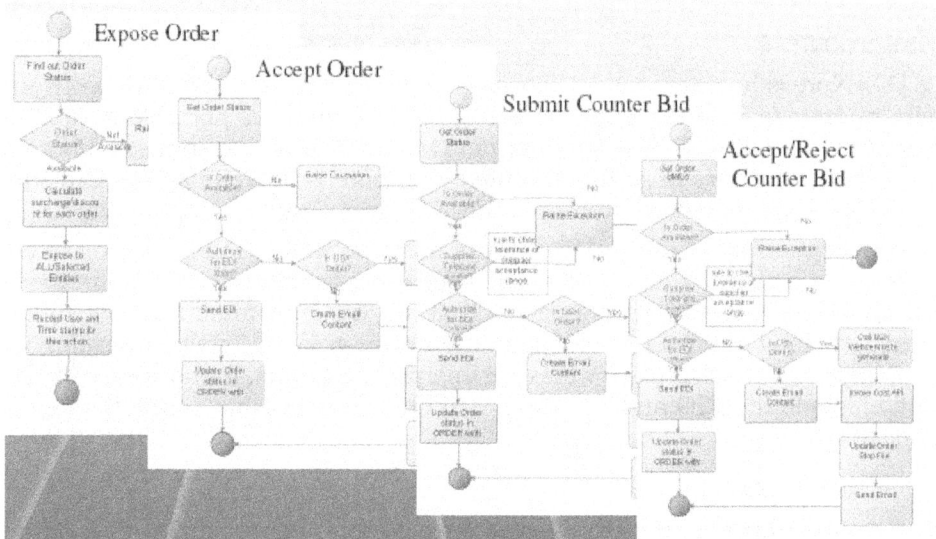

The impact of SOA based BPM centric development was apparent on both business and IT. First, instead of building solutions in a vacuum with little or sporadic interaction with the business, this approach bridged the gap between IT and business. Before, business only saw the system during user acceptance, and a slight change in the process became very costly and time consuming. After, business has become part and parcel of the solution enabling team, hence insuring the success of the project. Secondly, instead of business relying on IT to make changes in the process or modify the business rules, as a business requirement changes business is now empowered to make the changes just like they would do in Visio or a spreadsheet.

On the technology side, IT had to develop new governance and procedures to the solution that are not "built to last" but rather "built to change." It is a fundamental change the way IT thinks of developing solutions. Secondly, IT had to develop proper checks and balance to insure changes to business rules and processes are properly managed as they could be rolled to production in minutes instead of hours. Therefore the presence of a solution architect/gatekeeper became a real need to insure purity of a loosely couple layered architecture that shortens the testing time.

HURDLES OVERCOME

Change is never easy. Therefore management buy-in is a major success criterion. Management must encourage training of both in IT and business. Also, it is important both success criteria and risks are properly managed with realistic expectations. For example getting proper resource allocation in terms of skill sets is important along with willingness to breakdown/circumvent ingrained methodologies may be required.

Business becomes an integral part of the delivery team. Business must realize that their level of participation really determines the success of the project. They are no longer dropping in and out of the project to review the requirement or user interface - but rather must be sitting and designing, testing processes, business rules, etc. It requires the same level of commitment that is required for business to get fluent with a spreadsheet or Visio.

The strategy for organizational adoption is very simple. Start small instead of a big bang approach; show a success; establish a track record of success; and evangelize the benefit and success of the project. Once a particular business realizes the benefit of driving change with little IT help, it just catches fire.

BENEFITS

The savings to U.S. Xpress includes:

- With the real-time view into the Exposed Orders, overall reduction in average order processing time has decreased from hours to minutes
- More efficient visibility and monitoring of orders with clear, quantitative and factual data that was not available before - hence no more late response to Exposed Orders and unfulfilled orders
- Automating processes increases the overall bandwidth/efficiency of the well trained hard-to-find order processing resources
- Long term cost reduction in order processing as new trucking entities are added via a scalable solution
- Web based user interface insures remote connectivity for the remote operations, and escalation via email means very close monitoring of orders

The top down BPM centric development approach of the U.S. Xpress project, if properly executed using a SCRUM approach, is typically completed within 90 days assuming the BPM stack is already pre-integrated. In other words, ESB, BPM, BAM, Rules engine and MDM must be well integrated, otherwise lots of cycle time is invested in getting these various stacks to be integrated. It is a great competitive advantage for the organizations with slim profit margins.

The productivity gains of the U.S. Xpress are all around. Business becomes more productive by monitoring their own processes and relying less on IT. It provides IT greater room to focus on the operational efficiency of their system instead of constantly learning and supporting day-to-day business activities. In this specifically, business became more focused on improving existing processing and reducing order processing time instead of chasing and tracking orders manually. As for IT, its prime focus remains on assuring system availability, system performance and plumbing improvement in the backend integration.

Other examples include:

- Quick time to market – less than 90 days
- Seamless, scalable platform
- Reusable, process driven integration
- Increased value out of existing, disparate systems
- Cost reduction
- Rich user interface
- Executive dashboard that utilize Business Activity Monitoring
- (BAM) to monitor and manage processes
- Not just a single application but a platform that forms the bridge between IT and the business

Best Practices, Learning Points and Pitfalls

7.1 Learning Points

✓ *Engage business early and often*

✓ *Follow 80/20 rule for good enough instead of looking for nirvana; same goes for the best of breed tool set/approach where you spent majority of time making various systems work together instead of focusing business needs*

✓ *Top down analysis and design will greatly reduce unnecessary development and cycle time*

✓ *Develop web Services only for what is needed instead of developing services that perhaps may be needed in some distant future*

✓ *Let the process govern what services and backend systems are needed for the solution*

✓ *Insure your backend systems are capable of supporting extra load*

✓ *Get the security guideline early and talk to Operations as early as possible before technical architecture is finalized*

✓ *Do not under estimate testing and production rollout*

✓ *Get your SOA and BPM governance implemented as soon as possible*

7.2 Pitfalls

✗ *Avoid choosing too broad of a project with too long of a duration for your first BPM project; the project or first phase of the project should be scoped to allow for a "quick win"; success early and often helps keep executive support behind the project*

✗ *Avoid allowing the project to be viewed as an IT only project; the business has to be involved and take an active role in the project*

✗ *Avoid taking existing processes and placing them as is into a BPM tool; ineffective processes will still be ineffective processes after they are automated; be willing to examine and re-engineer business processes.*

Competitive Advantages

U.S. Xpress can now move more quickly than any competitor to bring on companies that they acquire an interest in during a merger or acquisition. Using a BPM tool allowed U.S. Xpress to act very quickly to bring subsequent companies onto their Load/Bid Board application.

Going forward, implementing projects using a BPM tool will allow U.S. Xpress to create an ongoing competitive advantage in the carrier industry. U.S. Xpress can now build applications that are more powerful, faster than before and with fewer developers. They are a more agile development organization and they are allowing the business to "self serve" in many areas.

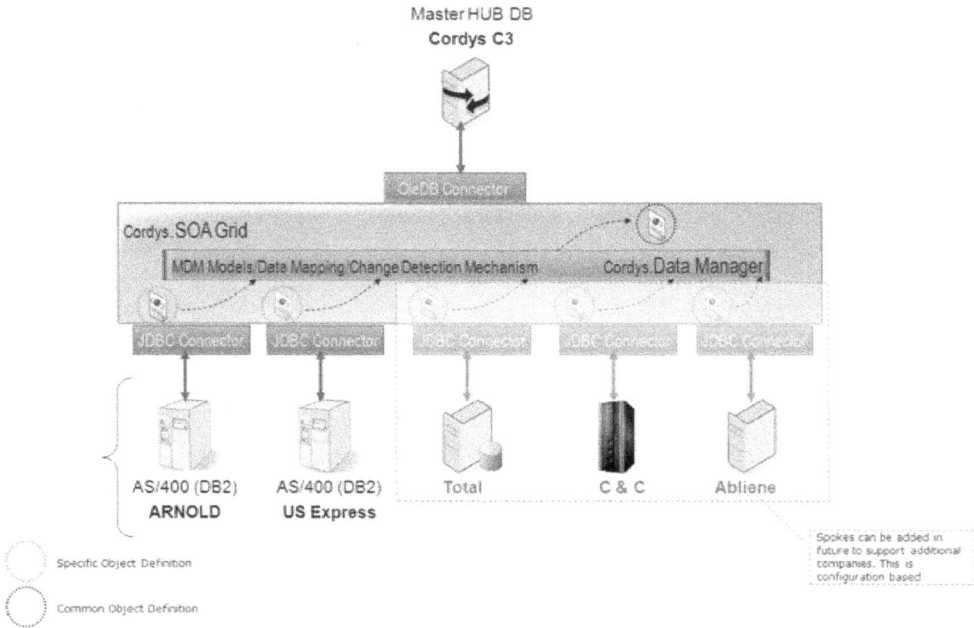

TECHNOLOGY

The U.S. Xpress goal was to develop a scalable solution that is not only standard based but also supports rapid delivery of application. Architecturally, the solution was divided into five major components:

- Backend integration of AS/400, EDI, e-mail and database
- Service enablement of various backend and business components of the solution
- Model driven Processes that support both Human-to-System and System-to-System processes
- Rules Engine to support dynamic price tolerance and acceptance criteria
- Web based user interface for single view of orders and dashboard to monitor various business parameters

In the initial phase of the project, the scope was limited to integrating U.S. XPRESS and Arnold AS/400 based legacy systems that maintain and process orders. However, the architecture remained flexible where any backend system from future trucking entities can be easily integrated without impacting any overlaying processes, user interface and business rules with very little effort. The technical team opted for Service Oriented Architecture where backend systems were integrated using Cordys SOA Grid (Enterprise Service Bus) and standard connectors.

Once the back end systems were connected to the SOA Grid and web Service enabled, the appropriate service were mapped to each activity on the processes. Similarly a set of services were created to display orders and the required detail on the User Interface.

The Cordys Rule engine was used to build a set of business rules Services to support dynamic rules related to Rate calculation and price tolerance. Using Cordys, rules engine interface business users were able to change the parameters as needed and hence instantaneously changing the behavior of any in flight or future process instances.

Finally, a dashboard was created using BAM on top of processes to provide real drill down visibility into processes.

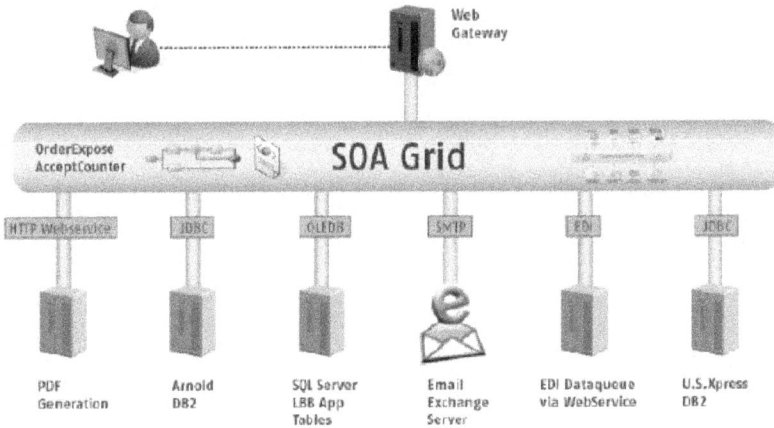

THE TECHNOLOGY AND SERVICE PROVIDERS

Cordys is a global provider of software for business process innovation and Enterprise Cloud Orchestration. The industry-leading Cordys Business Operations Platform (BOP) consists of a complete suite for next generation Business Process Management (BPM), Business Activity Monitoring (BAM) and innovative SaaS Deployment Frameworks (SDF), delivering a complete Platform as a Service (PaaS) solution. It includes an open, integrated set of tools & technologies including Composite Application Framework (CAF), Master Data Management (MDM) and a SOA Grid. The Cordys platform and its cutting-edge Cloud technology empowers customers to dramatically improve the speed of change, fundamentally altering the way they innovate their Business Operations to achieve a true customer-centric philosophy. Global 2000 companies worldwide have selected Cordys to achieve business performance improvements such as increased productivity, reduced time to market, higher security and faster response to ever-changing market demands. Headquartered in the Netherlands, Cordys is a global company with offices in the USA, the UK, Germany, China, India and Israel. For more information please visit www.cordys.com.

US Military Entrance Processing Command, US Government

Gold Award, North America

Nominated by Oracle Corp., USA

1. EXECUTIVE SUMMARY / ABSTRACT

The United States Military Entrance Processing Command (US MEPCOM) processes and qualifies individuals applying for military service in any one of five Armed Services (Army, Navy, Marine Corps, Air Force and Coast Guard) and their subcomponents (i.e. Reserve, National Guard). They are required to process over 1 million records a year with potentially spikes of 18,000 per day (5.6 million a year), and to maintain over 60 million current records across all the armed services. Their existing Enterprise Architecture (EA) was to antiquated and brittle to handle the growing requirements of its customer in an increasingly changing environment.

US MEPCOM chose to transform itself into a Net-Centric enterprise by implementing BPM and SOA. It chose this path to cut cost and risks associated with upgrading its existing EA. BPM and SOA enabled it to better abstract and govern its existing capabilities and allow external customers and partners better and more reliable access to its services. BPM and SOA enable MEPCOM to see significant Return-On-Investment across cost savings, speed to delivery of new services, reusability, risk management, and interoperability. Its new BPM / SOA EA now enables them to look forward to rolling out future systems that will enhance capabilities for the war fighter in the future.

2. OVERVIEW

The United States Military Entrance Processing Command (USMEPCOM) processes and qualifies individuals applying for military service in any one of five Armed Services (Army, Navy, Marine Corps, Air Force and Coast Guard) and their subcomponents (i.e. Reserve, National Guard). They are required to process over 1 million records a year with potentially spikes of 18,000 per day (5.6 million a year), and to maintain over 60 million current records across all the armed services. Each Service has its own, unique Recruiting System and the only interface to USMEPCOM was either a flat file or manual re-keying of data. The system is actively used by over 15,000 recruiters and 2,700 MEPS employees across the US (see Figure 1.1). Additionally, USMEPCOM exchanges data with a variety of Federal, state and private agencies such as the Social Security Agency, FBI, the Office of Personnel Management, Departments of Motor Vehicles and medical laboratories. Building and maintaining these capabilities in a secure and trustworthy architecture across such a broad set of internal and external stakeholders would be a challenge for a project team that on average totaled only 17.

The genesis of the Business Process Management (BPM) and Service Oriented Architecture (SOA) project was a business requirement to make the exchange of data more efficient and real time. The original project, named by the functional proponent was Data Exchange/Top Of System Interface Process (DE/TOSIP) was intended to address the interface with the Armed Services. The Office of the CIO saw an opportunity to expand beyond the Armed Services and to address all of the data interface requirements of the command.

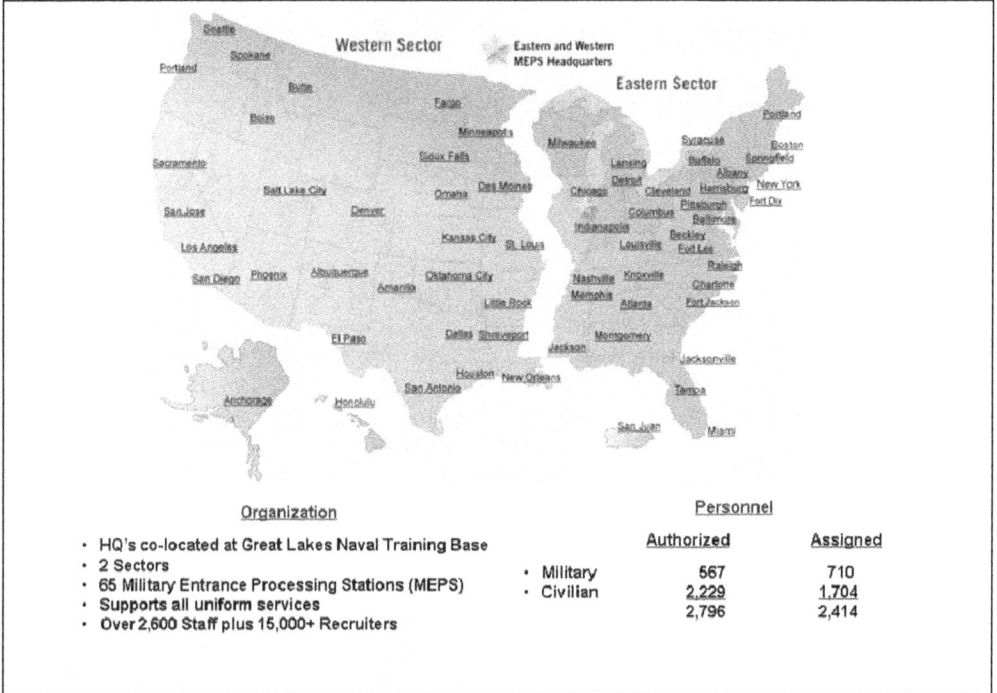

Organization

- HQ's co-located at Great Lakes Naval Training Base
- 2 Sectors
- 65 Military Entrance Processing Stations (MEPS)
- Supports all uniform services
- Over 2,600 Staff plus 15,000+ Recruiters

Personnel

	Authorized	Assigned
Military	567	710
Civilian	2,229	1,704
	2,796	2,414

Figure 2.1 US MEPCOM Operations

BPM and SOA were seen as a way to provide an agile and flexible architecture to meet this growing requirement, increase data quality, and reduce the cost and risk of adding new capabilities. Additionally, this would permit USMEPCOM to move to the future of Virtual Processing, with the goal of reducing processing time from about 2.6 days to 1 day or less.

Using BPM and SOA USMEPCOM planned on prequalifying 90% of the applicants for military Service without a visit to an actual USMEPCOM facility. Additionally, BPM and SOA was believed to provide standardization without having to reengineer all the legacy systems; more accurate estimates of project time / costs (key for budget planning, mission planning, accurate projections and auditing); better Governance and control; added agility due to Business Process Management (rapid development of processes, change control and management, error reduction or "six sigma" capabilities); reusability of BPM and SOA components once added to the SOA Architecture; and cost savings in development and support once a library of components are built. Collaborating across DoD, other government agencies, and even with some commercial entities (e.g. employment and credit verifications) would also be streamlined with an accepted standards based SOA interface. The BPM and SOA Governance structure would also be enhanced to a more robust model that would include the USMEP leadership, staff, customers (Recruiting Services), etc. Finally, the USMEPCOM CIO (J6) staff wanted to be compliant with the Defense Information System Agency (DISA) newly defined system requirements for the future DoD net-centric architecture.

3. BUSINESS CONTEXT

The Project Team consisted of Subject Matter Experts (SME) from the functional (business) proponent, the Information Technology (IT) Directorate, Resource Management Directorate (budget/contracts), and contractor engineers and architects. This team is the core of our Center of Excellence (CoE) which averages around 17 personnel. As projects start and progress the team may grow with the addition of SMEs from both internal business lines and / or external participants (e.g. Armed Force components, other agencies, etc.) that could be assigned either full or part time. The Team first meets to review and agree on the System requirements Specification (SRS). The Team was chaired by a senior IT manager. Meetings were held at least once a week to review designs, project progress, etc. All decisions were Team-based with no differentiation between Functional and technical issues. It was the responsibility of the Team to coordinate with external customers – i.e. Army, Navy, Air Force, Marine Corps and Coast Guard.

MEPCOM has also established a program chain of command that is key in project governance, control, and ultimate success. The ultimate Sponsor is the Secretary of Defense, but actual sponsorship is delegated to Mr. Bill Carr, the Deputy Under Secretary of Defense, Military Personnel Policy, then to The Commander, US-MEPCOM, further to The CIO for USMEPCOM is Mr. Kevin D. Moore and The Director of Operations, Navy Captain Sandra Haidvogel.

Additionally, MEPCOM set up a Governance structure to manage change control, budgeting, planning, etc. This was key to keeping the functional and line of business components from circumventing process.

As described in Figure 2.1, US MEPCOM, processes over 1 Million records a year to qualify and recruit quality personnel for the US Military. The challenge was that its existing IT Enterprise Architecture (EA) could not modernize to meet the growing demands of the US Military in its current form (see Figure 3.1). US MEP-COM was faced with two choices; build a completely new modern IT EA while still running the existing system and then change over, or "wrap" the existing EA with SOA and BPM and then manage the legacy resources either to migration or support scenarios. The obvious lowest risk and fastest path was to use SOA and BPM. It was not feasible to re-build the existing systems as this could mean waiting over 5 years for a new system to be in place. The new "Enterprise Service Oriented Architecture" (see Figure 3.2) provided the abstraction layer required for US MEPCOM to allow standardized access to its existing resources, while allow for new business interactions to take place without changes to the these legacy resources.

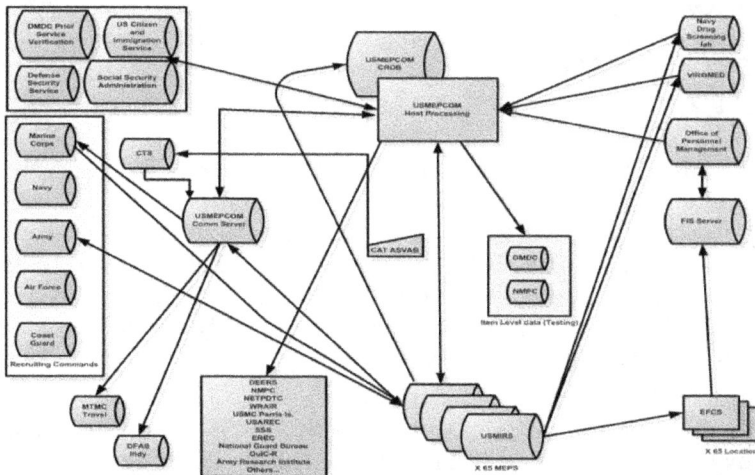

Figure 3.1 (Starting IT Enterprise Architecture)

Enterprise Service Oriented Architecture
(eSOA)

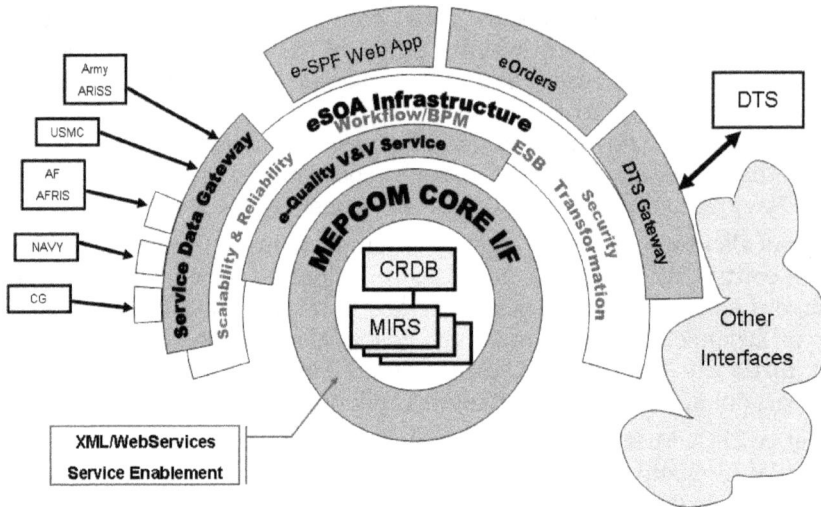

Figure 3.2 (New Enterprise Service Oriented Architecture)

4. THE KEY INNOVATIONS

A good example of how the USMEPCOM BPM and SOA has transformed the business of accessing young men and women into the Armed services is the case of the U.S. Air Force Reserve (USAFR). The USAFR is a small component of the Air Force from a accessions viewpoint. Their recruiters work from store fronts across the United States and us a proprietary system to track and process potential recruits. Prior to January 2007, if a USAFR recruiter wanted information on an applicant from USMEPCOM, he/she would call an Air Force liaison at a USMEPCOM facility and ask that the liaison look up the information in the USMEPCOM Information Resource System (USMIRS) and call back. This process could take anywhere from a half hour to three days depending on the liaison. Once the USMEPCOM BPM and SOA implementation was in place, the USAFR created the necessary SOAP calls to pull information from USMIRS through the SOA directly from the recruiters laptop. Now, any field recruiter can get the necessary information in under 30 seconds. The USAFR has estimated that they are saving around $350 thousand per year because of this. The USAFR accounts for only 2% of the total accessions number.

Additionally, US MEPCOM has gone from a 12 month development cycle for changes to the environment to approximately a two month cycle, depending on how fast the governance Board reacts. US MEPCOM has already experienced the efficiency of Reusability. As US MEPCOM readied the eSecurity (a $10 million project) project for Beta, we were able to create new composite service in a matter of two weeks to obtain and the store the necessary data. The original estimate for this work was six months without a BPM and SOA.

In another example, based on the analysis done by a third party, we have decreased the estimated project costs of the new Virtual Integrated Processing System (VIPS) (which is scheduled to begin deployment in FY2010) by $56 million just by having BPM and SOA in place.

Finally, MEPCOM has seen a not only a reduction in costs, but also a reduction in risk. As more BPM and SOA components are added to our inventory we can estimate project scope (time and costs) and even project scope variance a lot better. This is increasingly important as our projects get more and more complex and we are asked to do more with less. Allocating the correct amount of resources (neither too high nor too low), is a key measure of the success of our overall SOA governance initiative.

Everything that we built as part of the original BPM / SOA EA is being reused as part of the Recruiting Service Interface (five Armed Services, five different requirements. Additionally, all of the services built for the original deployment are being reused in one way or another in US MEPCOM's eSecurity Project, eRecords Project, eOrders Project and the Armed Services interface. US MEPCOM has managed to get four major projects (total cost was around $40 million) fielded in less than one year and only had to build three new services. The ROI came in 4 dimensions: cost saving, time to delivery, reuse of services, and decreased project cost variance (see Figure 4.1). Talk about efficiency!

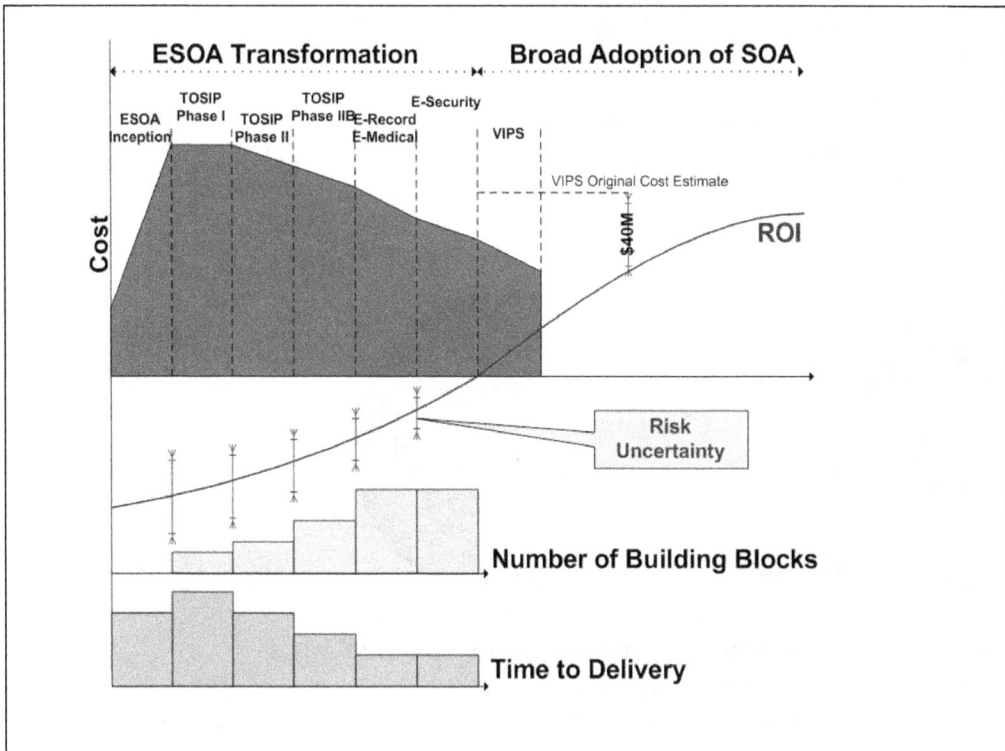

Figure 4.1 (BPM and SOA Return on Investment)

4.2 Business

- The US government and the US Military in particular have had to adapt to a much more interconnected, real-time environment with many new business challenges. US MEPCOM was unable to meet its mission to serve its DoD branch (Army, Air Force, Navy, Marines, Coast Guard) customers with its aging and inflexible systems. Additionally, many legacy systems were built in stove-pipes, lacked sufficient documentation, and/or were created by programmers that had left or were soon to retire. Add to this, US MEPCOM's business is dependent on highly interconnected, high volume processes spanning defence, civilian, and commercial entities with sensitive information.

- Transforming its EA to a SOA-based standard with automated processes and full SOA governance was the only path to successfully supporting its customers current and future requirements.

4.3 Process

- The project charter for US MEPCOM transformation to eSOA was to implement "system to standard" processes to save time and money in the recruitment US DoD personnel (see Figure 4.2). This is the highest level process where system to system interaction processes span MEPS, Recruiting Services, and Training Centers.

System-to-Standard Outcomes Fully Implemented eSOA

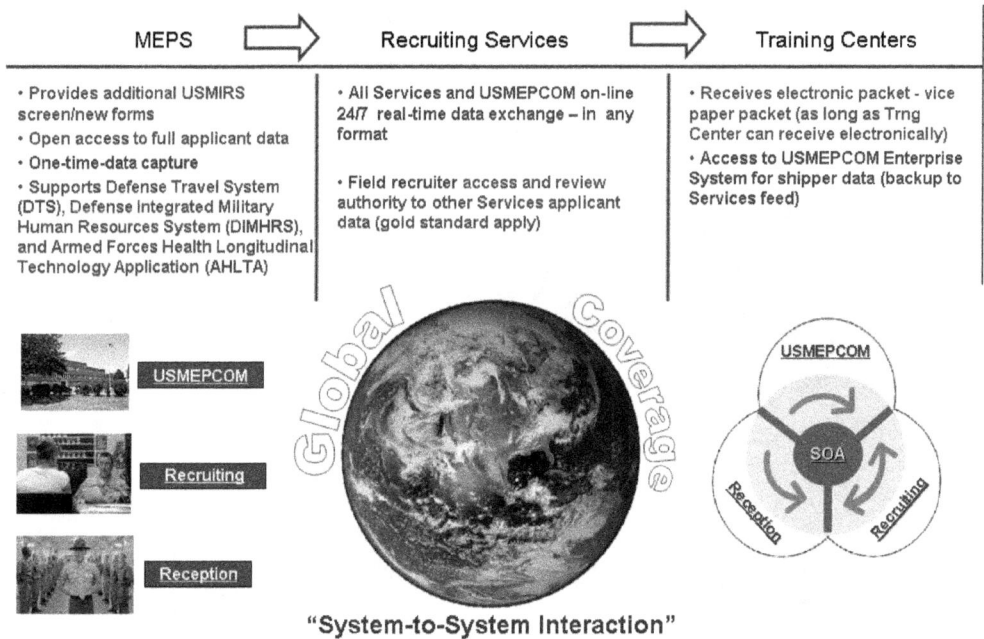

MEPS	Recruiting Services	Training Centers
• Provides additional USMIRS screen/new forms • Open access to full applicant data • One-time-data capture • Supports Defense Travel System (DTS), Defense Integrated Military Human Resources System (DIMHRS), and Armed Forces Health Longitudinal Technology Application (AHLTA)	• All Services and USMEPCOM on-line 24/7 real-time data exchange – in any format • Field recruiter access and review authority to other Services applicant data (gold standard apply)	• Receives electronic packet - vice paper packet (as long as Trng Center can receive electronically) • Access to USMEPCOM Enterprise System for shipper data (backup to Services feed)

"System-to-System Interaction"

Figure 4.2 System-to-Standard Fully Implemented

Additionally, more detail processes are being rolled out across the organization starting with e-Record/e-Medical and e-Security (see Figure 4.3 and 4.4).

System-to-Standard Outcomes Fully Implemented e-Record/e-Medical (Beta Test-Milwaukee Mar 08)

MEPS ⇨ Recruiting Services ⇨ Training Centers

• No more hard copy File Rooms • All archived files scanned • Daily processing documents scanned for MEPS/Service real time access • Data extracted from 3 Medical Forms direct database update – reduce data entry with increased accuracy • No lost packets/files • Scan DEP Packet day prior shipping	• Anytime Electronic access imaged data to Include shipper packet • Services can print any image • Services push Service forms for shipper packet • MEPS and Services same day access to support "Other MEPS Processors" • Eliminates Services Hard Copy Residual Packet	• End state complete electronic shipper packet • MEPS continue to provide hard copy shipper packets per Service request

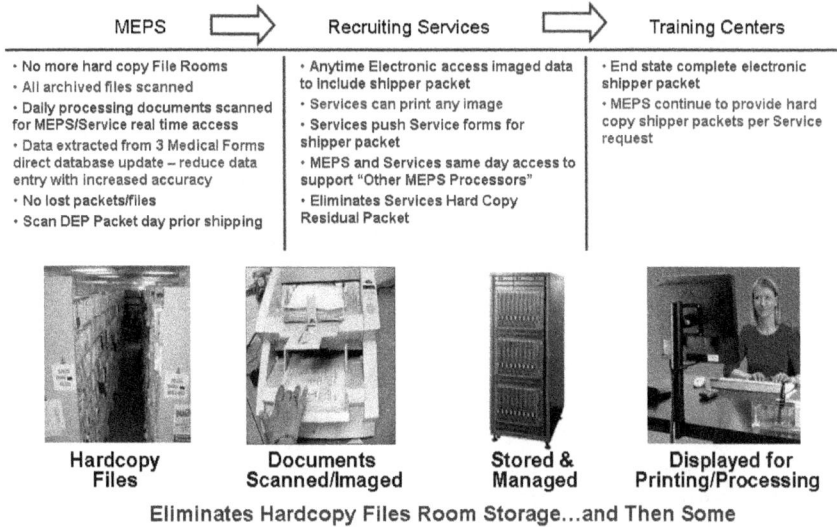

Hardcopy Files — **Documents Scanned/Imaged** — **Stored & Managed** — **Displayed for Printing/Processing**

Eliminates Hardcopy Files Room Storage...and Then Some

Figure 4.3 (e-Record/e-Medical process)

System-to-Standard Outcomes Fully Implemented e-Security (Beta Test-Baltimore Apr 08 & San Juan May 08)

MEPS ⇨ Recruiting Services ⇨ Training Centers

• Positive Applicant Identification • Electronically track applicant via Biometric and facial recognition photograph index/facial biometrics • DD Form 4 Contract signatures are index/facial biometrics • Enrollment requires 2 SSN source documents (680-3A-E plus other) • Reduce fraudulent processing	• Verify applicant identity "Cradle-to-Grave" • Applicant uses fingerprint to check-in/out • Services can access applicant location anytime to determine processing status • Biometric e-Signature DD Fm 4 • Project all applicant (MEPS/MET Site) • Continuous Verified Test Scores	• Same enlistee arrives at the Initial Entry Training Center • End state capability to verify new enlistee identification with Defense Manpower Data Center (DMDC) Common Access Card (CAC) issuance (biometric) • Receive biometric e-Signature DD Form 4

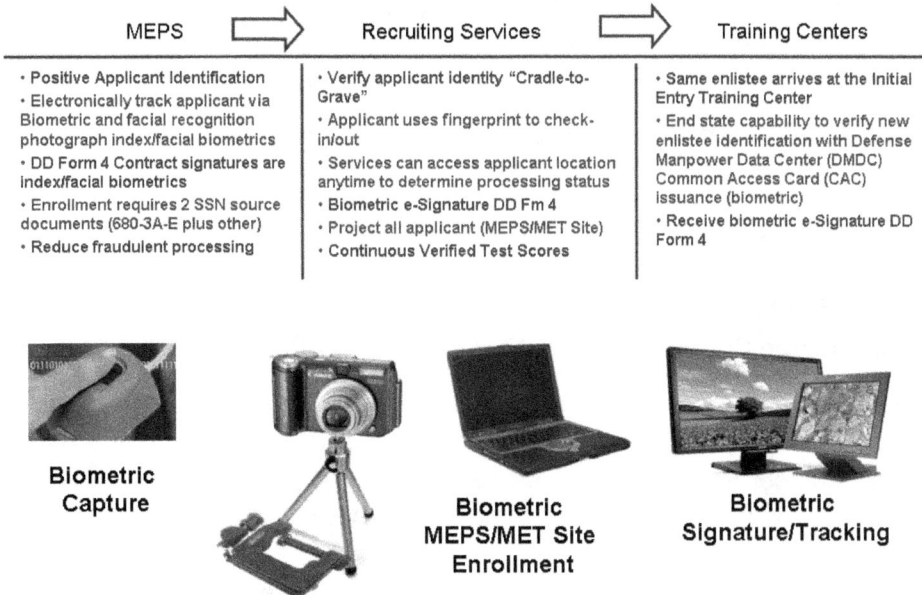

Biometric Capture — **Biometric MEPS/MET Site Enrollment** — **Biometric Signature/Tracking**

Figure 4.4 (e-Security process)

Currently, the overall system to system processes are fully implemented across the organization while, e-Record/e-Medical and e-Security are expected to be completed in 2009.

4.4 Organization

The implementation of the SOA was a new experience for USMEPCOM. Probably the biggest hurdle that had to be overcome was to stop people from thinking in terms of the legacy systems and to think in terms of services provided (business) and technical services required to support the business. It probable took six to nine months to educate the SMEs and to get them thinking in the right direction.

Establishing cross government collaboration early on is also essential (e.g. Social Security Administration, Homeland Security, the VA, etc.) as most processes span and require interfaces with these external partners. Additionally, it should not be expected that even if you are SOA "ready" that your external partners will be the same right away. A build and they will come philosophy should be avoided, and including your external partners in your project communications (e.g. updates and plans) is key in insuring that they will be ready when you are.

The Project Team consisted of Subject Matter Experts (SME) from the functional (business) proponent, the Information Technology (IT) Directorate, Resource Management Directorate (budget/contracts), and contractor engineers and architects. This team is the core of thier Center of Excellence (CoE) which averages around 17 personnel. As projects start and progress the team may grow with the addition of SMEs from both internal business lines and / or external participants (e.g. Armed Force components, other agencies, etc.) that could be assigned either full or part time. The Team first meets to review and agree on the System requirements Specification (SRS). The Team was chaired by a senior IT manager. Meetings were held at least once a week to review designs, project progress, etc. All decisions were Team-based with no differentiation between Functional and technical issues. It was the responsibility of the Team to coordinate with external customers – i.e. Army, Navy, Air Force, Marine Corps and Coast Guard.

US MEPCOM has also established a program chain of command that is key in project governance, control, and ultimate success. The ultimate Sponsor is the Secretary of Defense, but actual sponsorship is delegated to Mr. Bill Carr, the Deputy Under Secretary of Defense, Military Personnel Policy, then to The Commander, US MEPCOM, further to The CIO for US MEPCOM is Mr. Kevin D. Moore and The Director of Operations, Navy Captain Sandra Haidvogel. Additionally, MEPCOM set up a Governance structure to manage change control, budgeting, planning, etc. This was key to keeping the functional and line of business components from circumventing process.

HURDLES OVERCOME

Kevin Moore, the CIO of US MEPCOM, likened US MEPCOM's challenging transformation to "conducting open heart surgery on yourself with a knife, while running a marathon, where the only training you've had was from the discovery channel."

There are still not that many implementations of BPM and SOA at the sheer size and scale that MEPCOM is endeavoring. Add to this fact that their systems handles a huge volume (over 1 million records) and must have no downtime and you can see what he means.

Management

Key to their success was a proper chain-of-command with clear lines of authority and responsibility. Forming the CoE with core staff and representation from the customer (DoD branches) was the next step. Finally, the governance structure enabled them to control change, risk, and scope.

Business

The implementation of the SOA was a new experience for USMEPCOM. Probably the biggest hurdle that had to be overcome was to stop people from thinking in terms of the legacy systems and to think in terms of services provided (business) and technical services required to support the business. It probable took six to nine months to educate the SMEs and to get them thinking in the right direction.

Organization Adoption

Establishing cross government collaboration early on is also essential (e.g. Social Security Administration, Homeland Security, the VA, etc.) as most processes span and require interfaces with these external partners. Additionally, it should not be expected that even if you are SOA "ready" that your external partners will be the same right away. A build and they will come philosophy should be avoided, and including your external partners in your project communications (e.g. updates and plans) is key in insuring that they will be ready when you are.

BENEFITS

6.1 Cost Savings

There are several cost savings estimates for the projects implemented as part of the eSOA transformation. Examples are:

- USAFR automated access to USMIRS = $350, 000 / year
  - As USAFR is only 2% of the total accessions number, DoD wide savings could be in the $ millions.
  - Estimated Cost Reduction of VIPS of $56 million

6.2 Time Reductions

- Now able to provide accurate and timely data on applicant test scores, backgrounds and placement in 30 seconds instead of 3 days
- Many manual processes (e-Medical, e-Security) are now being automated. Measurements have not been finalized at this time.
- Changing business logic was nearly impossible in the past
  - Now changes can be done at different layers
    1. BPM / workflow
    2. Service Bus

6.3 Increased Revenues

US MEPCOM does not generate revenue from its activities, but instead has goals to comply with DoD standards and inter-operability.

- US MEPCOM is one of the 1st in DoD to implement a SOA Architecture for Net-centric operations
- Service enabled existing systems are now easily accessible to all customers (e.g. Branches of the military)

6.4 Productivity Improvements

- Development Spirals reduced from 12 months to 3 or 2 months.
- Project Variance (cost and time) reduced.
- Reuse of SOA components (including BPM).
- Abstraction of business logic from legacy systems.

BEST PRACTICES, LEARNING POINTS AND PITFALLS

7.1 Best Practices and Learning Points

- ✓ Think Big, Start Small, Move Fast

✓ *Don't assume customer and/or partners will modernize at the same pace as you*

✓ *Establish a clear Chain-of-Command, with appropriate sponsorship levels*

✓ *Establish a Center of Excellence (CoE) with a core team that includes SMEs from the customer(s) when possible*

✓ *Governance across the project and services is essential*

✓ *Processes (that matter) usually span and require interfaces with external partners or customers*

✓ *Include your external partners in project communication*

✓ *Know your "As is"*

✓ *Knowledge of legacy environment*

✓ *Skill sets, including SOA*

✓ *Get Buy-In (IT & Business & Leadership – Executive)*

✓ *Foster Business Desire for Change*

✓ *Push for the upfront investment – "not your father's system"*

✓ *Constant marketing*

✓ *Adhere to a Reference Architecture*

✓ *Take a phased approach to its implementation*

✓ *Phase I – Build Reference Architecture with initial business components*

✓ *Phase II – Technology pilot at select sites*

✓ *Phase III – Build out enterprise SOA services aligned with strategic plan and shareholder feedback and use metrics*

✓ *Maintain project management discipline*

7.2 Pitfalls

✗ *"Turning-off" legacy systems without understanding the business logic that connects it to other systems*

✗ *Don't have a build and they will come philosophy*

✗ *Don't underestimate challenge of changing thoughts from IT infrastructure to providing Business Services*

8. COMPETITIVE ADVANTAGES

As one of the first in DoD to implement a BPM and SOA US MEPCOM has established an agile and flexible infrastructure that can continue to streamline personnel processing for its customers (all branches of service).

The next phase of US MEPCOM's transformation is Virtual Interactive Processing System (VIPS). Its goals are:

- One visit, one accession
- Paperless processing
- Positive identification of applicants
- Enhanced data accessibility
- Validation of self disclosed information
- Continued Compliance with DoD IT mandates
  - Net-centric
  - Enterprise architecture

What is VIPS?

Current Concept of Operations

Current Process
FY07 Data

Enlistment Tests

522,000 Tests

Interest

Medical Exams

347,000 Exams

Background Check

315,000 Electronic Fingerprint

Qualified

DEP-In/Job Placement 276,000

Enlist/Ship 243,000

Complete Basic 230,000

Projected

464,000 applicants
997,000 applicant MEPS visits

"Qualify the Force"
Measure / Validate

VIPS Future Concept of Operations

250,000 applicants
250,000 applicant MEPS visits

Global Accessions Processing
Applicant Processing Tools Available On-Line

Interest

I-CAT Enlistment Test
Medical Pre-screen
Background Check
Waiver Pre-screen

Validate
Confirmation Enlistment Test
Tailored Medical Exam
Biometric Verification
250,000

DEP-In/Job Confirmation 240,000

Enlist/Ship 235,000

Complete Basic 230,000

External

MEPS

Projected VIPS Workload

Increased capacity – reduced workload

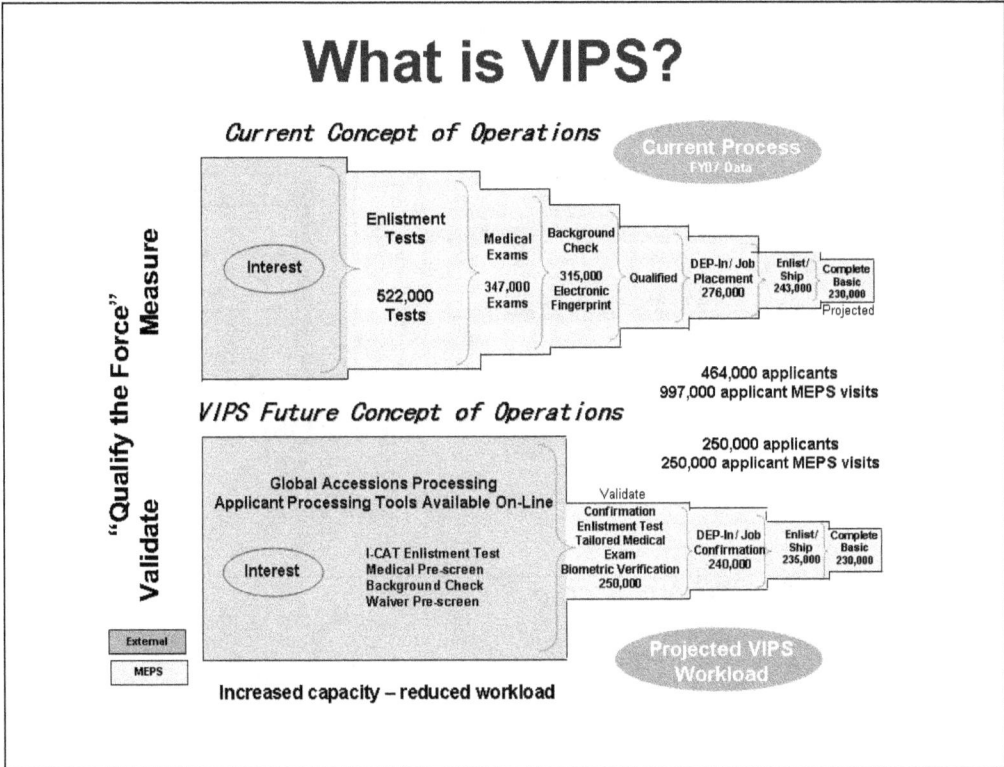

Figure 8.1: The Future VIPS

9. TECHNOLOGY

US MEPCOM implemented a BPM / SOA Enterprise Architecture (see Figure 9.1) that included Oracle Business Process Management Suite, Oracle Service Bus, Oracle WebLogic Application, Portal and Integration Servers, Oracle Forms, and Oracle Databases. This BPM / SOA solution integrated with various internal and external systems. Internal systems include MIRS built on Oracle Application Server (houses applicant qualifications), medical records system, and student testing data. Partner integration included all the Armed Services legacy systems; Defense Manpower data center; Office Personnel Management; Social Security Administration; State DMVs; and even the Selective Service System on mainframes. All of this complexity was increased by the security and privacy requirements necessary for the obvious sensitivity of the data used.

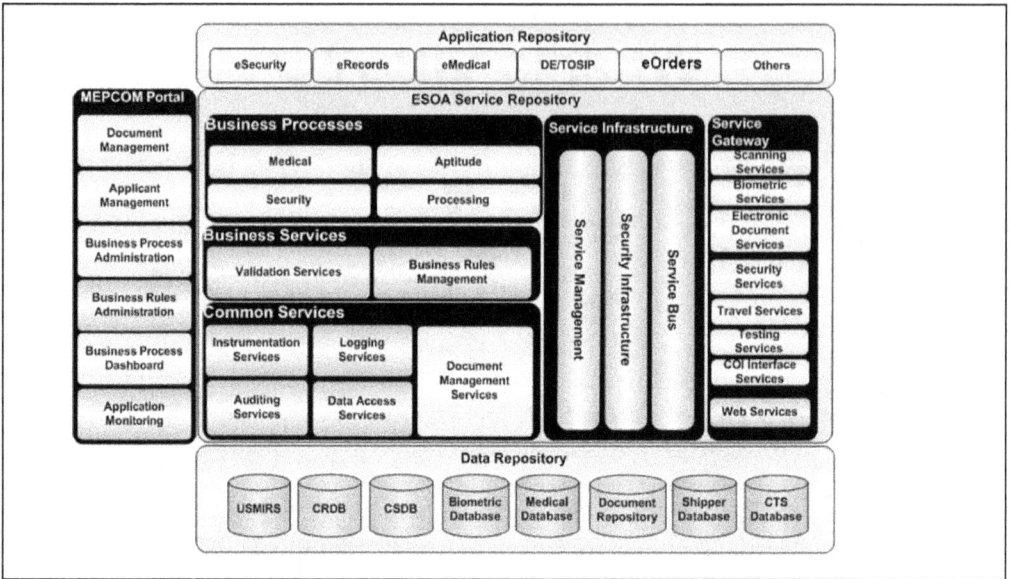

Figure 9.1 US MEPCOM Architecture

10. THE TECHNOLOGY AND SERVICE PROVIDERS

Oracle Software was used in this implementation: www.oracle.com

Section 4

Pacific Rim

AEGON Religare Life Insurance, India

Finalist, Pacific Rim

Nominated by Cordys, UK

1. EXECUTIVE SUMMARY / ABSTRACT

AEGON is a leading life and pensions company with more than 40 million customers worldwide and presence in over twenty markets throughout the Americas, Europe and Asia. Religare is India's leading financial services company. AEGON Religare Life Insurance is a joint venture promoted by AEGON, Religare and Bennett, Coleman and Co. The company specializes in life insurance, pensions and investment products. The biggest challenge faced by the business was to create and implement a successful, efficient and sustainable BPM model, incorporating real-time integration of systems and data exchange across its existing IT infrastructure.

AEGON Religare needed a user-friendly solution to automate existing business processes and to seamlessly integrate select systems to deliver optimal process execution, within an aggressive time-to-market.

The company aimed to launch operations across 14 independent systems, in real-time, at 25 locations on Day 1– this achievement would be a first in the industry.

2. OVERVIEW

Being a new player in the insurance and pensions market in India, AEGON Religare looked at putting in place a business process management solution to streamline its sales management process and the dissemination of information on the agency and customer portals.

To achieve this, AEGON Religare set out to build agility and adaptability into both process and technology in order to ensure the delivery of their promise of customer centricity and delivering need based solutions.

The key objectives/challenges for the AEGON Religare team were:

- Technology as a key driver for superior customer service
- Support for multiple sales channel and PAN India launch
- Web/portal as core information source for sales channel
- Single view front-end - independent of multiple back-end systems
- Faster time to market and improved productivity

AEGON Religare put in place a set of guidelines to meet these objectives:

- Clear process definition for every process area and standardized system platforms
- Clear process to system mapping – building in flexibility and scalability
- Focus on "single view" for specific channels – leave the "clutter" out
- All 14 systems functioning as planned from Day 1

For the core systems, AEGON Religare implemented established products like Future First/Asia from CSC for policy administration, a Distributor Management System from Mastek for agency compensation and AWD from DSTi for imaging and workflow of policy processes. The company also needed a solution to orchestrate and streamline its sales management process and the dissemination of information on the agency and customer portals. Initially, AEGON Religare looked at several solutions. First, they considered a simple packaged solution, but this was rejected due to the cost of license purchasing and the length of time it would have taken to customize the solution to meet the company's specific needs.

The company also considered developing its own bespoke application, which would have allowed AEGON Religare to design a solution that would meet its needs exactly and enable strict standards to be achieved. However, this would have taken a prohibitively long time to develop, potentially delaying the implementation and launch of operations. There were also numerous limitations on the scalability and flexibility of the solution.

AEGON Religare also looked at using several small applications within each department, which proved too complicated, before reaching the strategic decision to deploy the Cordys Business Operations Platform (BOP) for the Sales Management System, Portal, Cash Collection System and Procurement Management System.

Initially, the solution was planned and successfully implemented across three projects:

1. The first project was AEGON Religare's Sales Management System (SMS), which was created in order to increase sales productivity, manage and track agents, on-board new agents and enhance productivity. It eliminates the traditional manual tracking processes by implementing end-to-end management and visibility of inputs and processes. The SMS was required to integrate and interface with core systems.

2. The second project was the Agency Portal: providing a single window for all agents' activities that includes tracking of new business proposals, alerts and information regarding policy servicing, tracking of agents' commissions, and registering of complaints and requests. This project needed to be rolled out quickly, incorporating a customized look and feel for all channels and individual user IDs for each application.

3. The Incidence Management System, the third project, was devised with the aim to extend ROI using a single system to monitor all user complaints, helpdesk support and queries, and problems with tracking and service requests.

In order to ensure the success of these projects, AEGON Religare strictly followed three principles:

- "Robust" processes & "practical" technology only can deliver the right alignment & agility
- Process needs to be in sync with the technology solution
- "Engineer" it but don't "over-engineer" it - right talent and domain depth is key

The company's operation was successfully launched in July 2008, and the benefits AEGON Religare has realized include:

- Portal integrates with multiple backend systems (core policy administration, agency compensation, CRM, MIS, etc) and gives a single view to the user (i.e. sales team and customers)
- Faster deployment of process change due to
  - Model Driven BPM approach
  - Reusability
  - Standards based
  - Flexibility

- Increased business agility, clear processes and system architecture foundation
- Complete monitoring and sharing of real-time information
- Ease of use and fast implementation
- High productivity and scalability
- Fast time to market
- First mover competitive advantage
- After the successful implementation and roll out of these initial three projects, AEGON Religare has automated procurement management and further projects are being delivered within even shorter time frames.

3. BUSINESS CONTEXT

In 2006, AEGON, one of the world's largest life insurance and pension groups, partnered with Religare, India's leading integrated financial services groups, to create AEGON Religare Life Insurance.

Working with Bennett, Coleman & Co, India's largest media group, AEGON Religare received its license in the summer of 2008, enabling them to fulfill their business philosophy: to help people to plan their lives better.

Business dynamics

- •Focus shifting to non-metros and non-city market
- •Handling diversity - 21 plus languages, unique local cultures
- •Acquiring and retaining customers is a challenge
- •Scaling/adapting processes and systems to meet increasing volumes a challenge
- •"First mover advantage" a key success factor
- •Skilled talent and attrition a challenge
- •Customer "self service" model and "single view" is here to stay
- •Differentiated servicing by segment of population

In such a large scale and complex market, choosing the right solution was critical to the initial launch success of the business, which now boasts 13,000 clients.

AEGON Religare is a customer-centric business that endeavors to understand its customers' circumstances, and to provide needs-based solutions.

AEGON Religare realized that in addition to a portal and sales management system, they would be achieve greater competitive advantage by also incorporating escalation, routing, and calendar reminder capabilities.

With an ideal BPM framework in mind, for the portals and Sales Management System, AEGON Religare were faced with the choice of adopting a fixed, pre-made BPM system off the shelf, or commissioning a complete application built entirely from scratch. Ultimately AEGON Religare cherry-picked the best of both options by selecting the Cordys Business Operations Platform. This provides AEGON Religare with distinct competitive advantages, namely its agile responsiveness to a variety of eventualities. AEGON Religare has streamlined its business processes to such an extent that they were able to innovate with excellent customer service and policy servicing on the phone via Interactive Voice Response System on Day 1 of the launch: an industry first.

4. THE KEY INNOVATIONS

4.2 Business

In addition to the core policy, agency and workflow systems, the following bespoke projects have been successfully deployed which largely involved BPM in addition to business rules:

- Agency Portal
- Sales Management System
- Customer Portal
- Procurement Management System
- Cash Collection System
- Payment Gateway – part of the portal
- Global incidents management system

Agency Portal

The Agency Portal is aimed at giving the life agents and other sales groups on-line access to information about their clients, policies sold, premiums due, and commissions paid/payable.

It acts as single point of contact for the agent to track the pending proposals (for example, if a customer has outstanding requirements e.g. medical exam, document submission) and logs any specific complaints/requests.

Agency Portal access is based on unique allocated user-ID, and is tightly integrated with various backend systems.

These include:

- Operational data mart for policy information
- Agency management system for agency and commission information
- CRM for all complaints/issue tracking
- MIS tool for generating/displaying MIS reports.

The agency portal has helped in reducing the number of calls to the call centre as well as to the local branch offices.

It is beneficial for the agents in performing their jobs and being remunerated: previously, commissions were paid weekly following the submission of statements each week and quarter. Because all the details are now recorded on the website, commissions are paid more promptly, and the quarterly review is regulatory.

Sales Management System

The Sales Management System is one of its kind in the Indian Insurance industry, enabling the sales managers/sales team leaders to help the agent on-boarding process. It is similar to a customer lead management system, letting the sales team record lead of prospective agents, the conversion of prospective agent to company agent, and their productivity. This has enabled the company to implement an accurate system for tracking the number of prospective agents that the sales teams meet against their targets, and how they are able to convert the leads. Sales heads can thus manage sales more effectively.

Customer Portal

The Customer Portal is available to any policyholder of the company, providing them access to various details including:

- Their premium due and amount
- Their policy details
- Their unit fund value for those with unit linked policies
- Log in service requests.

The customer can also pay his premiums online using the on-line payment option. Once logged into the portal, the policy information is authenticated with the backend systems, and is connected to the payment gateway.

The Customer Portal is integrated with the MIS database, CRM, website and the payment gateway, thereby providing a single view of all policy holdings with the company.

In the near future, customers will also be able to get e-statements of premium notices and premium receipts, which will reduce printing costs. The Customer Portal has also helped to reduce the number of calls to the call centre as it offers a customer self-service option on the web.

Procurement Management System

The Procurement Management system is primarily aimed at:

- Reducing the headcount needed for all IT procurement
- Automate the IT purchase process
- Ability to accurately track payments and manage cash flow
- Maintain a tight inventory of all IT assets across the country, across the different branches
- Proactively manage policy renewals in advance thus helping in fund management and reducing headcount in these areas

Cash Collection System

The Cash Collection system helps the individual branch offices of the company to:

- Collect cash
- Issue receipts
- Generate cash register daily
- Generate cash deposit slip without any manual intervention

This system has helped to reduce the time per executive, per branch of between 1-2 hours daily, time previously spent on cash collection. Furthermore the cash counter can be opened for a longer period of time, as the system no longer has to be handed over for end of day processing. This system is integrated with the policy administration system, the quote system and the operational data store to obtain and validate all customer information before the premium is collected.

Payment Gateway

The Payment Gateway was launched on 1st January 2009 as an extension to the customer portal, enabling customers to pay the renewal premium directly on-line using a credit/debit card.

The main objectives are:

- To enable the customers to pay online and increase speed and efficiency of policy renewals
- To reduce the policy lapses by giving the customers more than one way to pay premiums

Global Incidence Management System

The Global Incidence Management system is an automated complaint/issue logging and tracking system. Once an issue is logged, it is routed automatically to the appropriate person by the system. It also tracks the time the person takes to resolve the query and depending on the delay, the system generates appropriate escalation mail to the next level. End users can log in and track the issue that they have raised. Once the query is resolved a mail is sent to the user.

At the moment the following projects are being reviewed for implementation: corporate Intranet and the off-line quotation system.

The biggest impact to date for AEGON Religare Life Insurance is the implementation of the Sales Management System and portal, which is aimed at the entire agent sales force and their customers.

This system is all about the process of identifying, short listing, and on boarding agents of the company. Agent activities—inputs, outputs, and end-to-end processes—are tracked, meaning that information is readily available at the fingertips of those who need them within the organization.

4.3 Process

As AEGON Religare was a start-up life insurance company, business processes were planned from the outset to be automated. The key areas where benefits were projected for the company on Day 1 were the automation of the process of the sales team's tracking of new agent hiring, as well as providing the key policy information to agents on-line. The BPM process below shows a sample key area in the Sales Management System in which the process has been streamlined. This has helped in reducing the potential headcount required for tracking agent productivity and on-boarding.

The process diagram for portal below shows the facility which was made available to the agents from Day 1 which includes comprehensive BPM features, resulting in reducing the load on the call center as well as calls to operations executives in the local branch offices.

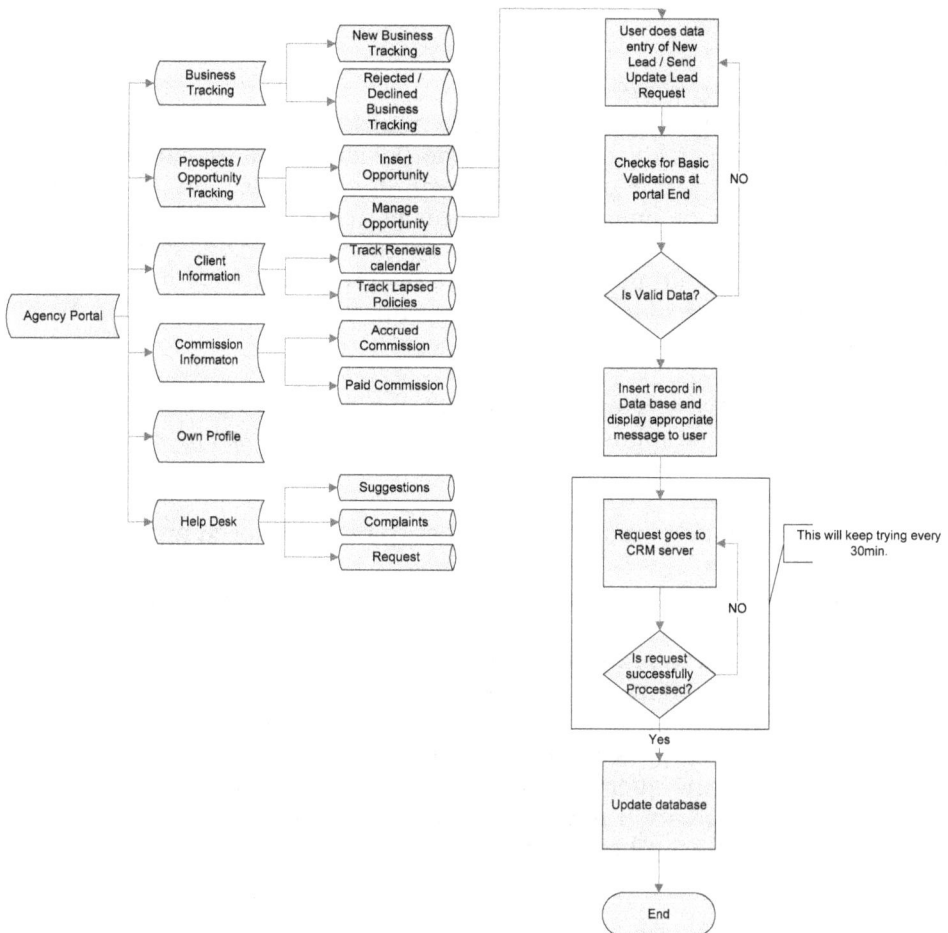

The unique advantage of having these systems in place was that the organization was able to rollout out optimized processes right from Day 1.

- For sales managers (called business manager) the system enabled AEGON Religare to enforce the recording of daily lead tracking and follow up, linked to the daily allowance for the business manager. This enabled timely updates and follow up without having to resort to reminders
- For business alliance partners, the portal has enabled tracking of the latest status on proposals thereby enabling them to get the completed requirements submitted on time without having to get a follow up from AEGON Religare. In addition to this, all commission information is available in the system, thereby reducing commission related queries to the life office
- For customers, this has enabled the tracking of all policies under "one login id" with the option to pay premiums online
- The subsequent systems launched, such as the Incidence Management System, has enabled company-wide tracking of issues whilst easily and measurably linking to resolution SLAs. This has also resulted in automated reporting of issues without the need for a person to collate all issues centrally
- The launch of the Procurement Management System has enabled the automation of the entire purchase process including inventory management of IT assets. This has allowed a reduction in headcount of 1 person since the launch of the project. The project will have paid for itself within the first full year and has led to complete accuracy of asset management
- The launch of the Cash Collection System has freed the branch operations from the need to complete all tasks by 5.30 pm (for the daily end of day batch) and helped extend the collections and processing till 8 pm. This has helped both the operations and agency work force

4.4 Organization

AEGON Religare has 51 branches across India, with at least one employee at executive level per branch.

The focus on process automation to help customers and the sales team has had the following impact on the employees (current and expected benefits in 2009).

Branch employees:

- Reduced support requests from the sales team due to availability of all information on the sales portal
- Operations portal has enabled just one or two branch executives to handle all request for policies of that branch
- Faster and accurate reconciliation and banking process (with the Cash Collection System) and at the same time allowing a longer time period for daily collections
- Automated call logging method (with the Incidence Management System) enabling the employee to track the issue all the way to resolution without having to follow up or actively seek status updates
- Branch sales leaders are able to track their team's performance from their desks, enabling them to focus on performance and productivity.

Head office team:

- HO sales: Reduced headcount otherwise needed to manage and track the agent lead management and productivity

- HO customer service: Reduced load on call center executives (thereby lower levels of incremental hiring)
- HO IT: Automated tracking and SLA based resolution of defects and issues. Reduced headcount that would have been needed for separate tracking

HURDLES OVERCOME

4. The following hurdles were faced during the project phase for two of the systems
5. Sales Management System: Understanding the complex validations and conditions for the daily sheet and tracking modules. These modules had complicated links to other screens within the SMS and also interlink with the backend systems (including the core agency admin and MIS system). This caused some delay during the testing phase with higher than expected defects. However, this was overcome by:

- Direct discussions with user, IT and the solution provider team
- Putting in a process flow chart for complicated screens to enable the technical team to gain a better understand the requirement or defect
- Strong project governance and defect tracking mechanism
- Additional support from the solution provider in issue resolution

6. Procurement Management System: As this project was implemented mid-year, getting all the back records into the system automatically was a challenge. In addition to this, capturing some unique processes of AEGON Religare for budget management was a challenge. This was overcome by:

- Making some minor modification to AEGON Religare process
- Sharing the old record formats right at the stage of designing the system
- Providing detailed sub-process level walk through with the solution provider team

5.1 MANAGEMENT
5.2 Business
5.3 Organization Adoption

The platform was well accepted by all users within the company. This can be attributed to the following:

- The applications were well planned and designed to ensure that the business requirements were correctly converted into the system (i.e. users got what they expected from the system)
- Benefits of single user-id and password for the group of applications (i.e. all applications developed on the Cordys platform accessed the same user-id and password but with restrictions at the application level depending on user groups)
- Development time was short, resulting in users getting the system delivery on or ahead of time leading to better acceptance of the system and solution
- Ease of use enabled faster adoption within the company without having to encourage usage

6. BENEFITS

The solution is reusable, flexible and scalable and provides effective BPM throughout the organization. It allowed the Sales Management System project to be smoothly implemented and integrated into the system infrastructure. The SMS interfaces with the underlying infrastructure and the Cordys Business Operations Platform, allowing the company to manage its input processes and drive the desired output via the platform, achieving consistency in performance.

The Agency Portal benefited from the re-usability of the codes required, resulting in rollout within a short time and customized access for each channel with minimal effort.

The Incidence Management System was integrated easily and drove the streamlining of IT infrastructure throughout the organization. The efficient implementation of the Incidence Management System means that the company is able to track performance to SLAs, managing escalation/reminders automatically through BPM, enforcing high-quality standards and increasing ROI through compliance.

Overall, the solution is easy to deploy, use and manage, with effective integration capabilities and sufficient scalability for use across the entire infrastructure in all 51 locations. The flexibility of the solution means that further applications and projects can be put into place on top of the existing platform, resulting in a sustainable long-term solution.

6.1 COST SAVINGS

Some of the actual and potential cost savings that AEGON Religare sees in these projects where the Cordys platform is used include:

Savings already realized:

- As opposed to the planned 2 server licenses, the applications are well managed within 1 server resulting in savings of 1 license
- Reduction of 1 headcount for the helpdesk team due to the implementation of the Incidence Management System (about INR 300,000 annual savings)
- The Cash Collection System has resulted in an increased collection window of 2 hours daily, as well as savings in reconciliation and checking time (conservatively 0.5 hour cost saving per day per branch @ INR 2,600 per day)
- Saving of about INR 550,000 due to development cost difference between developing the Cash Collection System in Cordys as opposed to developing this within the core policy system
- Saving of about INR 200,000 due to reuse of some existing code for developing the portal for other sales channel
- The total estimated savings are therefore well in excess of INR 1,000,000

Expected savings/WIP:

- At least 1 headcount reduction from the head office Sales team for monitoring sales performance (about INR 400,000 per annum)
- The Cash Collection System will result in a further 0.5 hour saving per day per person per branch, during this year taking into account an increased customer base
- 1 headcount reduction from the procurement team this year (INR 300,000 per annum) as additional headcount will not be necessary
- Reduced cost of additional Business Objects user licenses as the sales channel will get the reports directly through the portal
- The total additional projected cost savings in excess of INR 700,000

6.2 Time Reductions

The agent system has resulted in approximately 20% reduction in calls to the call centre. Agents are now able to find all information and query answers on the Agent Portal, saving AEGON Religare both time and costs.

Furthermore the company will now be able to post consolidated commission statements on the portal instead of posting physical statements. Apart from adding benefits on the "green policy", it is expected to save INR 750,000 in 2009 (2,500 agents, mailing cost INR 15 per letter, printing cost approximately INR 10 per agent, 12 monthly statements)

Global Incident Management System leading to a larger number of issues closed within the agreed service level agreement with an approximately 10% faster closure of cases to date. In the past this wasn't measurable. This, in turn, has resulted in the system paying for itself within the first year.

6.3   Increased   Revenues

These initiatives are more on the support side (i.e. cost reduction side) which in turn is expected to help frontline sales. However top-line impact cannot be measured at this stage.

6.4 Productivity Improvements

Please see the above sections.

7. BEST PRACTICES, LEARNING POINTS AND PITFALLS

7.1 Best Practices and Learning Points

✓ "Robust" processes and "practical" technology ONLY can deliver the RIGHT alignment and agility

✓ Process NEEDS to be in sync with technology solution

✓ "Engineer" it but don't "over-engineer" it - right talent and domain depth is key

7.2 Pitfalls

✗ Where the project requires BPM related enhancements, it is essential that the users and IT clearly document the process including the escalation charts before getting them developed. This will avoid defects and issues in the test stage.

8. COMPETITIVE ADVANTAGES

- The Portal is seamlessly integrated with multiple backend (core policy administration, agency compensation, CRM, MIS, etc) and gives a SINGLE view to the users
- The solution enables faster deployment of process change due to
  - Model driven approach to solution
  - Reusability
  - Standards based
  - Flexibility
- Faster time to market (15 days – 3 months per project)
- Business agility – adaptability and ease of use leading to increased speed of change and faster process innovation
- High productivity and scalability

The scale and complexity involved in AEGON Religare's launch of operations across 14 independent systems, in real-time, at 25 locations on Day 1 is unprecedented.

Future outlook – sustaining competitive advantage

Proposed systems planned to launch by July 2009 include:

1. A corporate intranet, which will enable users to

- Record attendance
- Log on to any system for doing their work where the access will be based on the user rights
- Get static information about the various functions of the company
- Enable each function to post their documents, messages, etc centrally
- Will be the default home page of the user whenever starting the system and will display calendar, tasks and appointments

2. Proposed re-modeling of the quote system to make it standalone
3. Development of a mobile based quote module

9. TECHNOLOGY

At AEGON Religare, there is a clear vision for not just the technology infrastructure but also for the key applications that will be developed in the first 2 years of the launch of operations. The core philosophy is:

1. Most routine activities to be automated
2. Any project delivering reduction in headcount/better self service for customer/ROI will be implemented first
3. Invest in "practical" technology and not just "latest" technology ... business benefits and lifespan of system are critical
4. Systems should be developed in J2EE (or compliant) platform except where the system involves a product purchase which is outside of the J2EE platform
5. For core policy administration and policy workflow processing, the regional platform product will be followed (e.g. Future First/Asia from CSC for core policy administration system and AWD workflow for policy processing workflow)

This focus on technology platform has resulted in the following benefits:

1. Tighter and maintainable integration between all the systems launched
2. Seamless data exchange between systems using Web services only (at least for all critical interface)
3. No major defect or issue reported from the production systems in the last 7 months (from date of launch) which is quite commendable
4. The core policy administration and agency administration systems will be hosted by the AIX servers and all other systems will be hosted on a Windows server. All other applications will have to be compatible with/run on Windows operating system.

This focus has helped AEGON Religare to host multiple applications optimally on a select number of servers, thus helping server consolidation at an early stage of company launch. This has also enabled resource hiring and effective redeployment of resources (as the platform/technology is similar). This has helped consolidating the applications amongst the select number of vendors, thereby helping vendor cost rationalization. For the core policy processing, a separate workflow based system has been deployed which is the regional platform of choice and where regional expertise can be commonly developed/deployed.

In addition to this, for every new application that is taken into consideration, a specific evaluation process is followed which begins with the requirement and its impact on business efficiency or strategic importance. This rationalizes the applications and also ensures that all stakeholders are on the same page about the requirement for an application.

The technology solution has led to the following business benefits:

- Reduced TCO – a highly scalable BPM platform that leverages existing IT investments and provides scalability
- The Portal is seamlessly integrated with multiple backend (core policy administration, agency compensation, CRM, MIS, etc) and gives a SINGLE view to users
- The solution enables faster deployment of process change due to
  - Model driven approach to solution
  - Reusability
  - Standards based
  - Flexibility
  - Faster time to market (15 days – 3 months per project)
  - Business agility – adaptability and ease of use leading to increased speed of change and faster process innovation
  - High productivity and scalability
  - Strong foundation for further process automation and innovation

10. THE TECHNOLOGY AND SERVICE PROVIDERS

Cordys

Cordys was chosen due to its expertise in Business Process Management (BPM), Rapid Application Development (RAD) and software integration. Cordys Business Operations Platform offered a model-driven approach to the development of the solution, based on standards and a single skill-set requirement, with a faster time-to-market than any other offering.

The Cordys professional services team worked in close collaboration with AEGON Religare to ensure the successful implementation and roll out of these BPM solutions, helping AEGON Religare to overcome challenges and meet their objectives and aggressive timelines. Skills and knowledge were transferred to AEGON Religare's in-house team to empower them to implement process change and further process innovation. This is an ongoing process.

About Cordys

Cordys is a global provider of software for business process innovation and Enterprise Cloud Orchestration. The industry-leading Cordys Business Operations Platform (BOP) consists of a complete suite for next generation Business Process Management (BPM), Business Activity Monitoring (BAM) and innovative SaaS Deployment Frameworks (SDF), delivering a complete Platform as a Service (PaaS) solution. It includes an open, integrated set of tools & technologies including Composite Application Framework (CAF), Master Data Management (MDM) and a SOA Grid. The Cordys platform and its cutting-edge Cloud technology empowers customers to dramatically improve the speed of change, fundamentally altering the way they innovate their Business Operations to achieve a true customer-centric philosophy. Global 2000 companies worldwide have selected Cordys to achieve business performance improvements such as increased productivity, reduced time to market, higher security and faster response to ever-changing market demands. Headquartered in the Netherlands, Cordys is a global company with offices in the USA, the UK, Germany, China, India and Israel.
www.cordys.com

Fullerton India Credit Company Limited, India

Gold Award, Pacific Rim

Nominated by Newgen Software Technologies Ltd., India

1. EXECUTIVE SUMMARY / ABSTRACT

Being a recent entrant in the retail-lending segment, Fullerton India Credit Company Limited (FICCL) plans for rapid rollout of branch network to reach a large customer base. The company's objective was to achieve lean but profit-oriented branches, reduce the turn-around-times, lower the operational costs and improve the customer experience.

Newgen offered FICCL a BPM solution based on Newgen® OmniFlowTM, which integrates with the core system, Flexcube. The solution covers the entire spectrum of loan process starting from loan initiation, de-dupe, credit verifications, deviation handling and approvals, loan booking by the back-office, and finally the loan disbursal process.

2. OVERVIEW

FICCL has two business lines, Commercial Mass Market (catering to self employed) and Retail Mass Market (catering to salaried class). FICCL provides all kinds of secured and unsecured loans to the two segments by offering various loan products suitable to the specific needs of the segments. The company planned to extend the portfolio to other financial services as well.

FICCL planned for rapid rollout of branch network to reach a larger customer base. The company's objective was to achieve lean but profit-oriented branches, reduced turn-around-times, lower cost of operations and better customer experience.

Newgen offered FICCL a BPM solution based on Newgen OmniFlow™, which integrates with the core banking system, Flexcube. The solution covers the entire spectrum of loan process starting from loan initiation, de-dupe (eliminating duplicates), credit verifications, deviation handling and approvals, loan booking by the back-office, and finally loan disbursal. The solution is integrated with a Software-As-a-Service offering for De-dupe, Customer ID generation and with Flexcube for Loan Booking. It is also integrated with another application called 'Dimension', for capturing the cash flow analysis. The solution offers comprehensive tracking and reporting of loan applications at multiple stages.

Bringing additional branches under the ambit of the solution, while ensuring performance of the system and that being done under highly squeezed time-lines is one of the major accomplishments of the project. The system is also capable of handling new business requirements, financial products and scheme launches in an agile and efficient manner.

3. BUSINESS CONTEXT

Being a recent entrant in the retail-lending segment, Fullerton India Credit Company Limited (FICCL) planned for rapid rollout of the branch network to reach a larger customer base. The company planned to open branches not only in A-class cities but also in B-class & C-class cities/towns and district headquarters.

The key focus behind the conceptualization of this project was that FICCL wanted to make every branch an independent profit center complemented by centralized operations and policy governance. This, the company envisaged, would effectively address the customer needs locally and, at the same time, help branches abide to the centralized policy guidelines and operations.

4. THE KEY INNOVATIONS

4.1 Business

The end customers for the company are people availing loans from them. Fullerton India offers financial products, which are tailor-made for the salaried individuals (Retail Mass Market), and the small-sized shop owners and entrepreneurs (Commercial Mass Market). The solution provided Fullerton India an efficient and reliable means to quickly reach out to a large number of potential customers. As the potential customer base of the company is spread across the length and breadth of India, the solution facilitated Fullerton India realizes this plan quickly.

4.2 Process

The solution automates a number of processes, some of which are as follows:

- Loan Booking Process (LBP): The Loan Booking process is initiated either directly initiated by the branch or through the input from Prospect Tracking process. After initiation, the loan application passes through various verification stages for credit approval. Once approved, the details are passed on to **Flexcube** for loan booking. In case of any exceptions the case is moved back to the relevant user who shall update the necessary details and clear the exception.

- Prospect Tracking Process (PTP): The solution also enables sales force to track their prospects efficiently and the management to gauge the effectiveness and efficiency of the sales and marketing efforts. The solution works as a precursor to the mission-critical loan process. Once the prospect has been converted, the details are moved to Loan Booking process for initiating the loan booking activity.

- Customer Referral Process: Users can refer the leads available with them to their business colleagues using the Customer Referral process. Based on the leads referred, cases are automatically assigned to Branch Managers or State Managers, who further allocates it to their subordinates.

- Early Warning Process: This process is used to reduce big-ticket defaults. Early Warning complements the Loan Initiation and Disbursement process by generating system alerts early into the system for big-ticket customers as regards their repayment capacity. Warning signals are acted upon through an escalation hierarchy structure.

- Collections Process: The Collections process enables the collection officer to enter the complete details of amount collected against the loan booked. The details entered by the collection officers are verified at Operations department.

- Once the Operations department verifies the details entered (Quality Check, Data Entry and Authorization), the solution generates a report on details of all verified collections and saves them into a folder. Flexcube uses these reports for updating the core system.

- Rural Loan Booking Process: Loan Processing at branch is handled by 'BRMFO', a customized core system developed by a third-party vendor.

Using a utility, the solution pulls all the details from BRFMO and initiates the verification of physical file. Various checklists ensure case details are verified before pushing for final processing.

- HR-DMS: At FIC, all the HR-related files were earlier saved physically at respective branches, except few important ones, which were maintained at the central location. Newgen implemented its Document Management System, OmniDocs™, to ensure all the HR documents are maintained centrally and retrieved at ease. Documents are captured and uploaded using OmniScan™. The employee master file is synchronized at regular intervals with OmniDocs™ to maintain the records of new joiners and re-signed employees.

4.3 Organization

The solution has been seamlessly integrated with the core application, Flexcube. The Flexcube integration framework enables users to complete entire transaction through uniform OmniFlowTM interface without the need to separately log into the core system. The solution also provides integration with certain other third-party modules, such as Cash Flow Analysis and Decision Tree, and leverages their capabilities through single, uniform OmniFlowTM interface.

The solution supports 1560 concurrent users, which enables a large number of users to simultaneously use the system. With the extension of network of branches, support for more number of concurrent users is planned.

5. HURDLES OVERCOME

The biggest challenge was to ensure that while opening the new branches throughout the vast geography, the branches are immediately enabled to process loans by bringing them under the ambit of the BPM solution, while ensuring performance of the system under highly squeezed timelines.

Users readily accepted the system. This was because by integrating with the Flexcube, the solution provided users the system as one integrated whole, wherein they can accomplish everything from a single interface right from entering/specifying the details, viewing document images, processing to underwriting loans.

6. BENEFITS

The biggest benefit obtained was rapid scaling up to a large number of branches (750) in a short span of 18 months.

Newgen solution offers FICCL continuous process improvement, rapid results, visibility and control to effectively manage the rapid growth in business. The major benefits accrued are as follows:

- **Reduction in end-to-end loan processing time:** FICCL has been able to sharply reduce the processing time due to optimal work distribution, immediate identification of bottlenecks and deviations, and parallel processing of loan application documents.
- **Efficient tracking of loan status and sales prospects:** Loan application and accompanying documents are efficiently managed and loan status can be easily tracked to quickly uncover and remove bottlenecks. The solution also provides FICCL's sales force agility to track the prospects.
- **Greater customer satisfaction:** Quicker end-to-end response times have lead to more satisfied customers of FICCL.
- **Tracking of Sales Prospects:** The solution helps generate 'cross-sell' and

'up-sell' opportunities for the sales force through the Prospect Tracking module and facilitates greater customer retention. Also, the system stores the history of interactions with a particular prospect, thereby ensuring a uniform experience for the prospective customer irrespective of the sales-person with whom he/she earlier interacted with.

- **Faster and informed decision-making:** Efficiency-effectiveness matrices generated from the system facilitate the top management to make the strategic decisions faster.

- **Reduced big ticket-size defaults:** The solution helps provide early warning signals for potential defaults; thereby ensuring decision could be taken well in time.

- **Cost Cuttings across the board:** The solution has resulted in reduced costs for setting up new branches and minimizing operational costs that includes document retrieval, underwriting, courier, etc.

- **Uniform user experience and reduced training needs:** The solution's tight integration, with Flexcube and other legacy & third-party modules, ensures uniform user experience throughout the process, ease of working and users being comfortable with the system without extensive training needs for geo-graphically dispersed locations. The single, uniform front-end of OmniFlow™ ensures highest level of user satisfaction.

- **Reduced bandwidth dependency:** Provision for off-line module at remote branches, where continuous network connectivity is not guaranteed, has reduced dependency on bandwidth. This has helped FICCL extend the solution to remotest of MGFL branches in southern part of the country, with further plans to implement the same for mainstream branches as well.

7. BEST PRACTICES, LEARNING POINTS AND PITFALLS

7.1 Best Practices and Learning Points

✓ *Establishing a method to provide early warning signals for potential defaults is an absolute must to ensure big-ticket defaults are avoided.*

✓ *Consistently tracking prospects opens new opportunities for cross selling and up selling*

✓ *Greater customer satisfaction, which demands immediate and informed response to their queries, is effectively implemented using a BPM solution*

✓ *A BPM solution establishes explicit and specific responsibilities with the stakeholders, thereby ensuring greater drive to accomplish work at their end.*

8. COMPETITIVE ADVANTAGES

This is one-of-its kind project in India. FICCL is growing at a rapid speed and has opened more than 750 branches across the country in a short span of around 18 months of its roll out. FICCL also has further plans to continue opening new branches at such a pace.

- Bringing additional branches under the ambit of the solution, while ensuring performance of the system and that too under highly squeezed timelines are one of the major accomplishments of the project.

- Another factor setting this project apart from other similar implementations is the use of BPM platform to build the entire Loan Origination System (LOS), which takes care of all the loan process activities e.g. Application Data Entry, Dedupe, Credit Verifications, Credit Approval, booking of loan as well as post-booking application and document tracking. BPM usage makes the process changes flexible, affordable to suite the agile business environment of FICCL. The system is capable to handle new business requirements, financial product and scheme launches in an agile and efficient manner.

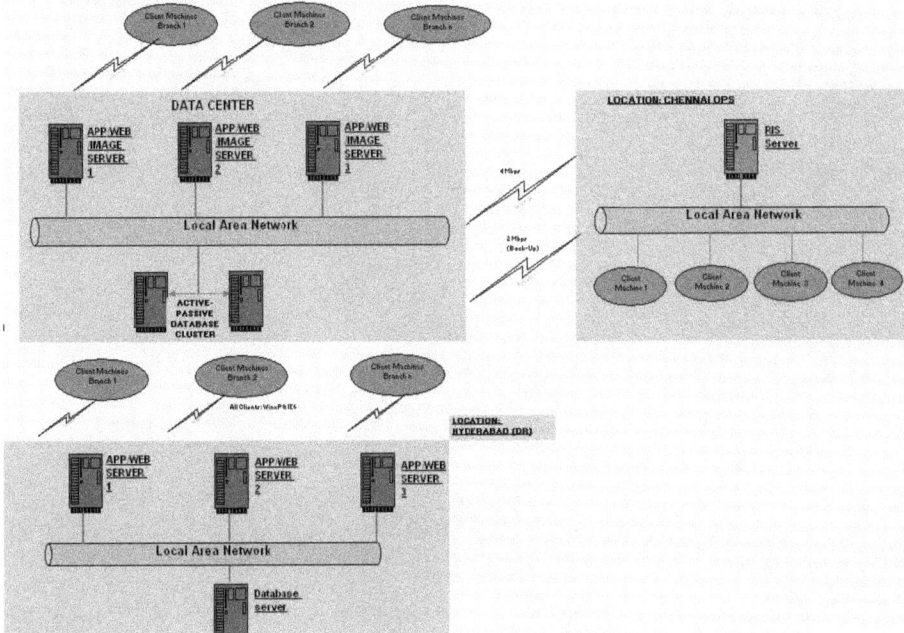

Solution Architecture Overview

9. TECHNOLOGY

The solution is built on Newgen's Business Process Management (BPM) platform, which constitutes OmniFlowTM, the workflow engine; OmniDocsTM, the Image-based Document Management System and OmniScanTM (earlier known as OmniCaptureTM), the production-grade scanning tool.

OmniFlowTM and OmniDocsTM are built using J2EE technology and use XML extensively to communicate to other systems (integration) and also within the system between different components.

Newgen BPM solution is installed on Windows 2003 Application Server. The Database used is Oracle 9i on IBM AIX server. Server-side components also include Java Transaction Server (JTS) and ODTomcat Apache web server.

The Hardware included Intel Xeon Servers for application, IBM pSeries servers for database, P4 PCs at the client side.

The Technology and Service Providers

- Newgen Software Technologies Limited. www.newgensoft.com
- Flexcel is the implementation partner to implement Flexcube (core system)

IMAN Australian Health Plans Australia

Silver Award, Pacific Rim

Nominated by Polonious Pty Ltd, Australia

EXECUTIVE SUMMARY / ABSTRACT

Australian Health Plans, a division of IMAN International Pty Ltd is a specialist provider of health plans for temporary residents working in Australia. Since 1981, the IMAN group has specialised in this niche market for health plans.

In 2004 IMAN had a problem; as their sales grew, their costs grew in proportion. Considering this, they made a strategic decision to embark on an IT improvement strategy based on implementing Open Source technology via their IT software partners Polonious Pty Ltd. Their main objective was being to control operating costs and stop costs increasing with sales as far as possible.

A side benefit of this approach has been to reduce the external systems to near zero and provide a single point of reference for all information pertaining to claims and plans within the core system. The approach has improved IMAN business processes so that their cost structure is now well below the industry average.

OVERVIEW

Polonious, IMAN outsourced IT partners have implemented open source in most areas of the operation. This diagram represents the whole-of-business view of the current IMAN 2008 implementation.

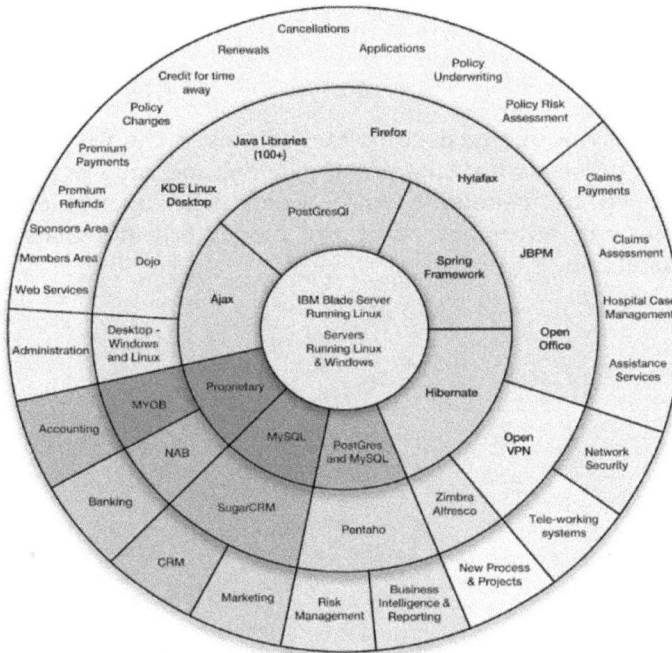

In each area of the business, the investment has been made with a view to long term productivity gains. The system depicted above has been developed for just under $1 million Australian which is a modest outlay compared with the cost of similar commercial systems.

By 2008, with the above system fully implemented, IMAN operating costs were only 40% of the health insurance industry benchmarks.

Benefits of this enterprise system are:

- Member at a glance. All Member details for Plans, Claims, CRM and accounts are presented on a page that renders in less than 1 second.
- The CRM is part of the core business application so that productivity is improved and the staff are service focused.
- Many of the lengthy documentation processes associated with plan membership and claims processing have been reduced to a click of a button.
- A comprehensive BI implementation ensures that the management team are able to review all parts of the operation from their level of interest, but drill down into the detail of data.

CHALLENGES:

With over 100,000 open source applications available, the implementation of open source software amounts to placing bets on the likely winners. After a few errors along the way we were successful in implementing the enterprise application.

BUSINESS CONTEXT

The initial state was a system built up over several years around a MS Access database supported by hundreds of spreadsheets. This became increasingly unwieldy, expensive and error prone. The driving motivation for initiating the change program was the increasingly stringent regulations introduced by the regulator the Australian Securities and Investments Commission [ASIC]. The aim was to create a single view of the enterprise within a low cost and error free environment.

THE KEY INNOVATIONS

Business

The single view of the business completely changed the way IMAN related to Members. "The person who answers the telephone answers the question". There is no need to transfer calls between departments e.g. plans and claims. This not only saves both time and money but increases Member and employee satisfaction.

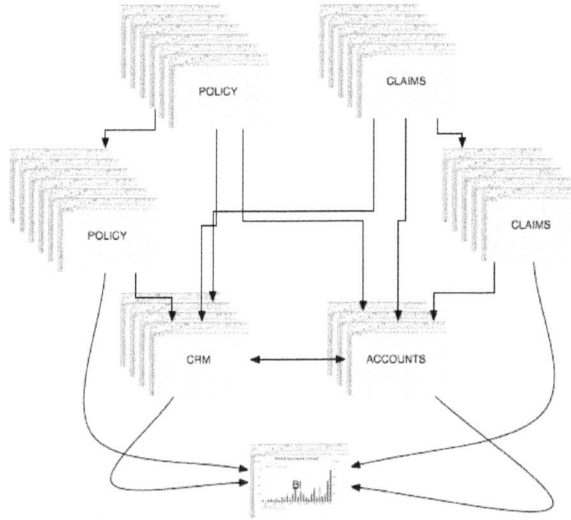

Process

This diagram shows the initial state of the IMAN business systems before the project began. Most sub-systems were actually spreadsheets or mini databases. This was symptomatic of the level of IT engagement. In an efficient IT operation, these mini-systems are part of the main application process. Not having them there means a massive error-prone task of synchronising spreadsheets and mini databases to establish the 'truth'.

Process improvements have been focused on servicing a Member request. To ensure this works well, considerable effort has been invested in functionality and performance of the main Member and Employer view. A Member's records are retrieved in less than a second and show all claims, historical plans, accounts and outstanding CRM notes at a glance. At the click of a button, Members and Employers can be emailed all their current plan certificates, claim forms, form letters of other sorts as well as templated sentences representing IMAN's policy responses on any service requests made.

The IMAN system is regularly updated ahead of legislation changes to ensure the Member records reflect current government requirements for this type of health plan. This prevents delving into sub-systems such as spreadsheets to find answers, causing delays in service.

Organisation

Prior to implementation, IMAN staff used a combination of spreadsheets, access databases and the main system to reconcile accounts, pay claims and ensure the operation kept running.

Due to the constantly changing insurance regulatory requirements combined with an insufficient IT operation, most new changes needed to be captured in office automation products such as spreadsheets rather than in the main system. This meant a 'high touch' environment for IMAN staff which lowered productivity and service levels for customers. Employees now have a total view of each Member's Plan membership and claims records from the day they joined a plan. No longer do they have to place a Member on hold or call back with information. This in turn boosts staff morale and satisfaction.

IMAN staff are now able to enter all transactions via the one common interface. Typing in a Member ID provides a 'whole-of-business' view. Transacting all common Member requirements has been reduced to a few mouse clicks. This has improved productivity and service for IMAN clients, benefiting not just the bottom line but also peace of mind of the users of the system.

This is represented in the low staff turnover rates at IMAN. When people join IMAN, they stay.

HURDLES OVERCOME

Not a problem as the CEO, with over 50 years experience starting with work on SILLIAC one of the first computers installed Australia in 1957, understood the opportunities offered by Open Source solutions.

Management

Unusually for this sort of project, there were no management hurdles to overcome.

Business

The business was ready for change and helped the process at all stages.

Organisation Adoption

The only resistance to change was with the last users losing Windows on the desktop. The final result has been a successful open source desktop deployment running at a lower cost of ownership than equivalents at other insurers.

BENEFITS

Cost savings

Overall, we know the IMAN system improvements have resulted in significant productivity improvements from these initiatives.

Percentage saved per annum

Area of Improvement	Time Saving %
Form Letter integration email and standard forms.	12.50%
Credit Card Processing	60.00%
Whole-of-Member view (30 secs to 1 sec)	12.50%
Response time improvements	20.83%

Without these savings, IMAN would not be profitable had they continued with their 2004 IT infrastructure.

Time reductions

Total Hours per annum

Area of Improvement	Original Hours per annum	New Hours per annum	Saving in Hours per annum
Form Letter integration email and standard forms.	7200	345	6855
Credit Card Processing	750	60	690
Whole-of-Member view (30 secs to 1 sec)	53997	13499	41248
Response time improvements	13499	2250	11249
Identified Savings	75446	16154	60042

INCREASED REVENUES

IMAN have experienced year-on-year premium growth of more than 40% over the last 4 years. The best year was 50%. Some of this growth is directly at attributable to the new systems and levels of service IMAN have been able to attain.

PRODUCTIVITY IMPROVEMENTS

The open source system ensures that the significant productivity improvements achieved over the last four years will continue into the future.

BEST PRACTICE AND LEARNING POINTS

Implementation

- ✓ Implement Open Source in a disciplined manner.
- ✓ Have an expert scout the field ahead before assigning significant resources to the project.

Risk Management

- ✓ Ensure you are not building into a dead end.
- ✓ Stick to recognised standards.
- ✓ Work out your exit plan should this component fail.

Budgeting and Timelines

- ✓ Expect some components to take longer to integrate commercial off-the-shelf. You are taking short term pain for the long term gain of no more silos of information.
- ✓ Trial on a small scale before committing considerable resources to the project.
- ✓ Agile methods are needed to control budget.

Pitfalls

- ✗ Open Source involves betting on likely winners. You need to support 'fast failure' if you place the wrong bet on software that does not become a market leader, and build a community base that ensures its long term survival.
- ✗ Using Linux on the desktop has meant that some printers and attachments are harder to integrate to than others. You can avoid this by picking products from companies that are 'good open source citizens'. Some companies do not issue Linux drivers or contribute enough information to the open source community to make their products useful in this state, avoid these companies if you choose this path.

Support

If you choose to implement and support the open source product, you will need to ensure that your team are good open source citizens. Contributing patches back and generally helping other open source users is a great way to get help yourself. Some companies even sponsor projects and this helps gain them kudos and assistance from open source users. For many OSS projects these days, there are known companies that can assist.

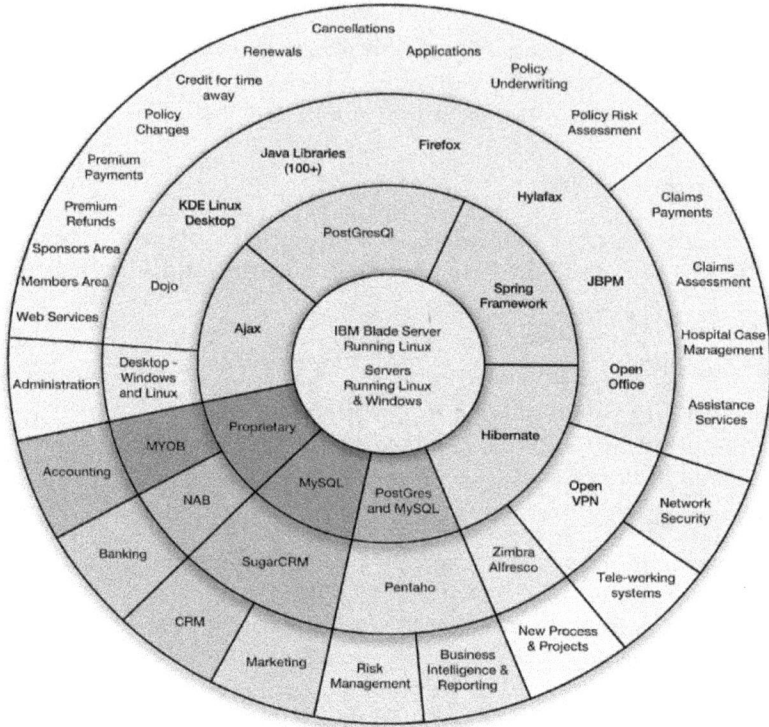

COMPETITIVE ADVANTAGE

Health plans are an error-prone industry. Our major competitive advantage is a culture of "zero errors". This is only possible with a single view of the Member. Immediate resolution of any problem is only possible when an employee has online access to all information about a Member. Today our Members are time-poor. They resent being placed on hold when they make a telephone call. They expect a seamless integration with immediate email to confirm a telephone conversation and to deliver information.

TECHNOLOGY

Open Source System Integrator and IT outsource provider: Polonious Pty Ltd
This organisation has 10 employees including 6 software engineers. They are responsible for continual improvement and the IT infrastructure at IMAN. Polonious is the company that has brought these components together into a deliverable whole. Stuart Guthrie, Director, Polonious Pty Ltd., already had 5 years open source experience prior to the service delivery at IMAN.
John Braithwaite, Owner, IMAN International Pty Ltd, Project sponsor
John has over 50 years experience starting with work on SILLIAC, one of the first computers installed in Australia in 1957. He understood the opportunities offered by Open Source solutions and also the requirements along the way.

Section 5

South and Central America

INMETRO—National Institute of Metrology, Standardization and Industrial Quality, Brazil

Silver Award, South America
Nominated by Cryo Technologies, Brazil

1. EXECUTIVE SUMMARY / ABSTRACT

Through directives which have already been named in its strategic planning, IN-METRO seeks to roll out a new process-oriented public administration model, focusing entirely on customer satisfaction and the efficiency of its processes. As an initial project, the redesign and automation of its Accreditation process, essential to guaranteeing the competitiveness of Brazilian industry, succeeded in substantially reducing the total time required to carry out this process, at the same time introducing a new paradigm for the way governmental agencies provide services in Brazil. This project's success now serves as the model for many other process automation initiatives within the organization.

2. OVERVIEW

The National Institute of Metrology, Standardization and Industrial Quality – IN-METRO is a federal agency linked to the Brazilian Ministry of Development, Industry and Foreign Trade. INMETRO's main objective is to strengthen national companies, increasing productivity through the adoption of mechanisms that improve the quality of their products and services.

One of INMETRO's main activities to achieve this objective is to plan and carry out the Accreditation process for certification organizations. Accreditation is the process of assessing and demonstrating that an organization has the technical competence necessary to carry out certification activities in the Brazilian market. This is essential to inform and protect Brazilian customers, particularly with regard to health, safety and environment.

Previously carried out by hand, each instance of this process used to take, on average, 13 months to complete, which is a long period of time when compared to similar accreditation processes in other countries, which usually take 6 to 8 months. For this reason, there was a high level of dissatisfaction among our clients seeking accreditation. Some of the difficulties we used to face were:

1 the existence of a variety of different systems to fill out the forms during the process;
2 use of paper accreditation forms;
3 a lack of information that might enable the management and control of accreditation processes by managers.

In order to resolve these issues, we adopted BPM (Business Process Management) management and technical principles. The project took six months to implement, from January to June of 2007, and was carried out by an independent consulting firm together with the INMETRO team responsible for the process. As it was carried out, we went through stages including the review, redesign and automation of the central process, creating the cultural and technological foundations for a new approach to management that was focused on customer service quality and operational efficiency.

Through this optimization, we reduced the number of activities in the process by 43%, going from 103 to 58 steps. In terms of automation, an application responsible for coordinating the process via Internet was developed, accessible by INMETRO and its clients from anywhere in the world. This application is based on Brazilian company Cryo Technologies' Orquestra BPMS (Business Process Management Software). Integrated with legacy systems, this BPM application makes it possible to trace and monitor the whole process cycle, making it possible to not only optimize costs but to make information more transparent as well.

Using only 0.025% of its annual budget, INMETRO was able to reduce its average certification organization accreditation process time by about 30%. In June 2008, only a year after beginning implementation, the process had already been reduced to 9 months.

3. BUSINESS CONTEXT

Initially, the stages of the process were controlled manually in a rudimentary manner by accreditation managers – the personnel responsible for every stage of the process. The client was required to fill out a great many paper forms and send them in by mail, along with detailed documentation. Control was carried out through individual spreadsheets, controlled by each participant. From these, dozens of analyses were made and reports were drawn up to evaluate the organization's capacity to satisfactorily carry out the proposed services. Visits and audits carried out at the organization's headquarters are, among others, mandatory activities during this process.

Information regarding the status of the internal processes needed to be gathered in a decentralized way, individually from each responsible party. This situation made managing the business and introducing improvements complicated. Moreover, it led to:

* Large volumes of paper and documents
* Difficulty in controlling the history of the processes
* Impossibility in supplying precise information and providing transparent service to the client.

With 800 processes carried out every year for a public of approximately 300 certification organizations across the country, the risk for errors and non-conformities was great. Significant delays in processes were capable of harming an entire productive sector or region of the country in need of evaluations in new segments.

4. THE KEY MOTIVATIONS

As a well-respected Brazilian entity in its field of activity, in recent administrations INMETRO has sought to reinforce its image as a model for public administration as well, seeking to apply technology and innovative processes that might be replicated, in the future, in other areas of the Brazilian Government. In this way, in recent years Inmetro's working model has been concerned with creating new managerial practices that are focused on results, customer service, quality service and process efficiency.

In 2006, during Inmetro's most recent Strategic Planning strategic objectives and performance indicators were mapped out for the coming years. Among the activities to be formally defined are those related to the development and implementation of an integrated management system concerned with the excellence of management processes.

These initiatives aim to achieve the following results:

- Reduce average time for execution of key-processes;
- Adapt to growing industry and citizen demands;
- Increase team production capacity.

The adaptation of the key-processes for Accreditation to international time, quality and team productivity parameters has shown itself to be an excellent opportunity to begin a new way of managing the organization.

The Key Innovations

It is almost universally accepted that public administration is a fundamental factor in making governmental action more efficient, aiming at improving the services it provides to citizens, and not just focusing on internal bureaucratic processes without leading to significant changes the population can feel. The adoption of BPM has come to provide Inmetro with a greater ability to generate concrete results for society and create the ideal conditions to gauge, in a significant way, the performance of the services we provide.

4.2 Business

During the execution of the project, we could see the great effort all those involved put into building awareness about the individual importance of each participant's work in the search to meet goals and improve the services we provide. Considering the fact that the Accreditation process is both extremely collaborative and quite complex, participation of most of the operating team during the mapping and redesign phase was essential in improving group work quality and everybody's commitment to the organization's strategic planning.

This intense participation made it possible for the *status quo* to be questioned and modified. Not only was the activity flowchart altered, but all norms, regulations and procedures were revised, one by one, aiming to make them leaner and increase efficiency.

By making the BPM software available online via Internet, clients also began to take part in the process, receiving and carrying out activities. As well as being able to follow the progress of their requests online, they also came to play an indispensable part in carrying out the process and achieving the goals.

4.3 Process

In simple terms, INMETRO's Accreditation macro process is made up of the following stages:

4 Service request
5 Documentation analysis
6 Evaluation of client facilities and structure
7 Evaluation of the organization's performance and competence in its activities
8 Final Decision - the General Accreditation Coordinator decides on granting accreditation or not by analyzing the results of previous stages.

Initially, these five stages were mapped out into approximately 103 activities, practically all manual and carried out by INMETRO's in-house team. Nine process managers and five administrative assistants were responsible for carrying them out, while end client contact was carried out over the telephone, by e-mail and conventional mail. Dozens of computer spreadsheets and paper forms were annexed to the process, in a procedure that physically involved many folders and digitally, a variety of different, disconnected systems.

With the roll out of the BPMS, it was possible to reduce the total number of activities to 58. A few of these were automated and many others were simply eliminat-

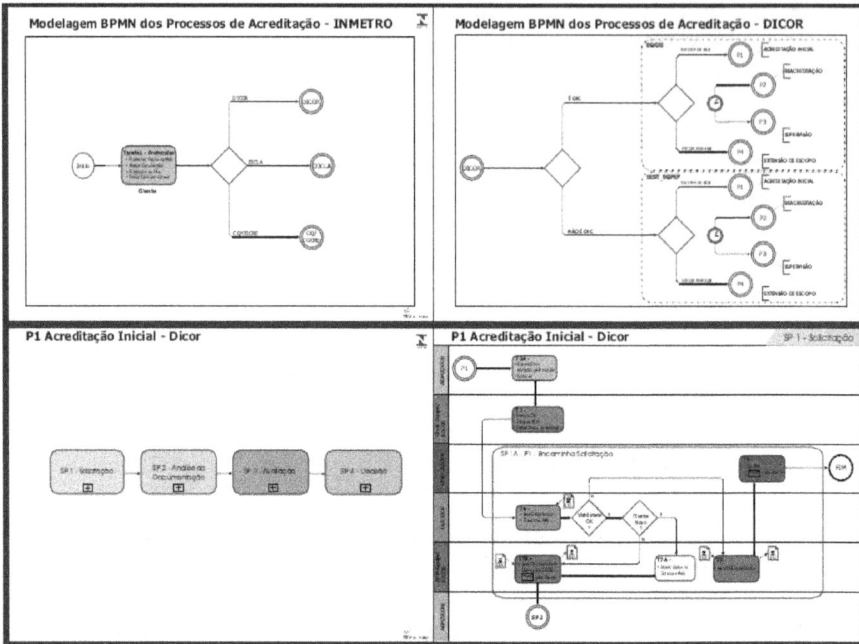

ed, in a great effort to reduce bureaucracy. In general, the activities that were automated were manual tasks, which had involved retyping information.

Picture – Drawing of the new part of the flowchart

After rolling out the technological platform, clients began issuing their requests from directly within the BPMS. Any company can request a BPMS access password and fill out the digital request form, which consists of approximately 100 fields of information. However, because of Brazilian legislation and the criticality of the process, several legal documents from the organizations must be sent. What is innovating is that now these documents can be sent in a computer for-

mat to INMETRO. Once a request has been submitted, the INMETRO team immediately begins to analyze the information.

Picture – Computer-based form (web) for submitting a new process.

The work is done using a simple, intuitive interface, giving special attention to the list of pending activities. Each step of the process which is begun will begin a se-

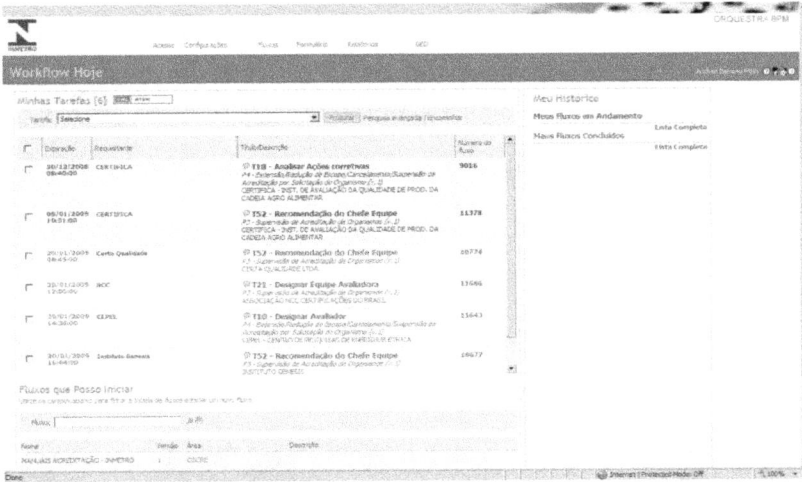

quence of activities with their given responsible parties and predetermined deadlines needing to be carried out.

Picture – List of tasks for a participant in the process

During the nine months that follow, our clients can monitor, at any time of the day or night, the current status of the process, as well as foresee the next activities that will need to be carried out.

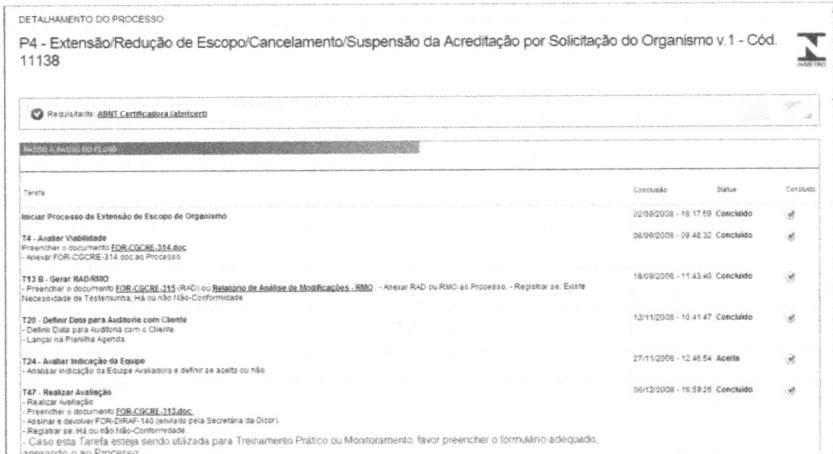

Picture – Clients monitor the process step by step

At the same time, Inmetro's managers now have access to performance indicators and reports, and will be able to immediately take corrective action and intervene in processes which may eventually encounter problems.

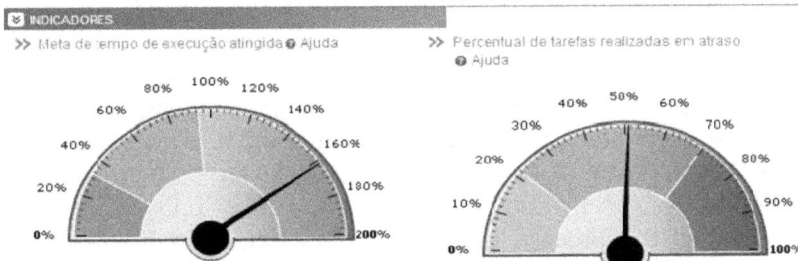

Picture – Manager monitoring performance indicators

4 - Índice de Tarefas em Tempo , nos processos Concluídos e em Andamento, por Tarefa, e tempo Médio por Tarefa, em dias

ATOR	CONCLUÍDO Total de atividades	CONCLUÍDO Atividades em tempo	CONCLUÍDO Atividades atrasado	CONCLUÍDO Tempo médio em dias	CONCLUÍDO Índice de Atividades em tempo	ANDAMENTO Total de atividades	ANDAMENTO Atividades em tempo	ANDAMENTO Atividades atrasado	ANDAMENTO Índice de Atividades em tempo
P1 - SP 3E - P1 - Encaminhar Diárias e Passagens	1	0	1	5	0.0%	1	1	0	100.0%
P1 - T1.1 - Corrigir Dados do Formulário	0	0	0	0		9	7	2	77.8%
P1 - T10 - Designar Avaliador	4	1	3	0	25.0%	12	4	8	33.3%
P1 - T11 - Aceitar Indicação de Avaliador	3	1	2	5	33.3%	11	4	7	36.4%
P1 - T12 - Aceitar Avaliador	3	1	2	1	33.3%	9	4	5	44.4%
P1 - T13 A - Avaliar Necessidade de Memo	6	2	4	14	33.3%	8	7	1	87.5%
P1 - T13 B - Gerar RAD/RMO	13	3	10	43	23.1%	26	25	1	96.2%
P1 - T14A - Preparar Memo e Encaminhar Junto com Documentos	7	7	0	6	100.0%	3	1	2	33.3%
P1 - T14B - Assinar Memo e Enviar à PROGE	3	1	2	1	33.3%	3	1	2	33.3%
P1 - T15 - Registrar Parecer da PROGE	3	3	0	25	100.0%	3	2	1	66.7%
P1 - T16 - Registrar Não-Conformidade da Análise da Documentação	4	0	4	0	0.0%	3	1	2	33.3%
P1 - T17 - Enviar Ações Corretivas	9	0	9	1	0.0%	1	0	1	0.0%
P1 - T18 - Analisar Ações corretivas	11	2	9	2	18.2%	1	1	0	100.0%
P1 - T2 A - Aguardar Chegada da Documentação via Correios / Scanner	5	1	4	13	20.0%	30	3	27	10.0%
P1 - T20 - Definir Data para Auditoria com Cliente	10	9	1	55	90.0%	2	1	1	50.0%
P1 - T21 - Designar Equipe Avaliadora	2	0	2	1	0.0%	2	1	1	50.0%
P1 - T22 - Avaliar Indicação de Equipe	1	0	1	0	0.0%	2	1	1	50.0%
P1 - T24 - Avaliar Indicação da Equipe	1	0	1	0	0.0%	1	0	1	0.0%
P5 - T25 A - Emitir FAU	1	0	1	0	0.0%	1	0	1	0.0%
P1 - T25 B - Emitir PCD	1	0	1	0	0.0%	1	0	1	0.0%
P1 - T26 - Aprovar FAU	1	1	0	1	100.0%	2	0	2	0.0%
P1 - T28 - Aprovar FAU (Testemunha)	0	0	0	0		1	1	0	100.0%
P1 - T27 - Corrigir FAU	0	0	0	0		1	0	1	0.0%
P1 - T29 - Gerar GRU	1	1	0	35	100.0%	1	1	0	100.0%
P1 - T29 - Gerar GRU (Testemunha)	0	0	0	0		1	1	0	100.0%
P1 - T3 - Designar TA e ADM Equipe - Prazo Avaliação	6	1	5	2	16.7%	25	6	19	24.0%
P1 - T30 - Elaborar Plano de Avaliação	1	1	0	13	100.0%	1	0	1	100.0%
P1 - T31 - Realizar Logística da Avaliação	1	0	1	0	0.0%	1	0	1	0.0%
P1 - T32 - Realizar Avaliação	3	2	1	29	66.7%	1	0	1	0.0%
P1 - T33 - Emitir Relatório de Viagem	1	1	0	3	100.0%	1	0	1	0.0%
P1 - T38 - Registrar Não-Conformidades (Escritório)	0	0	0	0		1	0	1	0.0%
P1 - T39 - Enviar Ações Corretivas (Escritório)	0	0	0	0		1	1	0	100.0%
P1 - T39 - Enviar Ações Corretivas (Testemunha)	0	0	0	0		1	1	0	100.0%
P1 - T4 - Avaliar Viabilidade	13	10	3	55	76.9%	21	10	11	47.6%

Picture – Manager monitoring reports

Process Design

From the beginning, it was known that, after the redesign stage, the Accreditation would be implemented through BPM software. Thus, the entire design stage concentrated on – besides achieving an optimized model for the process – surveying flows and information, aiming towards automation. To this end, the choice was made to use BPMN (Business Process Modeling Notation). This notation system, aside from being widely used, is also the standard notation system for the chosen BPM software. As this was INMETRO's first project, it was decided to start with a reduced number of the BPMN's elements, making it easier to use and understand.

The first impact that automation has on a process like this is on the level of detail that is to be worked. End users have a tendency to go down to the procedural level during the description of their activities, while with automation we need to work with the flowchart on a more macro level, more software oriented. This difference in vision was a frequent subject of discussion for the project team.

In the end, an architecture composed of four interconnected processes was decided upon, all related to Accreditation but carried out at different moments in the life of the client:

- Initial Accreditation
- Reaccreditation
- Extension of the process scope
- Supervision

All of the processes make up the Accreditation macro-process and are carried out in logical order, though at different times.

4.4 Organization

Decreasing the number of manual activities helped our team stay focused on the main tasks in the accreditation process - those involved in evaluating the organization. Parallel controls and many administrative tasks were eliminated, reducing mistakes and rework.

With the roll-out of the process management system, accreditation managers began to play a fundamental role in achieving our sector's goals - they began to truly manage the process, instead of just trying to monitor it through spread-sheets. At the same time, the accreditation department's head manager was able to dedicate him/herself to fewer operational activities. Their focus was no longer on solving specific problems, but on more holistic control of the service provided, always looking towards innovation and improvement.

However, the idea for a BPM Center of Excellence is still under construction. The knowledge acquired by the project team is, as we will see in the pages to come, being shared with other departments within the organization. A centralized corporate governance and BPM best practices team is slowly but steadily being put together.

5. HURDLES OVERCOME

Management

From the beginning, automation of the Accreditation process relied on the full support of INMETRO's top management, including the support and sponsorship of the President. Still, initial difficulties in the implementation of this new technology and new paradigm were apparent. The managers did not understand how the BPM worked and most learning happened on-the-fly. The answer was to carry out many process tests and simulations, at times involving those end clients with which we have a closer relationship. This made is possible to identify new possibilities for improvements as well as helping to improve users' opinions of the new software.

Business

One of the greatest challenges the project team confronted was reconciling significant changes in the process with strict national and international laws and regulations regulating certification activities and public institutions. For example, Brazilian legislation requires many documents and official reports to be stored in print, with the signature of the responsible manager, for a minimum of five years. The use of digital signatures has yet to be adopted by the Brazilian Government, and though an attempt was made, it was not possible to obtain the use of this resource for this project.

One of the solutions adopted was to postpone the printing and signing of these documents as much as possible. In this way, many documents are digitally attached to the process and are only printed out and signed at the end of the process. This prevents the paper documents from slowing the procedure down.

At the same time, support from top management made it possible to add flexibility to and revise many internal norms. We were able to cull the number of internal procedures discussing Accreditation from 38 to 18.

Organization Adoption

Considering that the automated process would come to be used as much by INMETRO's in-house team as it would by the organization's clients, another huge challenge was in promoting adoption of the software by such a large public. Since clients can request different accreditation processes (with different scope) over time, the majority were already used to the process and its previous procedures.

Regarding the internal public, the strategy was to involve them whenever possible from the very beginning of the redesign stage. As they helped to shape and improve the process, the entire internal public became acquainted with the new reality from early on.

As for the external public – the clients – these received training through seminars and presentations at industry events about the new technology and the new process. BPMS user manuals were also made available on INMETRO's own website, besides tests carried out with our closer clients.

6. Benefits

6.1 Cost Savings and Increased Revenues

Traditional models for measuring performance based on cost reduction and increased revenue are not directly applicable to INMETRO and the Accreditation process. As a public agency which is strategically important to Brazilian industrial development and market policies, the greatest challenge is in meeting, in a satisfactory and competitive way, demands from Brazilian society and industry in its realms of activity.

It is clear that reducing the number of activities in the process, the number of procedures and errors all have an important impact on the total cost of the process. Still, in the case of an organization where the main goal is centered on customer service and the service provided, basic cost savings are quickly reinvested in improving team training and improving infrastructure for conducting daily work.

Time Reduction

Certainly this project's most important objective, the results so far obtained in this regard were extremely satisfactory. We achieved our goal to reduce the average time for certification organization accreditations by 30%. Whereas in 2007 the average time for accreditation was 13 months, it is currently 9 (nine) months.

By the end of 2009 it is expected that the average time for certification organization accreditation will be reduced 50% in comparison with January 2007. This will lead to a status which is equal to or better than the majority of developed countries which have similar Accreditation processes. This will certainly be an important strategic advantage for our economy.

6.3 Improvements in Productivity

Our users can see a great difference in work done in an optimized job supported on a workflow platform. Each morning, the software tells each member of the group what they have to do (their list of activities) and what is most important to do (the priorities). Parallel controls, spreadsheets, databases in Access: these are all things of the past. The team can concentrate on those activities that add value to the process instead of wasting time on administrative and bureaucratic procedures. The number of telephone calls with clients has decreased, as they no longer need to call in to know the status of their process. The number of mistakes and rework has been reduced: the software validates the information entered into the process and certifies that everything is in order; the amount of information has itself decreased: revision of the process made an overall simplification of operations possible.

7. Best Practices, Learning Points and Pitfalls

7.1 Best Practices and Learning Points

Among the main best practices that could be observed during the implementation of the BPM project are:

- ✓ *Great effort during the process redesign stage was essential to the project's success. The initial version's flow was so large, complex and bureaucratic that integrating it into the BPMS in this state would be a great risk and might have a negative effect on the final cost of implementation.*
- ✓ *Support from management and top management was essential to guiding the project. Not only was it possible to question the status quo, it was also possible*

to overcome initial resistance and cultural barriers that might otherwise have been difficult to overcome;

✓ During the roll out, it was seen that the client, an integral part of the process, represented a separate challenge. With different profiles and realities, they would need to access the BPMS and carry out part of the work within the new system. Thus, it was crucial to simplify the software's screens as much as possible, leaving only essential information. Publicity at events and seminars were important in training a public that was spread out across the country;

✓ Correctly establishing end user expectations is a priority activity. Considering how out of step the technology had been, initially there were great expectations related to the resolution of a series of the organization's problems that were simply not part of the project's scope. It was always necessary to clarify the characteristics of a project of limited scope and function.

7.2 Pitfalls

The greatest pitfalls experienced during the project might be summarized as:

✗ Use of BPMN notation during the modeling stage was a challenge, due to the lack of end user experience with the notation system. In spite of having only used one, quite simplified subset of the notation system, users who had never been in contact with the methodology had a certain level of difficulty in understanding it, and as a result, the process as a whole. For the projects to come, seminars and trainings are being held on BPMN before consulting is done. A simpler initial alternative to BPMN is also being sought;

✗ The IT infrastructure department was not involved from the beginning of the project. After the initial usage of the software, technical obstacles were encountered and this initial distance made it difficult to find a quick solution to make an appropriate server available;

✗ Integration with legacy applications was very difficult, owing to security policies and to the legacy systems' being out of date. At the same time, internal users had the wrong expectations about several of the integration processes that, in the end, were not able to be developed for technical questions related to the existing platform.

8. COMPETITIVE ADVANTAGES

The roll out of this project and its automation software represents a revolution for the field of Brazilian accreditation. We are not only equaling our peers in other countries, but in many cases, surpassing them. INMETRO's automation in this area is strategically advantageous to our country's development, contributing significantly towards the improvement of the products we manufacture and sell in Brazil and export abroad. That strengthens our industry, our market and our consumers.

The usage of process management at INMETRO is taking on large dimensions. After automation of the Accreditation process, at the moment at least four other large scale redesign and automation projects are being carried out in other key INMETRO departments. In all cases, the Accreditation project has served as an example for teaching the managers in other departments. Above all, its success can be seen in the day-to-day contact with more satisfied clients and the possibility to truly manage the process, always finding opportunities for improvement. The Accreditation process is now entering into a routine of revision and periodic reflection. For the first semester of this year, a new, even more optimized version is set to be implemented.

Long-term plans to maintain competitive advantage

With the expansion of the project to other departments, now INMETRO is seeking to consolidate what was learned from the projects and from the best practices found in each department. Top management has already selected a team that will act, on the medium term, as a department of BPM excellence. This team will not necessarily intervene in the rules of the key department processes, but it will be generating best practices and maintaining knowledge on BPM.

INMETRO's goal on the medium term is for this department to also be trained in developing new BPM projects, without the direct support of external consulting firms.

9. TECHNOLOGY

We chose INMETRO for its usage of Cryo Technologies' "Orquestra BPMS". Cryo Technologies is a Brazilian company and its product was completely developed with domestic technology. Among the factors which led to the choice of this product are:

- Manufacturer located nearby;
- Product focus on human, collaborative processes;
- Microsoft platform, the same already in use by INMETRO;
- 100% web nature.

This last characteristic was essential to the project's success, since both the participants in the process and INMETRO itself are geographically dispersed across Brazil, a country of continental proportions. Regarding the technology architecture, Orquestra is currently integrated with other INMETRO corporate systems in such a way as to facilitate activity automation. Among these, we can mention the RECEITA (Finance) system and SIDOC (DMS). Regarding the characteristics of the hardware and software used in arriving at a solution, the following information:

Software:

Category	Model	Version
OS	Windows	2003
DB	SQL SERVER	2000
BPMS	Orquestra BPM	2.0

Hardware:

Category	Configuration
Processor	2 CPU
RAM	4 GB
MB	512 GB

10. THE TECHNOLOGY AND SERVICE PROVIDERS

Cryo Technologies' Orquestra BPM suite is award-winning software focused in human-centric BPM (Business Process Management), providing a complete set of tools to manage the entire process life-cycle. Orquestra BPM is helping leading South American organizations in both the private and public sectors to achieve greater control over and transparency in their primary business process, with cost reductions and better overall performance. Orquestra BPM is 100% web-based and empowers business analysts to design, automate, execute, monitor and optimize their business process, at great development speeds and a lower cost, using innovative and user-friendly features. Contact: www.cryo.com.br

ISAPRE Microsystem, Chile

Finalist, South America
Nominated by PECTRA, USA

EXECUTIVE SUMMARY / ABSTRACT

A process has been worked out allowing the ISAPRE - private institutions which capture workers' compulsory contribution payment and provide 18% of the Chilean population with their service – **to electronically manage audit processes of health affidavits.** This process is tailored according to the needs of each organization and exhibits **integration on two levels:** BPM solution integration with other components of documentary management and integration with each particular client's applications.

The developed solution offers innovations and benefits on a business level, in processes and in marketing models: It joins users from the entire national territory together, integrates applications on a unique virtual desktop, and is brought to the market under the **Software as a Service** modality. The latter has only been operating since May 2008 and already achieved the following:

- 35% of the ISAPREs in Chile are utilizing the service (including the country's biggest company for pre-paid medicine: **Banmedica, Consalud**).
- 1,460 active users.
- 20,000 processed transactions (DPS, for its letters in Spanish, health affidavits) every month.
- National coverage (Chile).
- Permanent traceability of the process, stages, people in charge, time.
- Reduction in the process length: before the implementation it took 3 work days; after the process automation it takes just one work day.

OVERVIEW

A process has been worked out allowing the ISAPRE - private institutions which capture workers' compulsory contribution payment and provide 18% of the Chilean population with their service – to electronically manage audit processes of health affidavits. Those processes are an exclusionary requirement when subscribing a health contract and form the basis of the ISAPRE business.

The developed process is modified according to each organization, the company structure, the profile of each user and the inherent tasks to each function. Those elements interact with each client's own applications; hence the developed solution exhibits integration on two levels: BMP solution integration with other components of documentary management to develop the mentioned process, and a second level of integration corresponding to solutions with every client's applications in particular.

The developed solution offers innovations and benefits on a business level, in processes and in marketing models: It joins users from the entire national territory together, integrates applications on a unique virtual desktop, and is brought to the market under the Software as a Service modality. The latter allows approaching the market with the BMP philosophy, offering great competitive advantages: Reduction of costs concerning licenses and void initial payments, flexibility in handling, purchasing and adapting the process in regard to the client's conditions, and the best possible management of identity and network access.

The process implementation has only been in use since May 2008 and has already achieved the following:

Metrics

- 35% of the ISAPREs in Chile are utilizing the service (including the country's biggest company for pre-paid medicine: **Banmedica. Consalud**).
- 1,460 active users.
- 20,000 processed transactions (DPS) every month
- National coverage (of Chile, spanning over more than 4,000 km from north to south)
- Permanent traceability of processes, stages, people in charge, time.
- Reduction in the process length: before the implementation it took 3 work days; after the process automation it takes just one work day

Business Context

At present the Republic of Chile retains a miscellaneous health system. The institutions of social insurance (ISAPRE) were set up in 1981, initiating one of the most significant changes in the sector, which was fully controlled by the state. This allowed private administration of workers' compulsory contribution payments, which currently manages 18% of the contribution (representing the total profit 2007 according to a balance of 1,600 million dollars).

The ISAPREs, tied to the regulations of market freedom and open health plans, are constantly seeking to increase benefits in order to provide the population with the best possible health service. Despite great advancements in legacy systems and the personal productivity in registering carried out activities, there used to be an area in the management of the ISAPREs which had not been automated. The process sets off when a client intends to activate himself within the organization until closure of this event.

All actions linked to this process are carried out based on present deeds, movements and exchange of ample physical documentation, committee dialogue, event registration in isolated systems and a high number of additional dealings. Just when registered, the clients entered into the world of digital management.

The manual process, which can be referred to as commercial pre-sale and control of health approval, was developed in a casual management setting, under little control and with minor optimization, and possibly under loss of commercial opportunities, without any vision on a systemic level within the organization and the business as a whole.

There was an obvious need for systematic and agile automation, control and management of this process. That's why a technological solution has been developed which - centered in a BMP solution - integrates applications functionalities for documentary management. This allows us to automate and to add value to the process. An innovative way of offering the service was found, based on a high growth trend: The Software as a Service modality.

Software as a Service is an evolution of traditional software models, which combines the main benefits of three different schemes: Client software, server software and online services. It represents a significant challenge: The PECTRA Technology Department of Research and Development identified this trend amongst those that are experiencing the highest growth rates on a global level. It is estimated that in the year 2011 a fourth of all business application offers for companies will be distributed under the Software as a Service modality. This trend will quickly transform the software market.

As the ISAPREs are required to offer more and better services, automating the process of commercial pre-sale and approval audit, and SaaS´s growth is uphold with its assumed benefits, it has been decided to implement the described process under the following main objectives:

Functional objectives

- Attaining a follow-up of electronic documents and images from the entry of a prospect in the branch or agency until the adoption of a resolution.
- Controlling time and state of a case in each stage of the process.
- Optimizing response time to clients and prospects.
- Optimizing commercial opportunities.
- Managing the entire process online on a national level.

Commercial objectives

- Offering the possibility to outsource non-client process automation with effective costs. This applies for savings in licensing as well as in hardware requirements. Reducing costs and investment risks.
- Making software incorporation more accessible. The client pays the cost per user and only for the time he actually uses the service, with no initial payments.
- Simplifying as much as possible the phase of software implementation. With the software situated on external servers, it is immediately available to the client.
- Offering flexibility to the user: It is possible to sign off at any time without being tied to initial investment in licenses or hardware.
- Decreasing client's costs for IT resources, as it is not necessary to have a specialized area for system support, functioning and performance.
- Offering improvements and updates for management applications, streamlining usability, functionality, performance and design.

THE KEY INNOVATIONS

Business

Regarding the impact on the ISAPRE business, there are three main innovations described below:

- Management of the commercial pre-sale process and health audit control.
- Integration of productive-operational processes in a single framework: virtual desktop.
- Utilization of the process as a service.
- Management of the commercial pre-sale process and health audit control.
- Based on the recent options new information technology provides as regards digital processing of documents, computer processes integration and process-flow automation, this project allowed optimizing time of registration. It also made fraud prevention more efficient by automating the medical certification process, a fundamental part of the ISAPREs' registration process.

In this respect, the process combines various profiles, which are physically distributed along the 4,000 km spanning from the north to the south of Chile.

Amongst them:

Profiles considered in the process	
Sales executives	They initiate the process, register the case and scan it at the branch.
Sales Supervisors	They do a first review of the events the sales executives of their group have entered (cost center).
Medical Controlling	It audits the case either to approve or dismiss it. Within the process the case might come back inquiring further evidence.
System Users	Consultancy tasks, reports, management, etc.

These profiles are incorporated through the following business model:

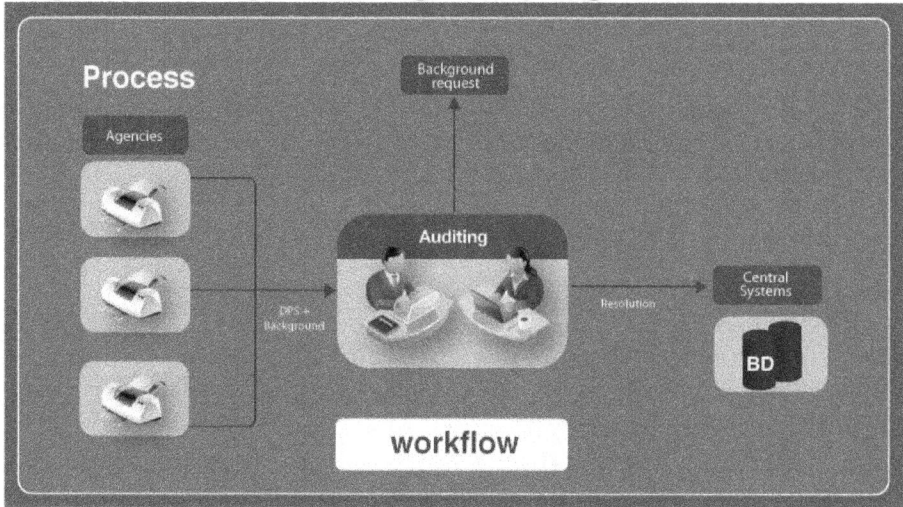

Additionally to the former, the solution is utterly transformed into a registration system built on company knowledge and the automated process is turned into an integration link with the Business Intelligence platforms.

Those are provided by the ISAPREs in order to achieve complete reports on sales success, quality process in sales production, productivity and several configured variables. Integration of productive-operational processes in a single framework—virtual desktop. A second innovation level is related to productive-operational processes. Apart from automating a great part of the productive activities entered within the process of account activation (clients, payments and others), the new solution is prone to integration within a single working framework – the virtual desktop – which assembles the actions that were previously supported by administrative procedures and the access to the company's multiple information systems.

This trend towards working desktop virtualization carries various advantages for the organization. Amongst others:

- Maximum utilization of available resources. Fast response in view of changes under demand.
- Business continuity and recovery in view of disasters. In case of physical system failure, included logical systems can be dynamically allocated to other systems.
- Scalability. Agile growth with cost mitigation.

- Improvement of service levels.
- Boosting business agility.

This second innovation level, connected with application virtualization and integration in a single working desktop, works together with the third central innovation, which is identified in relation to the impact on the ISAPRE business; the way of using the process as a service.

Utilization of the process as a service.

The offer of service modality frees the client from dealing with platforms of technological support and their latter adjustment and maintenance within the organization, which are related to complex technological products that go beyond the client's competence. The core concern of the implementation project consists of knowing and reformulating business processes considering the aptitude of these new techniques which allow the ISAPREs:

- To outsource automation and optimization of their commercial pre-sale process and of the audit of health affidavits at low cost and without initial investment.
- To customize the process according to their needs and integrate it into pre-existing applications.
- To improve operational agility, provide better service and maintain a high satisfaction level amongst users.
- To turn process-related tasks into virtual services, which are centrally managed and administrated but used and executed in situ and on demand.

PROCESS

A process has been worked out allowing the ISAPRE to electronically manage audit processes of health affidavits. This process is tailored according to the needs of each organization and exhibits integration on two levels; BPM solution integration with other components of documentary management and integration with each particular client's applications.

Condition previous to process automation

The activities linked to the commercial pre-sale process and the audit of health affidavits previous to process automation are characterized as follows:

- 100% manual activities. Attended deeds, extensive physical documentation movements and exchanges.
- Event records in isolated systems.
- Incongruent data.
- Delays in the process caused by geographic diversity; the process was initiated in Chile and the documentation material had to be shifted over long distances to get through all stages of authorization.
- Loss of documentation material as a consequence of various and extended regional journeys.
- Informal management.
- High rate in loss of commercial opportunities.
- Inconsistent criteria of approval, as it depended on regional audits each with their own separate criteria.

Implemented process

The implemented process optimizes and automates approval activities in the commercial flow, efficiently controls the queries for each task, substantially improves the organizations' productivity, digitalizes 100% of the documents implied and does not require the physical presence of auditors from all over the country.

The main characteristics and functionalities of the process are:

Characteristics and Functionalities	
Multiformat	Supports incoming paper images/electronic documents
Document administration	Reception, digitalization, indexation of corporate documents (reception/income). Enclosed documents.
Storage	Electronic storage of documents
Web-based	Operates over intranet web applications to manage the different flows.
System integration	Integration of the organization's diverse systems (e.g. ERP, etc.)
Data collection	Automatic information entry into external systems.
User administration	The solution allows defining and personalizing users and attributes.
Assignment of workload	Assignment of documents to users via the inbox.
Views	In their workstation the users visualize the images from the documents on which they can perform an action. They can consult the "folder" the client has defined, which contains their enclosed documents.
Control and follow-up	The solution makes each document's state and each action permanently available and maintains a historic record of them (variables: Document, time, status, and user).
Warnings	The solution provides the users with e-mail notifications, communicating current workload and delayed tasks.
Management control reports	Several variables such as: Statistics per process, per area, per user, etc.

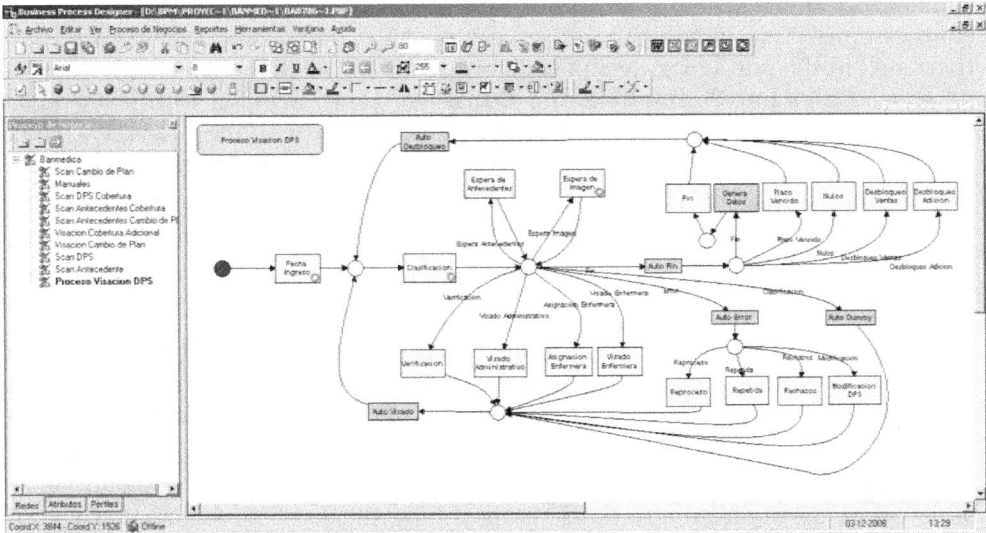

ARCHITECTURE

The general architecture of the solution is displayed below, making clear that in the case of the client **Banmedica** the solution is directly connected with the client's Oracle database. In the case of the client **Consalud** it is connected via web services.

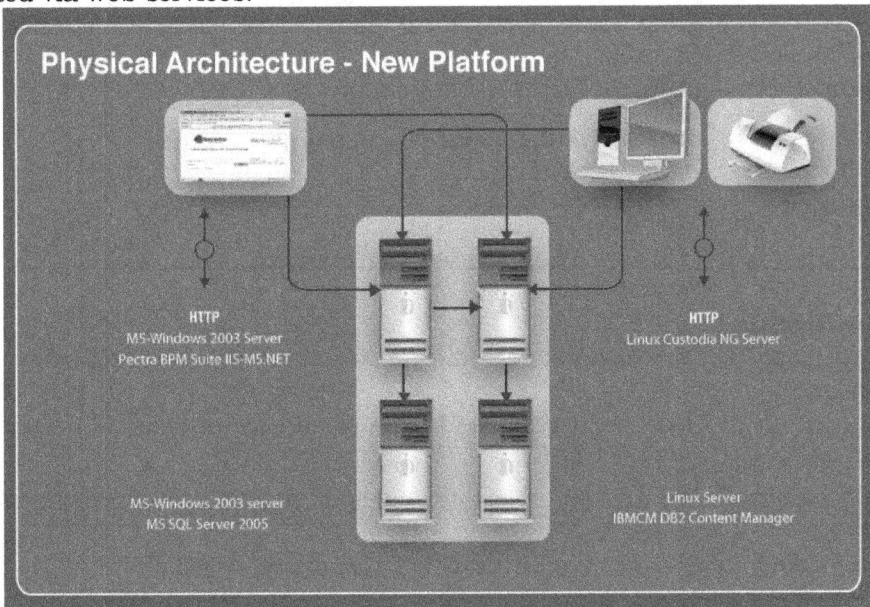

Organization

The impact on the organization has been significant, as the scheme has made a turn from a completely manual to a 100% digital one, comprising defined and controlled activities, time and people in charge. This has implied a great cultural change in the commercial areas, in which tasks and resources are currently being managed thoroughly, neatly and united within the entire national territory.

The process implementation has also deduced a radical change in the working habits of the ISAPREs, when offering new metrics of business intelligence. Acquiring centralized management information in order to take decisions and to plan commercial and marketing strategies and actions is one of the solution's main contributions. This is the general impact on all clients using the service. Furthermore, in the particular case of each organization, there are specific impacts to be seen, such as at **Banmedica** and **Consalud** where working with a regionally audited scheme has been replaced with a centralized working modality, which was considered a significant structural reorganization of the company.

The impact on business in terms of quantifiable benefits referring to time and cost reduction and to billing and productivity increase are shown in paragraph 6 "Benefits".

HURDLES OVERCOME

In general, the development of the project was successful and did not cause any significant problems. The developed process is offered as a service and is later tailored for each client according to their schemes of particular functioning.

In all implementations, there is a strong Change Management strategy, an accompanying cultural change, which entails the implementation of the solution on all levels of the organization. Particularly during the project of Consalud special emphasis was placed on this point, as in this account the implementation was accompanied by a significant reorganization that needed the support of a solid internal communication and awareness campaign.

BENEFITS

As an introduction all the ISAPREs that are currently using the service are described, including the most important company for pre-paid medicine of Chile (BANMEDICA): Main Clients

Banmedica	The country's biggest company for pre-paid medicine. 800 users in the DPS process. 10,000 DPS processed every month. www.banmedica.cl.
Consalud	Pre-paid medicine. 600 users. 10,000 DPS processed every month. www.consalud.cl

Cost Savings

Banmedica, Consalud	Average cost per transaction USD 1. 80% cost reduction.
General Process	Cost reduction due to loss or damage of physical documentation: 100%.

Cost reduction due to loss of opportunities / lack of process traceability: 100%.

Reduction of travel expenses (physical documentation): 100%.

Reduction of fraud risk: 80%.

Reduction of printing costs for physical documentation: 100%.

Time Reductions

Banmedica, Consalud	Reduction of total process execution time: 350% reduction. Before: 3 days / Present: Carried out within hours.
General Process	DPS approval: Reduction: 300%. Before: 1 day / Present: Minutes.

Access to centralized and online information from any place in the country.

Before: Delays in receiving physical documentation.

Increased revenues

General Process — Increase in number of commercial opportunities as a consequence of efficient management.

Productivity improvements

General Process — 100% electronic documents.

Reduction of unproductive time periods: 300%.

Centralized auditing. Before: Regional with their own criteria. Merge of approval criteria: 100%.

Fast error correction.

Improvement of action, people in charge and time control: 100% growth. Automatic control.

Permanent traceability of the process.

BEST PRACTICES

The process development has been carried out under international quality standards, such as ISO 9000 and PMI. The methodology measures guiding the project were the following:

Phase 1: Development of the business workflow

- Activities:
- Achievement of a flow diagram
- Validation of the proposed model
- Requirement gathering and analysis
- Requirement validation
- Defining profiles, flows, entities, documents, attachments, entry and exit formats
- Definitions of integration with the legacy system

Phase result

- Progress Report Phase 1

Phase 2: Implementation and tests

Activities:

- Enabling the platform
- Document configuration and parameterization
- Development of user tests
- Comparing obtained results
- Tests end
- Production start-up

Phase result

- Conclusion Report Phase 2

COMPETITIVE ADVANTAGES

The implementation of this process grants the ISAPREs a series of competitive advantages, especially deriving from the 3 levels of innovation regarding the impact on the business as described in this document:

- Optimization of the commercial pre-sale process and audit of health affidavits.

- Giving 300% efficiency to the process in comparison to the ISAPREs or state institutions that do not hold the automated process.
- Visibility and follow-up on commercial opportunities.
- Integration of applications in one single virtual desktop.
- Adoption of certain best practices which reduce the workload in IT and the cost in management of workstations and applications.
- Integral security management.
- BPM as a Service.
- Reducing the complexity and workload related to implementation, updating and application management.
- Reducing the total cost of property (TCO), improving service levels and responding in the simplest way possible to changes and new demands.
- Due to the success of this implementation, the following action plan has been elaborated in order to expand the solution over the year 2009.
- Development of new processes for the Chilean health industry.
- Development of new processes that answer to common problems in other industries; banking and finance as the next step.
- Regionally expanding the processes developed and implemented in Chile, projecting them on the whole of the Latin America region.

TECHNOLOGY

The developed process is tailored according to each organization, the company structure, the profile of each user and the tasks inherent to each function. Those elements interact with each client's own applications; hence the developed solution exhibits **integration on two levels:** BMP solution integration with other components of documentary management to develop the mentioned process, and a second level of integration corresponding to the solution with every particular client's applications.

Regarding the solution's internal integrations, the one of Business Process Management – PECTRA BPM Suite – with the proprietary documentary Microsystem manager stands out: Microsystem Content Manager MCM. While on the level of external integrations and de-pending on each particular client the integration with legacy systems is carried out, it might be either through direct connection to the client's database (e.g. DB Oracle-**Banmedica**) or via web services (e.g. **Consalud**).

TECHNOLOGY AND SERVICE PROVIDERS

The project was developed by PECTRA Technology together with its specialized partner in Chile: Microsystem. For more information, please visit: www.microsystem.cl.

PECTRA Technology specializes in Process Management, with more than 12 years of experience on the market and 200 successful implementations in the USA, Argentina, Mexico, Colombia, Spain and Chile. We have an extensive network of partners in the entire Latin American region and we offer services to more than 50,000 end users who, in turn, serve more than 6,000,000 users/ customers. For more information, please visit: www.pectra.com.

PECTRA Technology's IT Department along with its Marketing Department has accomplished this important document. Juan Chacón; PECTRA Technology's Marketing Manager- and Vanina Marcote; PECTRA Technology`s Marketing Coordinator, have planned the data searching and writing.

Produbanco, Ecuador

Gold Award, South America
Nominated by BizAgi Ltd., Colombia

1. ABSTRACT

Produbanco is one of the main financial institutions in Ecuador. In their search for a solution for the administration of credit applications they were looking for a simple system that was agile and able to integrate with their Core Banking systems as well as all areas involved throughout their organization. They decided upon BizAgi's BPM (Business Process Management) technology to automate the process of managing their consumer credit applications (personal, vehicle and credit cards) and mortgages.

Today, the system manages more than 4500 cases per month, all by means of a web portal that is programmed to disburse the loans at a national level in the shortest possible time. The levels of security and control are sufficient to ensure a healthy loan portfolio in accordance with the bank's guidelines. In terms of transactions, 80% are processed automatically and 20% are processed by risk analysts and a centralized, multi-product credit factory.

2. OVERVIEW

Banco de la Produccion S.A., Produbanco is the head of the 'Grupo Financiero Produccion', one of the most important financial conglomerates in Ecuador. Founded in November 1978, it now has a network of more than 100 offices which serve as the main channel for its consumer credit and mortgage business units.

In order to speed up the process from receipt of the loan application to final approval, including risk analysis, we built a strategy based on the credit factory process which is totally BPM technology. This allows automation of all activities, starting with the loan application, passing through the necessary approval and verification of information stages, until it is finally approved and disbursed to the client,.

After studying all the possible solutions, Produbanco decided upon BizAgi's BPM solution to automate all the human tasks and the business rules within the process.

The system invokes a specially designed business process by means of a web application. This delivers the relevant information to the appropriate user, at the right time and in the right place, activating applications as required, in order to control the execution of both human and automatic tasks and to generate alarm signals, when necessary.

The BPM system has enabled the bank to improve, considerably, the process time-cycle of an application, establishing not only service agreements with the various areas involved but also commitments from them. Also, the system has helped them to find bottlenecks, reintegrate departments that were previously isolated, eliminate manual activities that were the source of recurring errors, avoid reprocessing and automate policies and standards to enable approvals and rejections to be made objectively.

Thanks to the results obtained, they are planning to implement this solution for new business processes, taking advantage of the benefits that a BPM has brought together with the knowledge obtained from this first implementation.

3. BUSINESS CONTEXT

The previous system used for the approval and granting of consumer loans was Prometeus, which entailed passing the application through various phases and departments of the bank during the process. The main problems encountered with this system were delays related to lack of integration between the areas concerned, subjectivity in the approval, excess of manual activities, reprocessing and an excess of exceptions.

What the bank needed was a credit process that enabled them to measure the time delay at each point along the application process, create service agreements with the various areas and obtain their commitments, identify bottlenecks, reintegrate departments that had become isolated, eliminate manual activities that were the source of recurring errors, avoid reprocessing and to automate policies and standards to enable approvals and rejections to be made totally objectively.

Business and Process Innovation

Produbanco developed a consumer credit and mortgage process oriented towards efficiency and productivity. At the same time the process design needed to address the reduction in risk associated with each application.

The following diagram shows the 5 main divisions of the process:

The process begins with the completion of an application form by a retail bank officer, data entry clerk at exhibitions (vehicle, housing) or a dealer.

All stages of the process are performed through a web portal that enables the activities to be completed in real time either from the exhibition or directly from the dealers, by bank staff. Within five minutes from the time the application is entered into the system, a response is given to the customer. This is a major competitive advantage compared to other banks in the country.

Once the customer is identified, the first filter is to review the credit reference agencies and black lists, both internal and external. This is achieved automatically through web services not only with the Core Banking system but also with the appropriate external entities that specialize in this service.

All these filters are now concentrated at only one point and performed automatically whereas previously they were accomplished via external organizations such as credit reference agencies and external black lists by means of a SOA layer connection with the rest of the company's systems.

Having passed this first filter, the application automatically proceeds to calculate the customer's payment capacity depending upon his/her economic activity.

At this moment the officer who is inputting the information identifies the products that can be offered, assuming that cross sales are allowed and that there are no restrictions, the only limitation being the customer's payment capacity.

Following this activity and, again, automatically, all the information compiled so far is fed into the BPM system through a business rules engine that, with policies and standards already set, executes a decision matrix to produce an answer "application pre-approved", "pending" or "rejected". The main objective of this decision engine is to automatically pre-approve or reject the applications, eliminating the subjectivity of the risk analysts decisions, leaving only those that require manual intervention by the analysts or the various approval levels within the Bank.

Once an application has been pre-approved it enters a 'Call Centre' or 'Verification of Information' sub-process, where two main activities are undertaken: Reception of documents and verification of references. The first part of this process checks that all the necessary documents have been provided by the customer correctly and then proceeds to the Call Centre to verify all the applicant's references (personal, family and bank).

In the case of mortgage applications, a valuation to mortgage the property in favour of the Bank is made prior to these activities.

Thanks to the BPM system, only 20% of all applications are reviewed by the risk analysts, that is to say 80% are approved (or rejected) automatically. The approved applications are returned to the officer for the accompanying process documentation to be printed. This is generated and filled in totally automatically.

The application then passes through the legal department's system. Here, all the documentation is reviewed and the formalities of the guarantee are performed through the BPM system which provides all the associated information of the application. Once the guarantees have been legally established the next process is to review the insurance, input the payment method and finally the disbursement of the operation.

In case there are any changes to the original conditions of the application (e.g. rates, start date) the process documentation can be reprinted.

There are also processes specified to address different business processes, outside those of consumer credit, for example, within the Call Centre sub-process, current and savings accounts are managed. Similarly, the process for completing the formalities for guarantees and the disbursement of loans is also used for mortgages and corporate products.

Organizational Innovation

Many activities under the previous system were performed manually by the commercial department, resulting in many errors and reprocessing. Efforts have been made to automate as many of these manual activities as possible.

Those activities performed by the risk analysts were systematized so that an automatic response was provided for each application.

Some areas were always outside of the previous system and therefore it was impossible to verify response times in these cases. Under the new system all areas and departments of the Bank are included in the process.

Time to Market

BizAgi has given more autonomy to Produbanco business staff to efficiently manage important business criteria, in real time using the web portal, according to market dynamics and Produbanco strategies. This increased authorization has reduced the time to market for new ideas and business strategies. The adaptable criteria include:
- Products: Deadlines, Amounts, Fees
- Collateral Coverage % according to each type

- Waiting time for closing cases (applications)
- Levels of acceptance for Credit Bureau customers' risk factor.
- Conditions for automatic approval of products.
- Amount levels for assigning approval tasks to a higher organizational level.

4. OBSTACLES SURMOUNTED

One of the main challenges facing a BPM project is to convince staff from different areas to think as one; establishing targets and objectives that traverse the project, that are shared between them and that they are working in a global project with one end, not competing against one another.

In order to achieve this, people have to see it as just one process. One that has many different elements, each as important as the other, but to achieve success they all have to be managed correctly.

Equally, to be able to reach agreements among the business staff and those of risks, in respect of policies, standards, controls, decision matrix, etc., in a manner that was acceptable to everyone, and thereby used and applied, was a significant achievement throughout the project.

In order to surmount these barriers an internal 'evangelistic' approach was taken which was developed to generate sufficient expectations by means of presentations, manuals and multimedia animations to promote the concept of a credit factory.

As with any new process there exists the element of resistance to change, especially when this involves monitoring. In order to mitigate this, each user was approached directly with the aim of solving individual problems in an efficient manner.

Business Benefits

This new way of approaching process allowed Produbanco to innovate in both: inside the organization, changing the way the employees entail their jobs; and outside the organization changing the way the bank engage its customers. These achievements can be summarized as follows:

- Increased reputation as the most efficient bank to handle credit applications. Thanks to the implementation of BizAgi's BPM, the approval time for all products is now only 5 minutes.

    1. Call Centre verification time – vehicle loans 0.36 days.
    2. Call Centre verification time – other products 1.84 days.
    3. Approval time for credit factory – vehicle loans 0.79 days
    4. Approval time for credit factory – mortgages 2.37 days
    5. Approval time for credit factory – consumer loans 0.98 days
    6. Approval time for credit factory – credit cards 0.88 days
    7. Almost all of the automated processes take less than one day on average.
- Unified Credit Factory for handling all applications independently of the type of product. This has increased the efficiency and optimization of resources in the process operation in the Bank.
- New ways of engaging customers. Thanks to the BPM solution the Bank has been able to use new channels of distribution for vehicle loans like auto shows or car dealers where the bank has its own live operation. This has been possible replicating the bank process with BizAgi and the booth staff composed of a commercial sales person, an analyst and legal/ disbursement people.

- The new schema has given more autonomy to business people to change product policies in real time according to the business dynamics and the changes in strategies.
- Automatic Loan Approval. Thanks to the BizAgi business rule engine and the system integration Produbanco is now able to give automatic loan approvals directly in the branch offices if the conditions or business policies are complied (credit bureau, payment capacity, etc.).

5. COMPETITIVE ADVANTAGES

The response to a credit application can be made while the customer is present which brings added value and credibility to the institution.

We can install mini-bank branches with our own personnel in car-dealers and exhibitions, enabling us to generate applications and have the same response times as those in a normal branch office.

It is equally possible to interact with third parties involved in the application, for example, when establishing a mortgage. In this case the process model was designed in such a way that if one branch was unable to perfect a mortgage, they could forward a mail to an external solicitor of the bank, attaching a copy of the guarantee, for him to process it. Later, he would return the information to the bank.

6. TECHNOLOGY

BizAgi configured the SOA functions, based on the human processes designed for Produbanco, with the scheme and order of tasks of the process and the business requirements. BizAgi's BPM system interacts with the main Core Banking systems not only to extract information but also to send information to the transaction systems. The main performers of the architecture are:

BizAgi Work Portal: An application by which users involved in the process have access to the functionality of the credit process.

Prometeus: Prometeus's Core Banking system developed and implemented in-house.

According to the aforementioned description of the architecture, each user accesses the BizAgi portal and, when required, BizAgi makes use of the options available in Prometeus by means of a service layer (remoting and web service) to make the various inquiries based on the execution of the process and the information obtained.

The following diagram shows the different systems integrated with BizAgi:

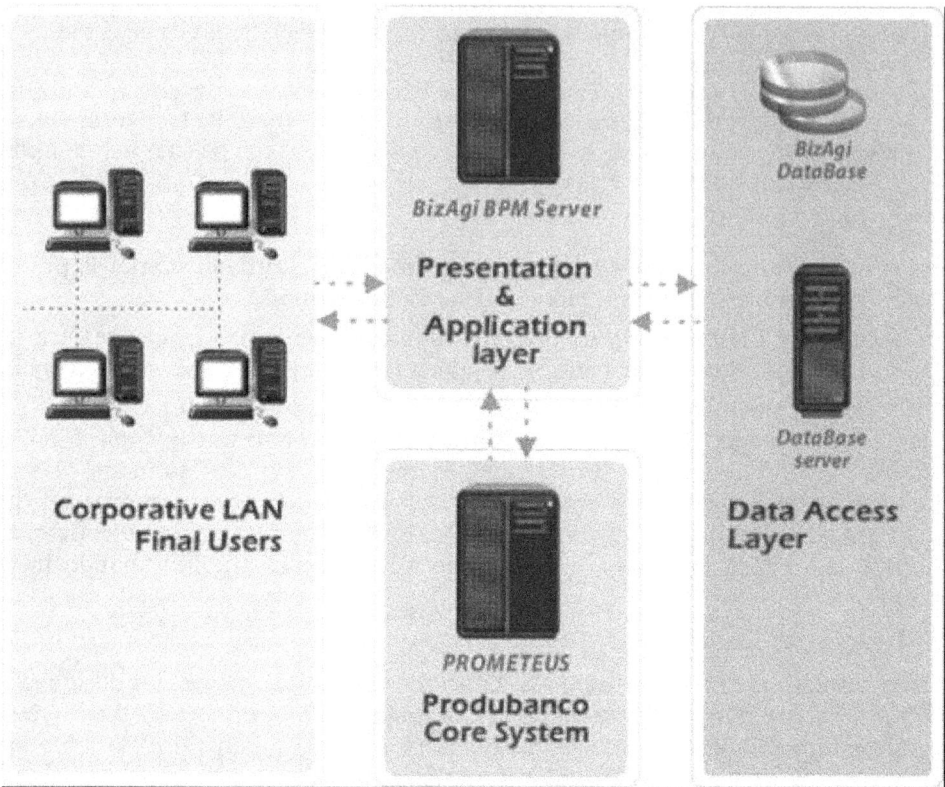

7. THE TECHNOLOGY PROVIDERS

Since its foundation in 1989, BizAgi has been focused on the development of technologies and methodologies to support the continuous improvement of our clients' business processes. Our name stands for Business Agility: we aim to empower business people and provide them with unprecedented adaptability to changing market conditions. Our BPM Suite is the result of more than 20 years of experience delivering process automation and optimization solutions. Start your BPM project small and inexpensively and once you have proven BizAgi's capabilities and experienced its business impact, you can scale it up to support even the most demanding enterprise wide BPM initiatives. Download now our Free 30 day Trial at www.bizagi.com and you will quickly discover how easy it is to create and manage processes with BizAgi.

Transfiriendo S.A., Colombia

Finalist, South America
Nominated by TYCON S.A., Argentina

EXECUTIVE SUMMARY / ABSTRACT

Transfiriendo S.A., a Colombian company with headquarters in Bogotá focused on providing transaction services through technological solutions related to the exchange of digital documents, has successfully implemented **BIZUIT Agile Business Suite** as a platform for information exchange and management of business processes that manage the issue, printing and delivery of insurance policies called **SOAT** (Compulsory Insurance of Motor Vehicle Accidents)

BIZUIT allowed us to count - in a very short time - with a technological platform that manages approximately 70% of **SOAT** policies that are issued throughout Colombia, managing information from the largest and most important insurances companies in the country.

The success of the business carried us to become a leader in the industry and replicate our business in Ecuador, with an overwhelming success. The BIZUIT SOA platform allowed us to reuse the majority of services and existing business processes.

OVERVIEW

When SOAT was created by Act 33 of 1986, Colombia has structured a mechanism to ensure the coverage required by the people if they were victim to traffic accidents.

This social insurance constitutes a scheme of risks management, under the insurance contract figure by which society, in solidarity, provides resources to pay the costs incurred for the care or compensation - the latter only in case of death – to people who suffer a traffic accident, regardless of the element of 'fault'. This implies structural differences compared to other insurance policies, either for vehicles (voluntary insurance) or the health care of people, to the extent that SOAT is the first instance payer and act even in cases where there is no insurance policy.

Transfiriendo S.A. is a Colombian company founded in 2006, to meet the needs of interaction and communication between different actors in a given business through non-invasive technology solutions related to the exchange of digital information of its customers in order to optimize their business processes, increase sales and add value to their supply chain.

The first business unit created had the objective to integrate all the actors (Insurance Companies, its Branches, the Intermediaries and the Points of Sale) that are part of the value chain in the SOAT policy emission process.

Our entry in the insurance market marked a turning point in how insurance policies are emitted in Colombia. In a matter of months, more than the 70% of the Colombian SOAT policies emissions were managed by our company and its platform of BPM and EAI through BIZUIT Agile Business Suite.

We offers services to 4 of the major insurance companies that emit SOAT in Colombia, which collectively manage 70% of the market for insurance policies

(About 1.800.000 insurances policies per month), for a total of U.S. $ 360.000.000 per year.

The success of the process based SOAT Management business model allowed us to also participate in the emission of the SOAT in Ecuador, with also a majority market-share.

Now we are using the same platform provided by BIZUIT Agile Business Suite for the handling of health transactions, managing audits and authorizations of medical practices.

BUSINESS CONTEXT

The sale of SOAT insurances policies was carried out in any shop in the country (drugstores, gas stations, etc), outside of the insurance companies, where the customer had to fill out a form provided by insurance companies and then the shop owner had to ship that form to those insurances companies. These stores were distributed all over Colombia, and the insurance companies did not count on a suitable control on those who sold their products, nor the amount of money these stores owed to them.

One of the main drawbacks was that the shipment was not on a regular basis and, depending on the area of the country, could spend weeks without reporting sold policies, thus the insurance companies were unaware of the policies sold and there were cases of accidents where the policy was not reported as sold.

This situation was exploited by some people who falsified insurance policies or scams such as selling the same policy to multiple customers.

With a vehicle park of 5.500.000 units approximately (1 vehicle each 8 people), and a high degree of fraud it was imperative to find a solution to this problem.

Our company created a new business model that allows to diminish the fraud and to make the scheme more efficient. This model consisted in launch a new electronic system of sale, validation and registry of the insurance policy.

This new system was implemented in the second quarter of 2006 and allowed ourselves and our customers to obtain great benefits observables since the first quarter of 2007, among which are:

A drastic diminution of the paperwork used in the process of acquisition of the SOAT insurance policy.

The securing that the emission of a SOAT insurance policy, in any point of sales in the country, is validated and registered in the backend transactional systems of the insurance companies in a matter of seconds.

- Decreased fraud
- A greater control of the emitted policies and the pending portfolio.
- Lower operating costs

THE KEY INNOVATIONS

4.2 Business

Our customers are in the markets of insurances, health, financier, and therefore they count with hundreds of points of sales, brokers and branches scattered in all the national territory.

All the transactions made by those customers happen through BIZUIT, who works like a switch or connector online between these points: end customers, points of sales, brokers, money collection companies, and the insurance companies' headquarters. Therefore it is vital that the communication links with all issuers and carriers of files and data and the processes of administration and management of the information that we receive is supported by a solution of high availability, effective, scalable and reliable.

With the implementation of business processes, and integration of information systems through BIZUIT Agile Business Suite, we were able to achieve very short response times, allowing us to implement quickly a new customer, a new point of sale, a new business rule as well as the ability to manage and charge for every transaction; integrating directly with the information systems of the money collector and insurance companies, all of this independently of software or hardware used by these and without the necessity to program, using the Zero-Code technology provided by BIZUIT Agile Business Suite.

In addition, through a unified web portal called "Transfiriendo Center", BIZUIT Agile Business Suite allowed us to provide to our clients real time and detailed information of the emitted policies (geographic distribution, amount, periods of purchase, etc.), and also access to the activities of the businesses process, becoming a true B2B.

4.3 Process

The development process used was provided by BIZUIT platform and followed the basic guidelines for SOA: Model, Assemble, Distribute and Manage.

Because in every process there is a component of knowledge of business issues that the process tries to solve, the used methodology suggests a top-down approach starting from modeling in a conceptual level close to the business problem to resolve. This modeling had different forms based on the process that was being developed. Thus, if a given process is a business process with human tasks, the modeling process involves defining the logical sequence of tasks, their roles, resources, and alternative and exception paths. If the process consisted of a series of steps required to obtain a system-to-system integration process, it was modeled to a high conceptual level, creating the great functional blocks that integration will implement to solve a business issue.

Once the process was modeled from a business point of view, we started the task of implementing (to assemble) the way in which the system would behave, the system is formed by the process logic and a set of activities that make atomic tasks as to be interaction with data bases, connections with systems in heterogeneous platforms, transformations of data, interaction with users, calculations, etc.

Once implemented (assembled) the model, the test and debug stage started. When we ended this stage, the process and its components distribution stage begun, which was made in a totally automatic way with the technology provided by the platform.

Finally, once the business processes were put into operation, it was necessary to monitor the implementation, using a tool provided by the platform to analyze performance, cost, timing, exceptions and other characteristics necessary to improve the efficiency of the process. The methodology follows incremental and iterative process where in each iteration the four stages must be fulfilled. At the end of each iteration a new version of the process was released.

The main innovation launched by our company was to implement a set of distributed workflows, in which the points of sales, brokers, insurance companies, banks and Transfiriendo S.A., are integrated into a great distributed business process, forming the links of the value chain.

SOAT information system consists of several business processes. Some of them are Human-Centric workflows and others are System-to-System workflows.

Through a Web Application, the points of sales emit the insurance policy and send the transaction to our web servers where the web services that initiate workflows are published. These workflows are exposed on a SOA platform, provided by BIZUIT Agile Business Suite, which allows its reusability by other businesses processes of our company and/or the insurance companies.

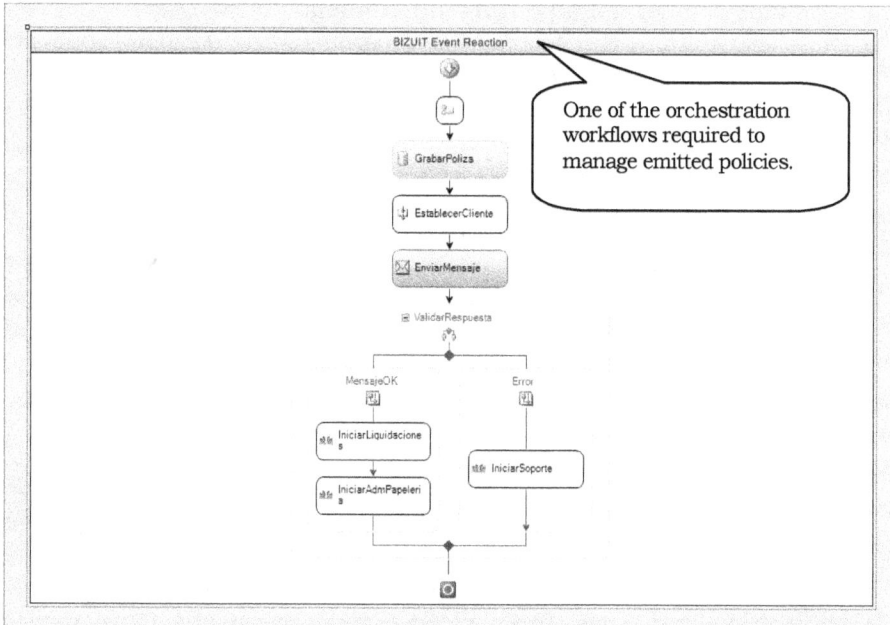

Because each insurance company has its own technological architecture and type of backend transactional system, the main workflow detects the insurance company to which the policy included in the transaction belongs, and invokes asynchronously the data-transformation and information storage workflow located in the insurance company servers. This distributed workflow is in charge to interact with the insurance company's backend transactional system and register the operation.

Web User Interface to sale a policy

When the insurance company's distributed workflow sends back a successful transaction message, the main workflow in our servers wakes up and takes the control again, starting businesses processes in which interacts our staff and also staff of the insurance companies, branches, brokers and points of sales. One of these processes is the Commission Clearing process. This process is executed when the transaction was successfully received and stored in the insurance company.

The process calculates and distributes the fees or commissions of all the participants of the sale (Broker, Point of sale, Branch of the insurance company and insurance company). Each sale's participant receives a task, and its corresponding notification, indicating the calculated values, with the fee to view reviewed

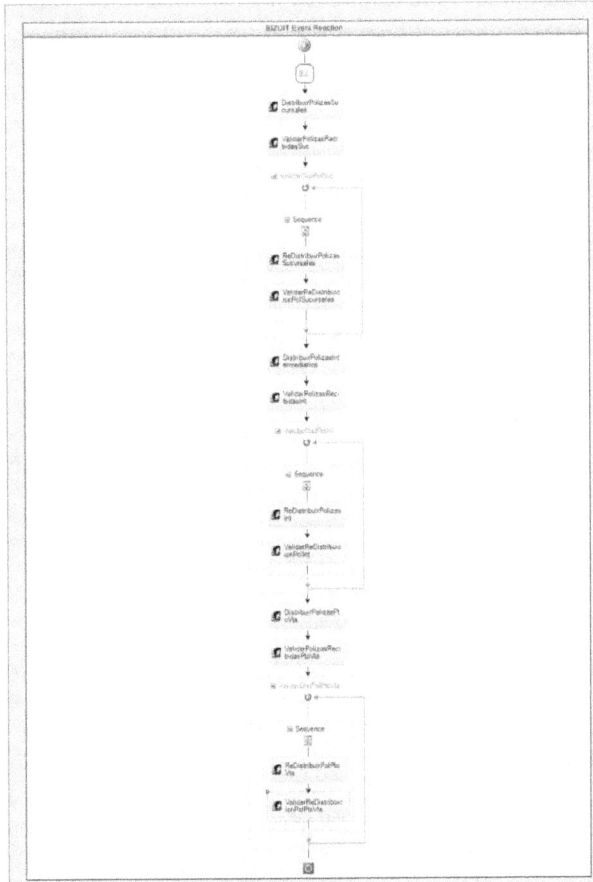

and, in case of not being in agreement with the calculated commission, to be able to reject the same one, in which case the task returns to the executive of sale for its review. The process continues when biweekly, the insurance company makes a cut in sales, and proceeds to the payment of the commissions.

The second executed process is the Stationery Store Management one. The stationery store contains the paperwork documentation that the point of sales gives to the customer who buys the policy. The paperwork distribution follows a process that starts from the insurance company, which sets the amount of paperwork to be delivered to each branch who receives the notification and the physical paperwork and distributes it to the broker, who in turn distributes it to the points of sales. When the sales report is made, the process in opposite sense is followed, controlling the sold policies with the given paperwork.

There is a third process that is occasionally executed and manages the exceptions that may occur. For example, when the distributed workflow located in the insurance company sends a message in where it reports that the policy could not be stored, the main workflow initiates the Exceptions Management and Support process for the customer support area to analyze the error, make the necessary corrections - that they can be in our processes, the Insurance Company processes or in both - and then proceeds to re-send the transaction manually to be processed. One of the exceptions that can occur can be due to a possible difference in the value of the money collection. When the points of sale make the payment of the sold policies, either through a bank or other money collection entity that makes up our chain of value, they use a published business process to send the received payments in batch. If the system detects that a difference exists between which it was due to perceive, and what really was received by the bank, it initiates a process of validation and authorization of the payment, where an account executive receives the task and its respective notification and validates or he rejects the transaction. In this process take part our staff and the insurance company and the money collecting organization staff.

The status of the BPM system can be summarized as follows:

Total Users	10.000
Concurrent Users	1800 (average), 4500 (Peak Time)
Installation location	Transfiriendo S.A. headquarters , 4 insurance companies and 4.500 point of sales.
Annual Total Completed Transactions	3.500.000
Average monthly pending transactions	120.000

4.4 Organization

From the beginning of its operations, we had the vision of its business on the basis of a platform of BPM and Workflow. Thus we grew up under a Processes Management philosophy. After careful consideration of various commercially available BPM solutions, we selected TYCON's BIZUIT Agile Business Suite platform and began implementation between August 2006 and January 2007.

Moreover, although our business has a high technological content, the technology provided by BIZUIT allowed us more rapid changes of business processes or rules, because they are not performed by traditional programming, but in the model, avoiding the need for staff with advanced technical knowledge or programming.

This allowed our IT department to reduce by 80% the response time to a new request from the business area. In the same way we were able to reduce significantly the time to market of new vertical applications, which are SOA-enabled, sued for different projects.

The insurance's market has a great dynamism, reason why constant changes take place. At present, the changes experienced by the market force us to do, steadily, various actions that directly affect the business models of our customers. Thanks to the BIZUIT implementation, our business and technical areas shares an only language. This allows a quick understanding of the processes involved in each new project and an effective reaction to the events arising from them. The solutions we offer tend to optimize processes, costs and resources for the sole purpose of meeting in a timely manner the needs of individual links that make up the sales network and therefore the end user, giving the optimum safety in the handling of his information. BIZUIT amply fulfills these requirements.

HURDLES OVERCOME

The Businesses Processes Management methodology was taken in count from the very start-up of the company when this kind of organization and enterprise strategy was envisioned. At the same time, the incorporated staff had experience in BPM and Workflow, so the acceptance was natural and without major complications, only a very small learning curve on the tool was observed. Coupled with the joint work of TYCON S.A. consulting area, the design, implementation and put in operation of all the processes that comprises the solution was conducted in six months.

BENEFITS

Cost Savings

The time reductions and increased productivity explained below allowed to each insurance company to obtain a ROI of 3 months.

The paper used for the printing of the policy is a special paper that has high costs. The implementation of the Stationery Management process allowed to the insurance companies to send to the points of sale the exact amount of paperwork that the point of sale needs, before the implementation of this process the paperwork was shipment without knowing the amount required by the point of sale, that many times asked for paperwork than the necessary one or asked for paperwork having still available a great amount. The implementation of this process reduced 45% the cost in paperwork.

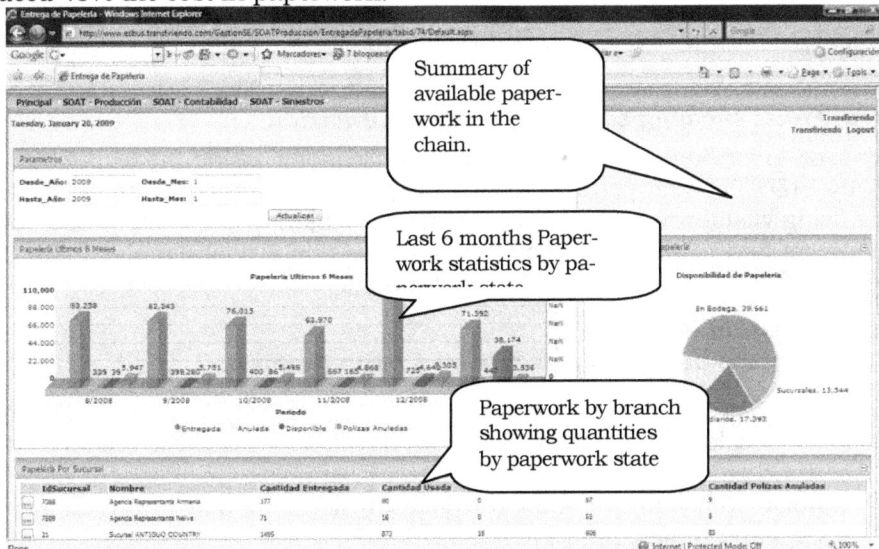

Control Panel showing some paperwork information

6.2 Time Reductions

A change in a business rule is made in a matter of minutes modifying workflow and publishing the change, whereas before, to inform to all the chain of sale of this new rule took approximately 5 days.

Considerable reduction of times for the integration of the different technologies used by the different links that compose the chain of sale, as well as for the description of processes that are involved in each transaction. The average time to integrate the backend systems of an insurance company with our processes, where in many cases it is necessary to implement new processes, has been drastically reduced. This integration tasks now takes a maximum time of 15 days when our competitors makes those tasks in not less than two months.

Drastic reduction of the money collection times. Before the implementation of the project the insurance companies had a delay of between 60 and 90 days to receive the cashing of the policies. This average time was reduced to 7 days, with the possibility of configure each point of sale by insurance agency, indicating the limit of days, quantity or amount of sold policies in which the point of sale must make the money deposit.

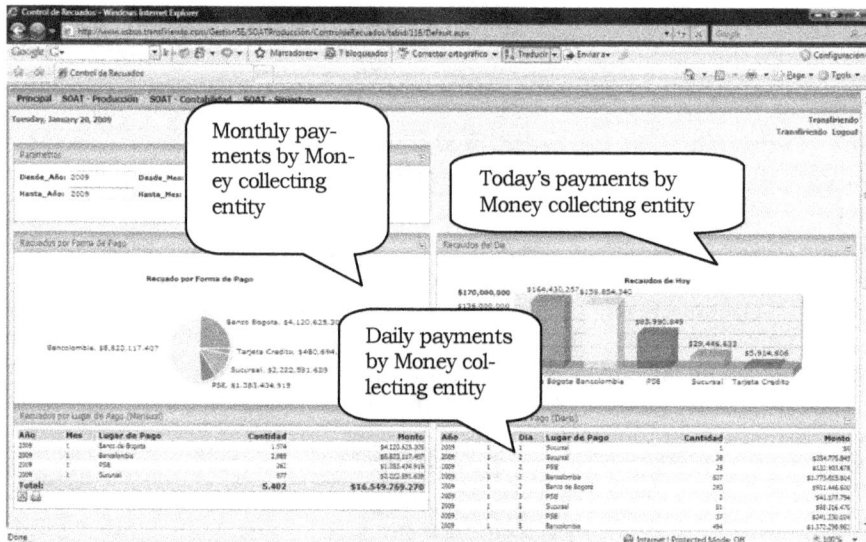

Control Panel showing some payments information

Better time-to-market of new process and applications, using the technology provided by BIZUIT it was possible to build those process and all the applications' layers using visual and reusable components, achieving a 50% reduction of the development and testing times compared to traditional programming, and at the same time obtain more maintainable applications.

6.3 Increased Revenues
The increase in profits was due by 4 main factors:

- Before the implementation of this project, insurance companies had 2500 points of sales all over Colombia. Now, having controlled the points of sales' network and automated processes, it was possible to increase the sales points to 4500 with the same resources, which obviously meant an increase in sales and profits.
- Elimination of fines set by the government, who monitors insurance companies, for not complying with the times and ways for the issuance of the policy.
- Reduction of fraud, because now is not possible for the points of sales to sell two or more times the same policy, and it is not possible to sell a policy to an amount of a motorcycle, and charged it to the insurance company as a policy of a truck.

- The implementation of a control panel led to a better knowledge of the network of intervening actors, to measure it, to control it and therefore to improve it. Before the project's implementation, the insurance companies evaluated the yield of the points of sales according to the quantity and the amount of sold policies. But in some points although the quantity and the amount of the policies were high, there was a high degree of accidents, thus the insurance companies had to pay much money and the utility was minimum or often it did not exist. Now, having a system integrated with the health agencies that charge the insurance, the points of sales are measured by the generated profits, which changed the map of points of sales, allowing insurance companies to concentrate on those that generate more profits.

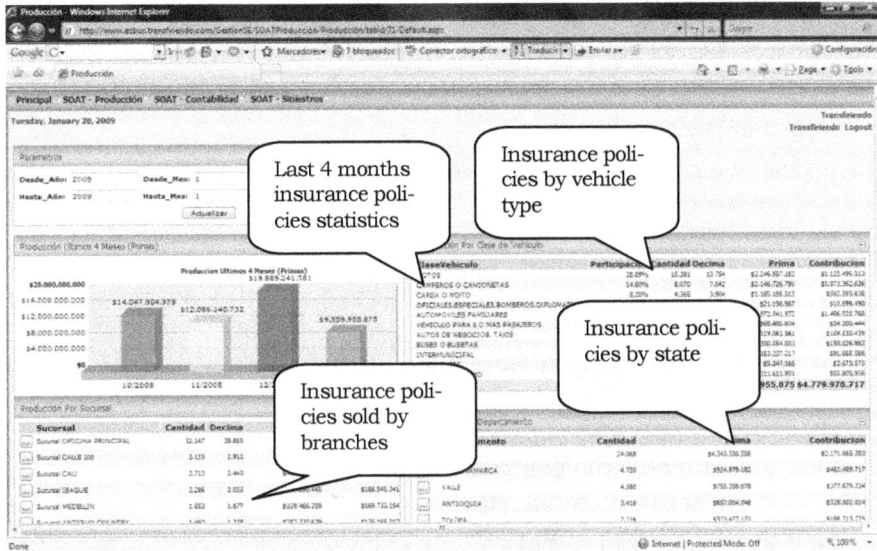

Control Panel showing some insurance policies information

6.4 Productivity Improvements

Constant awareness of the portfolio state, even if the insurance companies did not have received the documentation of policies sold.

Unification of security mechanisms for the data transportation.

Decreased the time of filing an insurance policy. Insurance companies used to receive documentation from 30 to 45 days after the sale of it. We reduced it to seconds, without mattering in which point of sale of the country the sale was made.

Possibility of offering to the insurance companies useful and critical information in real time (statistical, alerts and reports) for the decision making.

Reduction of the data entry time. The insurance companies had a group of people who were in charge to enter to the system all the policies that arrived from the points of sale. Now this procedure is automatic, since each point of sale is the one in charge to register the policy, diminishing in a 60% the operative costs of this task.

BEST PRACTICES, LEARNING POINTS AND PITFALLS

7.1 Best Practices and Learning Points

✓ To work from the beginning with a Processes Management methodology, allowed us to work in an ordered way, having a total control and improvement of the processes.

✓ To have the documented, automated processes and with the traceability of each one of the made tasks, contributed to a great extent to certify ISO 9000:2000 norm.

7.2 Pitfalls

✗ With the objective to reuse processes and Web Services, in the first stages of the implementation we constructed workflows with very fine granularity, that later were improved and consolidated where necessary

COMPETITIVE ADVANTAGES

Through our workflow and BPM platform developed with BIZUIT, we introduced a radical change in the way of issuing insurance policies in Colombia, becoming pioneers and leaders in electronic commerce. Any new business process or enterprise integration can be developed easy and quickly with the BIZUIT platform, being able to respond in a matter of hours to the customer's requirements and to the changes that the market imposes.

BIZUIT offers us a versatile and essential tool for their business, which also allowed us to create new units of business with the same philosophy in other sectors like health and finances.

To maintain and enhance the competitive advantage to their competitors, we are currently working on the following points:

- Integration with mobile devices where end customers may check the status of an insurance policy and begin the process of renewing the policy.
- Incorporate more collection money entities using BIZUIT in banks for an online and native integration.
- To extend the amount of processes automated within the companies that comprise of the value chain, but mainly within the insurance companies.

TECHNOLOGY

BIZUIT Agile Business Suite is a technological platform designed to provide a solution to the information needs of organizations. The BPM, EAI, BI and ERAD characteristics provided by BIZUIT used throughout the SOAT project's implementation provided us the following benefits:

Business Management Benefits:

Implement a Process-Based Management with BIZUIT allowed us to have a very flexible tool to make hot changes at any level of the process, allowing us to respond quickly to change from customers, market or the government, and providing a very short time-to-market, which proved a critical advantage over our competitors.

Enterprise Integration Benefits:

The ability to quickly and easily connect with different transactional systems under different operating systems and platforms offered by the BIZUIT Designer tool allowed us to not only do the integrations with insurance companies at a time less than our competitors, but also as an added value to the offer it was allowed to the insurance companies to have a graphic tool to monitor the traffic and the result of integrations as well as the possibility of making modifications to the processes by people with knowledge of the business and low technical skills by means of a GUI that allows the modeling and visual mapping of data and provides predefined activities for common tasks (connection to any Database in any OS, execution of web services and .NET, COM and JAVA components, Flat Text transformation to XML, File Transfer, etc) and the corresponding debug, publication and management.

Enterprise Rapid Application Development Benefits:

The constant changes of business rules in the insurance market required a tool that would allow us not only quickly adapt business processes and integrations with transactional systems of insurance companies, but also modify the software applications that support those process and integrations. With BIZUIT's Zero Code technology, it was possible to dispense with traditional programming to develop or make changes to user interface, services, processes, business rules, data access and applications' integrations; minimizing reliance on business with our IT department, because the changes are not made in the code and normally they do not need advanced programming skills or technical knowledge, and allowing the IT department to respond much more quickly and efficiently to the requirement of our business area, building interfaces, prototypes and applications without the need to write code, focusing exclusively on the business problem.

The BIZUIT's E-RAD features provided an IDE for the creation of all layers of the SOAT application quickly and easily, allowing the generation of user interfaces (Web and Windows), web services, business components and data access using rules, functions and predesigned components in a fully visual way, being able to use data, services, components and business rules from different sources in an intuitive graphical interface and, in a matter of minutes, transform those data into robust SOA-enabled applications at the same time that allowed to count on a documentation always updated with the application distributed, since when doing without the traditional programming in BIZUIT the source code is the model, which enormously increases the malleability of the applications and provided us a key benefit to offer better time-to-market and change time than our competitors.

Business Intelligence Benefits:

With the processes started up, the last stage of the project consisted of putting into operation the key process indicators (KPIs) and monitoring the business activities, exploring the data that was generated and making intelligence on the information available.

One of the clearest examples of how the use of BAM and BI characteristics of BIZUIT allowed us to increase the utilities of the insurance companies, was to have a Control Panel that not only reflected the volume of invoicing of the brokers and points of sale, but taking advantage of that we were counted on information from all the actors in our value chain, it was also possible to cross the volume invoiced in a region, with the amount destined to the payment to the health care services. In many cases it was found that although the volume of invoicing was high, so was the amount paid to the health organizations that took care of the casualties produced, thus the utility was very small, or in many cases there was no utility. With the aid a set of web parts providing graphs, reports and OLAP cubes features, each user who participates in the processes visualizes through BIZUIT Dashboard the information in clear and timely manner, which collaborates in the making decisions quickly and diminishing the risk of that decision. The configuration of those web parts is made easily and online from the Administrative Console of BIZUIT Dashboard allowing to an administrator make changes and offer new information to the appropriate user very quickly.

Architecture

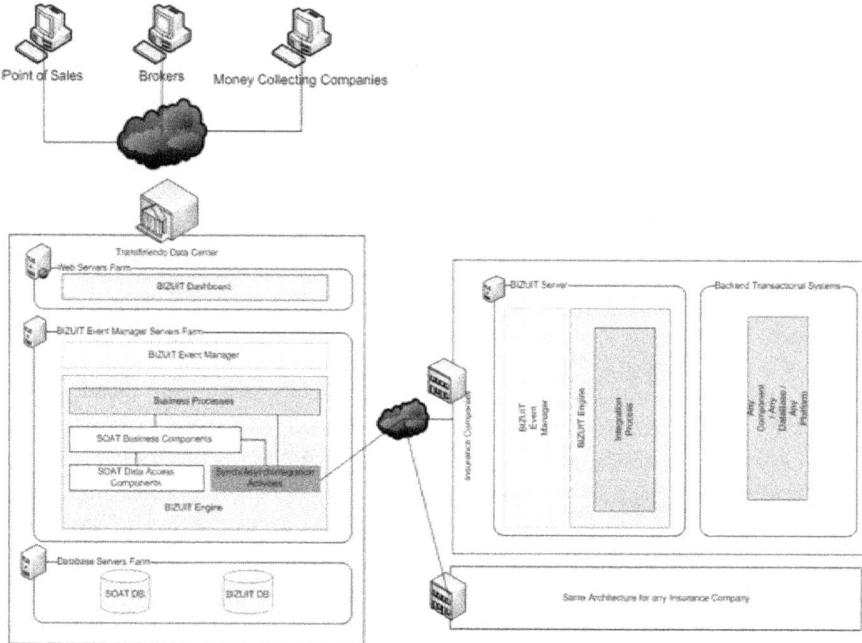

Project Architecture

BIZUIT Agile Business Suite is composed by four main components: BIZUIT Designer, BIZUIT Event Manager, BIZUIT Engine and BIZUIT Dashboard

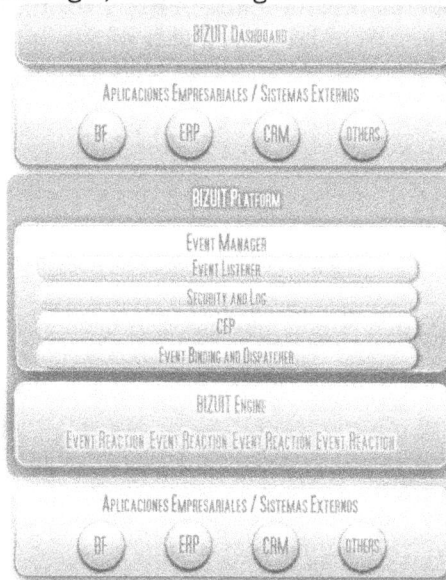

BIZUIT High Level Architecture

BIZUIT Designer:

Is a key element in the BIZUIT's architecture providing an IDE at a higher level of abstraction than the traditional IDEs, where the code is not written but that is modeled, thus shaping faster and easily the intentionality of the program, from its interface it is possible to design, to prove and to distribute processes, GUIs (Web and Windows), services, components and business rules, as well as the mechanisms of data access and integration networks ; enabling to achieve drastic time reductions.

BIZUIT Designer enables that the model built becomes source code, which allows

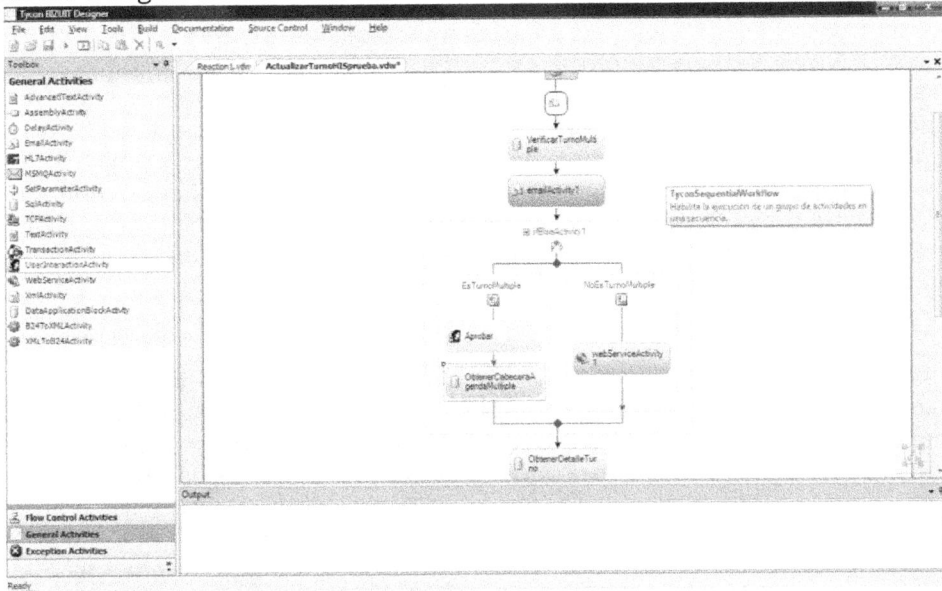

a number of advantages over traditional programming which include: developing speed, flexibility and adaptability to change and always in sync with the source code. That model is transformed into executable code. NET automatically by the platform BIZUIT, but the end-user always works with the model, not with the source code.

BIZUIT Designer Modeling Tool

BIZUIT Event Manager:

Is one of the BIZUIT's architecture founding components and provides the ability to communicate with BIZUIT from different platforms and technologies. Its main function is to provide a layer of technology for the reception of events under different communication protocols, using for it the features of Windows Communication Foundation. An application or user that wishes to interact with BIZUIT raises an event, which is received by BIZUIT Event Manager using a wide variety of protocols, like being TCP, HTTP, FTP, SMPP and MSMQ. Some of these events can be raised by a user from a legacy interface or made using the BIZUIT Designer, whereas others can be raised automatically from existing applications available in the organization. The events received by BIZUIT Event Manager cause a reaction; which can represent the execution of businesses process, integration of existing applications or the execution of logic and businesses rules.

Once an event arrives at BIZUIT using some of the protocols previously mentioned, the layer of security of BIZUIT Event Manager performs authentication and authorization tasks, and then a layer called "Event Binding and Dispatcher" is executed, which is responsible for inspecting the definition of the event and determine the reaction to run. Once determined the reaction to execute, the control passes to BIZUIT Engine, who will be responsible for providing the execution environment to the configured reaction.

BIZUIT Event Manager allows reception of asynchronous events by means of queuing mechanisms native to Windows platform (MSMQ), which allows the asynchronous reception of events, routing and guaranteed delivery by an efficient and scalable architecture.

BIZUIT Engine:

It is the component in charge of executing the reaction modeled by BIZUIT Designer. It is the responsible of the execution of the services, logic and business rules, businesses and integration process. It has a robust platform 3,0 100% .NET based on Windows Workflow Foundation and with support to the main standards. It has robust mechanisms for information logging, persistence and tracking that can store all this information and then carry out monitoring, process optimization, compliance with SLAs matrixes, etc. By means of extensibility mechanisms and configuration is possible to extend this functionality and change the place where this information is stored.

BIZUIT Dashboard:

Web Presentation Layer for the SOA Architecture provided by BIZUIT, it offers customized business information. Based on the popular framework DotNetNuke, combines scalability, security and Content Management features. An administrator can use BIZUIT Dashboard to define users, roles, and pages and web parts permissions, creating a custom site for the enterprise incorporating a set of predefined web parts or reusing third parts components to make a mash-up of information. Is the end-user interface from which it is possible to interact with the business process using a Task List web part, to monitor and manage the process and with a set of web parts providing graphs, reports and OLAP cubes features, offer the necessary information for the decision making in real time, administering the KPIs (Key performance indicators) predefined and providing alert when those PKIS need attention.

THE TECHNOLOGY AND SERVICE PROVIDERS

The BPM platform was provided by TYCON S.A., who was also responsible for the training of our staff, and collaborated in the survey, design, construction and release to production. TYCON S.A. – www.tycon.com.ar

Section 6

Appendix

APPENDIX

Award Winners, Nominees and Nominators

GUEST CHAPTERS

Clay Richardson
crichardson@forrester.com
Senior Analyst, Business Process Management,
Forrester Research, USA.
Clay delivers strategic and tactical guidance to Business Process & Applications professionals seeking to automate processes and integrate structured and unstructured information into business processes. Clay specifically helps enterprises establish BPM strategies, governance standards, establish BPM centers of excellence, identify lean and agile methodologies best suited for BPM projects, and identify vendors and technologies that help them optimize mission-critical business processes. Prior to joining Forrester Clay served as BPM practice leader at Project Performance Corporation, a global system integrator based in Washington, D.C., where he launched and managed the company's business process management practice. Prior to that, Clay directed a diverse team of consultants, trainers, and support engineers in delivery and support of BPM solutions, as the director of professional services at HandySoft Global Corporation, a pure-play BPM vendor. Clay is active with several BPM industry associations, including the Workflow Management Coalition, where he served as founder and co-chair of the organization's Public Sector chapter.

Lewis Carr
lewis.carr@oracle.com
Senior Director Global Public Sector Marketing,
Oracle Corporation, USA
As Senior Director for Global Public Sector Market Research at Oracle Corporation Lewis performs research, develops solutions and manages globally deployed market-driven initiatives in the Public sector including Government, Defense, and Public healthcare. Prior to joining Oracle, Lewis was a Senior Director for Global Public Sector and Commercial Industry Marketing at BEA Systems, Inc for 4 years and Sun Microsystems for 7 years before that as a Director and Group manager in product marketing and management, and industry and market development, covering Telecom and Enterprise hardware and software. Lewis developed his international business skills at Motorola working in Tokyo, Japan for 3-1/2 years. Lewis Carr started his career as a Research Engineer at Stanford Research Institute (SRI) International, designing, testing and managing large applied research projects for laser-based remote measurement systems used in a variety of government-sponsored applications including environmental monitoring, monitoring for battlefield contamination as well as other monitoring purposes.

ACERTI
Camino real de la plata 106 4to. Piso B., Col Zona Plateada
Pachuca, Estado de Hidalgo, 42083, Mexico
Luis Alfonso Ramírez Vega, CEO
lramirez@acerti.com.mx, 52 (771) 7195468

ACTION SOLUTIONS AG
Bahnhofstrasse 12,
Zug, Zug, 6300, Switzerland
Jürg Schenkel, Chairman
jschenkel@in-action.ch, 0044 41 720 37 00

ACTION TECHNOLOGIES INC.
P.O. Box 39,
San Leandro, California, 94577-0139, U.S.A.
Bill Welty, CEO
bill.welty@actiontech.com, 001 510 638 8300

ADOBE SYSTEMS
601 Townsend Ave,
San Francisco, CA, 94103, US
Melinda Campero, AE
Melinda.Campero@ar-edelman.com, 650-762-2852

AEGON RELIGARE LIFE INSURANCE
2nd Floor, Paranjpe B Scheme, Subhash Road, Near Garware House,
Vile Parle (E), Mumbai, 400 057, India
Srinivasan Iyengar, Director
srinivasan.iyengar@aegonreligare.com, +91 99870 44664

BIZAGI VISION SOFTWARE
Carrera 7 # 71-52 Torre B Oficina 1302,
Bogotá, Colombia
Federico Ramírez, E-Marketing Coordinator
federico.ramirez@bizagi.com, 571-3170049 Ext 132
As the result of over 18 years of experience in process automation technologies, our company developed the BizAgi® Business Process Management System. BizAgi® is now a leading BPM Solution specialized in the financial sector with a strong presence in Latin America and Europe where it is being used by some of the most important financial institutions. BizAgi® allows process owners to automate or modify complex and dynamic processes faster and more flexibly than any other solution in the market. This is due to a concept called The Relational Process Model. This model fuses the relational data model with modern process theory allowing BizAgi® to automate processes without programming using a Model Driven Architecture and a Data Driven Process Engine.

CITY OF EDMONTON
17th Floor Century Place, 9803 102A Ave
Edmonton, Alberta, T5J 3A3, Canada
Jacob Modayil, Product Manager, Desktop and Workflow
jacob.modayil@edmonton.ca, 7809445407

COMPUTRONIX LTD.
200, 10216 – 124 Street,
Edmonton, Alberta, T5N 4A3, Canada
Jim den Otter, VP Product and Sales

CORDYS
Abbey House, Wellington Way, Brooklands Business Park

Wellington Way, Surrey, KT13 0TT, United Kingdom
Lisa Solberg, Marketing Director
lsolberg@cordys.com, +44 7789 223 734

CRYO TECHNOLOGIES
Av. Joao Abott, 473, cj 305, Petropolis
Porto Alegre, RS, 90460-150, Brazil
Rafael Bortolini, Project Director
rafael@cryo.com.br, +55 51 30193532

DICKINSON FINANCIAL CORPORATION
Armed Forces Bank Data Center
1111 Main Street - Suite 200
Kansas City, MO 64105
Josh Laire, Application Development Integration Manager
jlaire@dfckc.com, (816) 472-0081 ext. 2488

FULLERTON INDIA CREDIT COMPANY LTD.
Mail Room, Fullerton India Credit Co Ltd, Building No 11, Second Floor,
Solitaire Corporate Park, Andheri - Ghatkopar Link Road,
Chakala, Andheri (East)
Mumbai, Maharashtra, 400 093, India
Pramod Krishnamurthy, Executive Vice President - Head Technology
pramod.krishnamurthy@fullertonindia.com, +91 - 22 - 67491150.

IMAN AUSTRALIAN HEALTH PLANS
Suite 1, 39 Albany St
Crows Nest, NSW, 2065, Australia
John Braithwaite, Managing Director
jb@iman.com.au, +61 2 84372888

INMETRO
Rua Santa Alexandrina 416- 5° andar,
Rio de Janeiro, RS, 20261-232, Brazil
Aldoney Freire Costa,
Chefe da Divisão de Acreditação de Organismos, DICOR
afcosta@inmetro.gov.br, +55 21 2563-2869

ISAPRE MICROSYSTEM
José Miguel de la Barra 536 P.3-5-7,
Santiago de Chile, Santiago de Chile, 8320000, Chile
Carlos Espinoza, Technology Manager
cespinoza@microsystem.cl, 8 56 2 460 6400

KPN
Maanplein 128 (TP13),
Den Haag, Zuid Holland, , The Netherlands
Michiel Valk, Program Director
michiel.valk@kpn.com, +31 70 3437019

MIGROS BANK
Industriestrasse 17,
Wallisellen, Zurich, 8304, Switzerland
Stephan Wick, Executive Board Member
stephan.wick@migrosbank.ch, 0041 44 839 81 00

NEWGEN SOFTWARE TECHNOLOGIES LTD.
D-152, Okhla Industrial Area, Phase 1
New Delhi, Delhi, 110020, India
Hareish Gur, Vice President, Sales & Marketing
hareish@newgen.co.in, -40773620
Newgen Software Technologies Limited is a leading vendor in Business Process Management (BPM) and Document Management System (DMS), with a global footprint of about 750 installations in over 35 countries. More than 100 of these implementations are large, mission-critical solutions deployed at the world's leading BFSI, BPO and Fortune Global 500 companies.

NSI
Chaussée de Bruxelles 174A,
B-4340, BELGIUM
Didier Rossetto, Project Leader
Didier.Rossetto@nsi-sa.be, +32 4 239 91 50

OFFICE OF THE UNDER SECRETARY OF DEFENSE (OUSD) FOR ACQUISITION, TECHNOLOGY & LOGISTICS (A T & L)
eBusiness Center
241 18th Street South, Suite 301
Arlington, VA, 22202, USA
Ousd.atl.portal@osd.mil +1 703-602-2626

ORACLE CORP
3015 Nicosh Circle, 2204
Falls Church, VA, 22042, USA
Linus Chow, Principal Consultant
linus.chow@oracle.com, 703-203-2178
Oracle (NASDAQ: ORCL) is the world's largest enterprise software company. Oracle delivers the unified SOA platform for business transformation and optimization in order to improve cost structures and grow new revenue streams. Oracle BPM Suite and SOA Suite are market leading software suites that allows enterprises to integrate modeling, execution and measurement of end-to-end business processes involving complex interactions between people and IT systems. Oracle customers across the world have achieved greater efficiency, control and agility by optimizing the business process lifecycle and improving the alignment between business and IT.

PECTRA TECHNOLOGY
2425 West Loop South, Suite 200.,
Houston, Texas, 77027, USA
Martín Sola, CEO
msola@pectra.com, (713) 335 5562
PECTRA Technology's award-winning Business Process Management system, PECTRA BPM Suite, is a powerful set of tools enabling discovery, design, implementation, maintenance, optimization and analysis of business processes for different kinds of organizations. PECTRA BPM Suite is an application that automates the processes and the most critical

tasks in the organization, generating optimum levels of operational effectiveness. It fulfills all requirements demanded by today's organization, quickly and efficiently. Furthermore, it increases the return on previous investments made in technology by integrating all existing applications. Based on BPM technology it incorporates the concepts of: BAM (Business Activity Monitoring) providing management with user-friendly graphic monitoring tools, to follow up any deviation in the organization's critical success factors, with capabilities to control and coordinate the organization's performance by means of graphic management indicators; WORKFLOW offering powerful tools to automate and speed the organization's business processes, improving communication and work-flow between people working in different areas; carrying out the work more efficiently and producing customer satisfaction, lower levels of bureaucracy and cost-reductions in day-to-day operations; EAI (Enterprise Application Integration) enabling integration with all existing technologies in the organization, regardless of their origin or platform, coordinating them to help the organization achieve its goals more efficiently; and B2Bi (Business to Business Integration) enabling the control and coordination of each and every link in the organization's value chain, providing robust tools for business process management, and enterprise application integration, making it possible to totally integrate suppliers, clients and partners in an easy and flexible way.

PEGASYSTEMS
101 Main Street,
Cambridge, MA, 2142, USA
Brian Callahan, Director, Public Relations
callb@pega.com, 617-866-6364

POLONIOUS PTY LTD
Suite 1, 39 Albany St
Crows Nest, NSW, 2065, Australia
Stuart Guthrie, Director
stuart@polonious.com.au, +61 2 9007 9842

PRODUBANCO
Av. Amazonas N35-211 y Japón, Edificio Produbanco , Piso 4
Quito, Ecuador
Lenin Landazuri, Productivity Manager
landazuril@produbanco.com, (593) 2999-000 Ext 2627

PRU HEALTH
155 West Street,
Sandton, Gauteng, 2146, South Africa
Paulo Dos Santos, Chief Information Office
paulod@discovery.co.za, +27 (0) 11 529 2035

TECHSPACE AERO
Route de Liers, 121,
Herstal (Milmort), , B-4041, BELGIUM
Catherine PAULMIER, Archiving and Document Management Manager
cpaulmie@techspace-aero.be

TIBCO SOFTWARE
23/25 Rue Delariviere Lefoulon, Paris La Defense 9
Ile de France, Paris La Défense Cedex, 92064, France
Catherine Lynch, Snr Product Marketing Manager
clynch@tibco.com, 33 1 42 91 92 69

TIBCO Software Inc. (NASDAQ:TIBX) provides enterprise software that helps companies achieve service-oriented architecture (SOA) and business process management (BPM) success. With over 3,000 customers, TIBCO has given leading organizations around the world better awareness and agility—what TIBCO calls The Power of Now®. TIBCO provides one of the most complete offerings for enterprise-scale BPM, with powerful software that is capable of solving not just the challenges of automating routine tasks and exception handling scenarios, but also the challenges of orchestrating sophisticated and long-lived activities and transactions that involve people and systems across organizational and geographical boundaries.

TRANSFIRIENDO S.A.
Calle 98 Nro 22-64, Oficina 810
Bogota, DF, , Colombia
Ruben Duri, Operation Manager
rduri@transfiriendo.com, 571 691 0810

TRIBUNAL SUPERIOR DE JUSTICIA DEL ESTADO DE HIDALGO
Mexico - Plaza Juarez - Palacio de Gobierno,
Pachuca, Estado de Hidalgo, 42083, Mexico
Alma Carolina Viggiano Austria, President
carolinaviggiano@pjhidalgo.gob.mx, 01(771)717-9000 ext. 9114

TYCON S.A.
Donaciano del Campillo 1760, Barrio Cerro de las Rosas
Cordoba, Cordoba, 5009, Argentina
Ariel Schwindt, CEO
aschwindt@tycon.com.ar, -4822823

U.S. XPRESS ENTERPRISES INC.
4080 Jenkins Road,
Chattanooga, TN, 37421, USA
Jeff Seibenhener, VP of IT
jeffs@usxpress.com, (423) 510-3306

US MEPCOM
US Military Entrance Processing Command, 2834 Green Bay Road
North Chicago, IL, 60064-3094, USA
Kevin Moore, CIO
kevin.d.moore@us.army.mil, Commercial: (847) 688-368

W4
4 rue Emile Baudot,
PALAISEAU, 91873, FRANCE
Francois BONNET, Product Marketing Manager
francois.bonnet@w4global.com, +33 1 64 53 19 05

Additional BPM and Workflow Resources

NON-PROFIT ASSOCIATIONS AND RELATED STANDARDS BODIES ONLINE

- AIIM (Association for Information and Image Management)
  www.aiim.org
- AIS Special Interest Group on Process Automation and
  Management (SIGPAM)
  www.sigpam.org
- BPMN (Business Process Management Notation)
  BPMN.org
- BPM Focus (previously WARIA)
  bpmfocus.org/
- IEEE (Electrical and Electronics Engineers, Inc.)
  www.ieee.org
- ISO (International Organization for Standardization)
  www.iso.ch
- Object Management Group
  www.omg.org
- Open Document Management Association
  infocentrale.net/dmware
- Organization for the Advancement of Structured Information
  Standards
  www.oasis-open.org
- Society for Human Resource Management
  www.shrm.org
- Society for Information Management
  www.simnet.org
- Wesley J. Howe School of Technology Management
  attila.stevens.edu/workflow
- Workflow Management Coalition (WfMC)
  www.wfmc.org
- Workflow Portal
  www.e-workflow.org